CLASSICAL MYTHOLOGY

FROM MOUNT OLYMPUS TO THE UNDERWORLD

NANCY CONNER

New York

FALL RIVER PRESS

New York

An Imprint of Sterling Publishing
387 Park Avenue South
New York, NY 10016

ACKNOWLEDGMENTS

The book you hold in your hands is the product of many people's hard work. I'd like to thank Lesley Bolton for writing a well-organized, well-researched first edition upon which I built this new edition. Thanks also to senior development editor Brett Palana-Shanahan for answering my questions and shepherding the book through the publication process.

I appreciate the top-notch work of the book's production team: including Casey Ebert, Mary Beth Dolan, Robin Witkin, Elisabeth Lariviere, and Deb Baker.

FALL RIVER PRESS and the distinctive Fall River Press logo
are registered trademarks of Barnes & Noble, Inc.

© 2010 by F+W Media, Inc.

This 2013 edition published by Fall River Press by arrangement with F+W Media, Inc.

Jacket design by Patrice Kaplan

Interior design by Gavin Motnyk

ISBN 978-1-4351-4471-2

Distributed in Canada by Sterling Publishing
c/o Canadian Manda Group, 165 Dufferin Street
Toronto, Ontario, Canada M6K 3H6
Distributed in the United Kingdom by GMC Distribution Services
Castle Place, 166 High Street, Lewes, East Sussex, England BN7 1XU
Distributed in Australia by Capricorn Link (Australia) Pty. Ltd.
P.O. Box 704, Windsor, NSW 2756, Australia

For information about custom editions, special sales, and premium and corporate purchases, please contact Sterling Special Sales at 800-805-5489 or specialsales@sterlingpublishing.com.

Manufactured in the United States of America

2 4 6 8 10 9 7 5 3 1

www.sterlingpublishing.com

CONTENTS

INTRODUCTION

 hy learn about classical mythology? You've picked up this book, so perhaps you have your own answer to that question. Or perhaps you're curious why anyone alive today would care about stories created 2,000 years ago.

Classical mythology comprises a group of stories circulated in Greek and Roman cultures in ancient times, starting somewhere around 900 to 800 B.C. and flourishing until Christianity became the official religion of the Roman Empire in the fourth century A.D. As you'll read in Chapter 1, the myths served several purposes: to reveal the origins and order of the universe, to explain natural phenomena, to explore human behavior, to praise the deeds of illustrious heroes, and to form the basis of ancient religion and ritual. Even after Christianity replaced Greek and Roman paganism as a religion, the myths themselves lived on, as Chapter 22 will show.

In many ways, classical mythology has shaped—and continues to shape—contemporary life. It's present in the language you speak. For example, the names of planets and constellations, the months of the year, and many plants and animals derive from classical mythology. If you call a conceited person a "narcissist," a long journey an "odyssey," or a weakness an "Achilles' heel," you're referring to classical mythology. Psychologists such as Sigmund Freud have studied myths to gain insight into human behavior. Western literature, art, and music of all ages have been influenced by classical mythology. In fact, when you become familiar with the myths of the ancient Greeks and Romans, you start to see them all around you: from television shows to comic books, from novels to cartoons, from pop songs to video games.

Classical mythology also fascinates those who are interested in history, allowing a peek into the everyday lives of the people who lived in Greek and Roman societies thousands of years ago. By reading myths, you can learn about the cultures, beliefs, and religious rituals of the people who created, heard, and retold those myths. Woven into the stories are clues about how they lived and what was important to them.

This book begins with a look at what myths are and what purposes they serve within a culture. After an overview of the best-known poets, playwrights, and authors of classical mythology, the discussion turns to the myths themselves. You'll read mythological accounts of how the universe was created and ordered, as well as struggles for control among the early gods. Next, several chapters introduce the twelve great Olympians who dwelled on Mount Olympus and had control over the universe's various domains. In these chapters, you'll read about Zeus, the king of the gods; his jealous wife, Hera; Hades, who ruled the Underworld, home of the dead; Poseidon, who ruled the oceans; Aphrodite, the goddess of love; Ares, the god of war; and many others. Aside from these powerful gods, the ancients saw gods and goddesses throughout the landscape—in woods, fountains, and rivers, for example. You'll get to know the most important of these lesser deities. You'll also meet the monsters that threatened the people's well-being and the heroes who challenged them, including those who fought in the Trojan War. Although the Romans borrowed much of their mythology from the Greeks (simply changing the names of the players), a chapter details specifically Roman myths about the founding of Rome. Finally, you'll see how classical mythology continued to influence Western culture after its own decline.

Above all, the myths are stories, full of daring exploits and passion, danger and intrigue. Whatever kind of stories you like—romance, adventure, military, horror, fantasy—classical mythology is sure to have something that appeals to you. After all, the myths have thrilled, entertained, and inspired people for centuries.

CHAPTER 1

WHAT ARE MYTHS FOR?

lassical mythology is brimming over with stories of passion, tragedy, war, and heroism. To get the most out of these adventures, you need to start with an understanding of what myths are and why they exist. Even if you're reading the exploits of gods, heroes, and rulers for pure entertainment, at some point you're likely to wonder how and why these stories were created. This chapter answers those questions, giving you a greater understanding of what mythology is.

WHAT IS A MYTH?

In popular usage, the word *myth* usually refers to a fictitious story or a half-truth. For example, you might see a report in the media that uses *myth* for some commonly held belief that the reporter wants to prove is untrue. But myths go much deeper than false beliefs or made-up stories. Scholars of mythology have struggled to agree on an exact definition, one that encompasses everything *myth* can mean. Myths may deal with questions of origins —who you are and where you came from. They may teach values or attempt to explain natural phenomena. Myths are often intertwined with religion, and some look ahead to the end of time. No wonder scholars have trouble settling on a single definition.

This book focuses on Greek and Roman mythology, but these are not the only myths. Other cultures—such as Japanese, Native American, Indian, Chinese, Norse, African, Celtic, Aboriginal, and Egyptian—have their own myths. Although the stories may be wildly different, all myths share certain characteristics. Looking at these similarities offers a starting point for developing a working definition of *myth*.

WHAT MAKES A MYTH?

The myth has several characteristics that set it apart from other kinds of stories. One characteristic is how a myth is created. Unlike most works of fiction, myths are not the creation of a single author. A myth evolves as it's told, over and over again. Scholars explain that the mythology of a culture is created through the oral renderings of its people. Someone tells a story, and then the audience tells it again, and their listeners tell it again—and on it goes. Because myths are told and retold, passed from one person to the next, there is often more than one version of the same story.

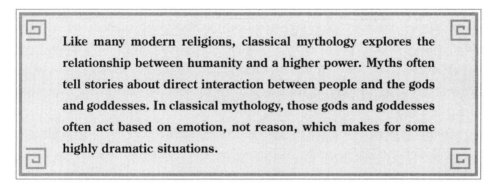

Like many modern religions, classical mythology explores the relationship between humanity and a higher power. Myths often tell stories about direct interaction between people and the gods and goddesses. In classical mythology, those gods and goddesses often act based on emotion, not reason, which makes for some highly dramatic situations.

A myth is a religious story that involves a higher power or entity. The gods, goddesses, and other supernatural beings who appear in myths are worshiped or revered. Within the culture that created it, the myth is considered sacred and believed to be true.

A myth may attempt to explain the unknown, such as how the universe or Earth was created. It also attempts to answer the broad, fundamental questions all people ask themselves about the meaning and purpose of human existence.

Any individual myth is part of a larger mythology, a group of stories that belong to one culture. The myths that make up a mythology may be tied together by shared characters (such as the gods and goddesses involved), historical events (such as the Trojan War), or common themes (such as love and sex). A culture's mythology contains socially accepted truths that provide a sense of identity, shared values, and purpose.

These characteristics comprise the essential elements of a myth. In addition, a few other elements—not necessarily essential to all myths—may appear. For example, many myths highlight activities that break the laws of nature: People change into inanimate objects, the dead rise and live again, and so forth. Also, myths often convey different planes of existence and the interaction between them—heaven and hell, for example, or the future and the past.

LEGENDS AND FOLKTALES

You may hear the words *myth, legend,* and *folktale* used interchangeably. Although each of these words refers to a type of story and all three share similarities, each has its own purpose. As you've just read, a myth evolves in its telling; addresses questions of origins, natural phenomena, or values; has a religious element; and expresses a sense of purpose and identity for its culture. Legends also evolve in the telling, as they are handed down from one generation to the next. Although a legend is presented as true (relating to a specific person, place, or historical event), there is little or no hard evidence to back it up. Examples of legends include stories about historical figures such as King Arthur or George Washington, many ghost stories, and contemporary "urban legends"—widely circulated stories that are purportedly true and often contain an element of horror. A legend may not have all of the elements of a myth, however. For example, although the legends of Robin Hood are full of adventure, they have no religious significance and don't attempt to answer any "big picture" questions. A myth can be a legend, but a legend is not necessarily a myth.

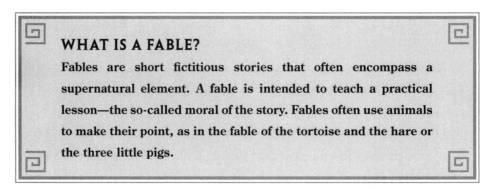

WHAT IS A FABLE?
Fables are short fictitious stories that often encompass a supernatural element. A fable is intended to teach a practical lesson—the so-called moral of the story. Fables often use animals to make their point, as in the fable of the tortoise and the hare or the three little pigs.

A folktale, as its name suggests, is a story circulated among the common folk. Folktales are simple, timeless stories that convey the customs, traditions, and beliefs of ordinary people. Like myths and legends, folktales are told orally and may change in the telling. Folktales, however, usually do not attempt to explain natural phenomena, and they tend to be pure fiction; that is, they are not founded on a particular person, place, or event. In fact, folktales are often set in a distant time and place, beginning with a phrase such as "Once upon a time in a faraway land. . . ." The fairy tale, including stories such as "Cinderella" and "Hansel and Gretel," is a kind of folktale. Like legends, folktales do not have all of the essential elements of myths, so a myth can be a folktale, but a folktale is not necessarily a myth.

THE SACRED MYTH

For the ancient Greeks and Romans, myths served several purposes, one of the foremost being religion. As you know, an essential element of myth is religious significance. In classical cultures, the myth explained religious beliefs and justified religious rituals. In fact, the sacred element of mythology heavily influenced the behavior of the ancient Greeks and Romans.

PROTECT YOURSELF—PRAY!

The Greeks and Romans were religious people who believed that the gods and goddesses, and even the lesser deities, held vast powers over people and the world. The myths defined which god or goddess to turn to in times of need. For example, for a safe sea voyage, they would pray to the Greek god Poseidon or the Roman god Neptune; for a successful hunt, they would pray to the Greek goddess Artemis or the Roman goddess Diana; soldiers who wanted victory in battle would pray to the Greek god Ares or the Roman god Mars.

With so many deities, the ancients had to take care to keep them all straight. If a prayer intended for the god of justice went to the god of wine instead, for example, the outcome could be disastrous—or so people believed.

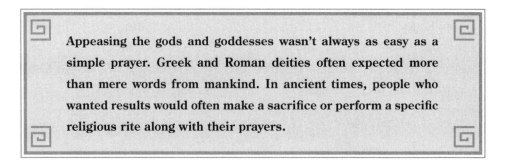

Appeasing the gods and goddesses wasn't always as easy as a simple prayer. Greek and Roman deities often expected more than mere words from mankind. In ancient times, people who wanted results would often make a sacrifice or perform a specific religious rite along with their prayers.

The majority of today's religions usually understand God as steadfast and just. Greek and Roman deities weren't like that. They could be downright moody, and they didn't always have the best interests of humankind in mind. The ancients accepted the gods' inconsistent behavior and temperament and altered their own behavior to try to please the gods. After all, the deities wielded the powers of creation and destruction; it was best to be on their good side as much as possible.

READ YOUR RITES

The ancients developed religious rituals that went beyond prayer. The myths gave these rites meaning; sometimes, they even spawned new practices. One important ritual explored in several myths is sacrifice.

Prometheus, a Titan who was friendly to humans, devised the ritual of sacrifice. He was asked to settle a dispute between the gods and humanity concerning which portion of the sacrifice should be given to the gods and which kept for the people. Prometheus divided a sacrificial bull into two packets. The first packet contained the animal's flesh, wrapped in its skin and stomach lining; the second had the animal's bones, wrapped in its fat. Prometheus then offered the packets to Zeus (ruler of the gods) and told him to choose which portion he wanted. Zeus chose the fat-wrapped packet because it looked richer and more appetizing. Of course, upon discovering the packet contained inedible bones, Zeus grew furious, but his decision had been made. Thanks to Prometheus's cleverness, the ritual of sacrifice would require people to burn the bones of an animal, letting them keep the flesh for themselves.

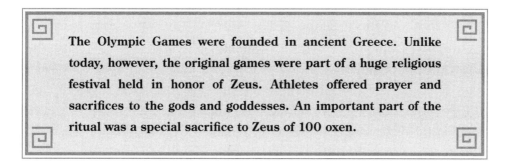

The Olympic Games were founded in ancient Greece. Unlike today, however, the original games were part of a huge religious festival held in honor of Zeus. Athletes offered prayer and sacrifices to the gods and goddesses. An important part of the ritual was a special sacrifice to Zeus of 100 oxen.

Of course, myths describe other rituals besides sacrifice. Some of these rituals were even created because of myths. Furthermore, certain rituals honored only one deity. For example, rites associated with the worship of Dionysus, the Greek god of wine, were unlike those of any other god. These Dionysian rituals were kept secret, so not much is recorded about them. However, allusions suggest that they involved much drinking, dancing, and wild behavior. (Chapter 16 tells you more.)

Religious rituals were also important to social order. Because myths explained and justified these rituals and actions, the ancients relied heavily on myths to guide them along the correct path; they needed myths to tell them how to appease the gods and to maintain an orderly society.

ANSWERING THE UNKNOWN

An important function of the myth is to explain the unknown. It is human nature to pose questions rather than to accept things blindly. People always want to know "why." Today, many mysteries of the universe have been explained through science. The ancients, however, did not have today's scientific knowledge or sophisticated technology. Instead, they relied on myths to give them the answers they sought.

THE QUESTIONS

The ancients hungered for knowledge. They wanted explanations for the phenomena they encountered in their daily lives, such as where thunder and lightning came from or why the sun appears to cross the sky. They also wondered about the structure of the universe. Curiosity drove people to ask questions, and myths evolved to explain these otherwise unanswerable questions. For example, the creation myth (discussed in Chapter 3) answers huge questions such as "How were the universe and Earth created?" and "Where did people come from?" Another explanatory myth deals with the Underworld, answering the question, "What happens after we die?"

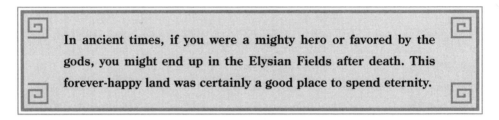

In ancient times, if you were a mighty hero or favored by the gods, you might end up in the Elysian Fields after death. This forever-happy land was certainly a good place to spend eternity.

Myths also answered smaller everyday questions. For example, where does the hyacinth come from? According to a Greek myth, Apollo, god of archery, fell in love with a youth named Hyacinthus, who was accidentally killed when he and Apollo were throwing a discus. Apollo was so heartbroken that he transformed the youth's blood, as it fell to the ground, into a new flower. That flower, the hyacinth, returns every spring to honor his memory.

Here are some other subjects explored in ancient myths:

- Where certain constellations come from
- Why the sun disappears at night
- Why creatures behave as they do (for instance, why the spider weaves a web)
- How bad things such as sickness, death, and grief came into the world
- How fire came to humanity
- Why the seasons change

THE ANSWERS

A myth's explanatory element is important to its structure. Like any other religion, classical mythology sought to provide definitive answers to seemingly unanswerable questions. Because the ancients were not constrained by scientific and technical knowledge, they were free to develop stirring, sometimes outrageous tales to explain these phenomena. If you think about it, this freedom was beneficial in many ways. Myths were entertaining, so people wanted to hear them and remembered them after they'd been told. The oral tradition of the ancients thrived in part because of the people's interest in these stories. People listened to myths, retold them, and eventually wrote them down—and that's why they are still in existence today.

ESTABLISHING ORDER

Another important function of myths is to maintain natural and social order. Although the creation myth begins with Chaos, the story works to provide a specific order to the universe. After order is created within the cosmos, order is then brought to the lesser beings—people and their societies. Establishing order is an orderly process in itself.

NATURAL ORDER

Most myths affirm that Zeus, ruler of the gods, was responsible for creating order in the natural world. By the time he came to power, however, some sense of order already existed. Earth, heaven, seas, sky, and space were already set in their respective places. So Zeus shouldn't get all the credit.

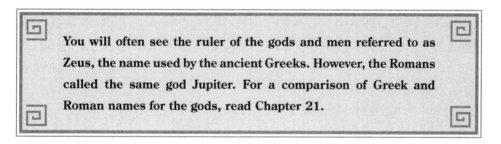

You will often see the ruler of the gods and men referred to as Zeus, the name used by the ancient Greeks. However, the Romans called the same god Jupiter. For a comparison of Greek and Roman names for the gods, read Chapter 21.

The affairs of the universe were within the domain of Zeus, who presided over the natural world. The ancients believed that Zeus placed the stars and planets in their individual places, but he didn't stop there. Also referred to as the weather god, Zeus gave rain, snow, thunder, and lightning to Earth.

Although Zeus held highest command, other gods also maintained order in the natural world. The universe was divided among the gods (the goddesses were left out of this part), each having jurisdiction over a particular domain. Zeus ruled the heavens, Poseidon the seas, and Hades the Underworld.

Other deities helped ensure the ultimate order of things. For example, Zeus had children who helped to establish the natural order. The three Horae were the goddesses of nature: Eunomia (Discipline), Dike (Justice), and Eirene (Peace). Zeus also fathered the three Moirai—Atropos, Clotho, and Lachesis—who represented destiny. These three sisters, sometimes called the Fates, determined the length of an individual's life by spinning a thread, then measuring it, and then finally cutting it.

These deities were aided by various lesser deities. River gods, nymphs, satyrs, sirens, and the various gods and goddesses of light, darkness, and dawn—whom you'll read about in Chapter 17—all played a role in maintaining the natural world.

SOCIAL ORDER

After bringing order to the universe and organizing the natural world, the gods had to make sure that lesser beings, such as humans, understood and kept their place. Myths worked to maintain order in society by showing what behavior was acceptable—and what was not.

Again, the burden of creating order fell upon Zeus. To reign over immortals and mortals was a huge responsibility, and Zeus took this responsibility seriously. He came to be known as a god of justice, creating laws that were fair and sensible and maintaining order. Zeus often used diplomacy to settle disputes through compromise, and he watched closely to ensure that his laws were not broken, especially those governing oaths and hospitality. Because Zeus never really warmed to humankind, however, it was easy to lose his favor. Therefore, it was best to abide by his laws; no one wanted to experience the wrath of Zeus.

Zeus set the laws and often meted out harsh punishments against those who broke them, but he wasn't the only deity concerned with maintaining order. All of the gods and goddesses placed demands upon humankind, most of which concerned sacrificial rites and due respect. Crimes never went unpunished. The thought of escaping a deity's anger was almost laughable. The ancients had many rules to follow, but they did so willingly because they wanted to avoid the wrath of the gods.

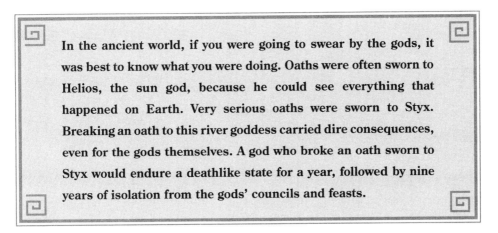

In the ancient world, if you were going to swear by the gods, it was best to know what you were doing. Oaths were often sworn to Helios, the sun god, because he could see everything that happened on Earth. Very serious oaths were sworn to Styx. Breaking an oath to this river goddess carried dire consequences, even for the gods themselves. A god who broke an oath sworn to Styx would endure a deathlike state for a year, followed by nine years of isolation from the gods' councils and feasts.

EMOTION OVERLOAD

Everyone, even the most stoic person, feels emotion; it's an important part of what makes a human human. So it's not surprising that the myths, which evolved to help the ancients understand themselves and their place in the world, covered the wide range of human emotions.

In the ancient world, the gods and goddesses were superior beings who wielded powers beyond human ability (and sometimes comprehension). But even the gods, in all their glory, could not escape emotion. Classical deities reached extreme levels of emotion far beyond the range of ordinary human feelings. If you've ever been in the grip of overwhelming feelings, you'll relate to myths in which mortals and immortals alike allow an emotion to take control. As in real life, this situation sometimes ends in disaster; at other times, it works out for the best.

Myths' endings are often unpredictable, so if you are expecting to learn a lesson about the destructive power of jealousy or the brighter side of sadness, think again. Although myths involve emotion as part of human (and divine) nature, rarely do they offer lessons or teach morals. Lessons aren't spelled out as they are in fables. Instead, myths provide insights into human nature and human experience.

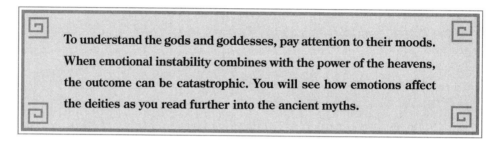

To understand the gods and goddesses, pay attention to their moods. When emotional instability combines with the power of the heavens, the outcome can be catastrophic. You will see how emotions affect the deities as you read further into the ancient myths.

THE IDEAL

Because myths are created collectively, as they are told and retold by count-less people, they evolve and change, depending on who's telling the tale and who's listening to it. Therefore, a myth reflects not only the views and ideas of a culture, but also of individuals.

Myths paint a portrait of ideal human behavior, illustrating what the peo-ple of a particular culture valued in action, thought, and deed. Myths may also explain social hierarchy, why some people have higher status than others.

MAN'S SHINING MOMENT

In myths, ideal human attributes shine most brightly through the character of a hero. The hero plays an important role in classical mythology. Among all the grandiose stories of gods, goddesses, and other deities, a few humans earn praise and admiration for their feats. These human heroes became models for good and admirable behavior. (Chapter 19 presents some of the heroes of classical mythology.)

How did these men emerge from the shadows of the gods to become heroes? Why were they singled out as exemplary? What actions did their peers admire?

GOOD BEHAVIOR REWARDED

The ancients admired many characteristics that people today also find admirable. For example, when you think of a hero, you probably imagine adventure. In ancient times, adventure stories were highly popular. A classical hero, however, had to display certain traits to be considered heroic. A hero had to be not just brave but fearless. A hero had to be supremely confident and full of ambition that drove him to meet all challenges. Classical heroes were so confident that they might seem like egomaniacs to modern readers.

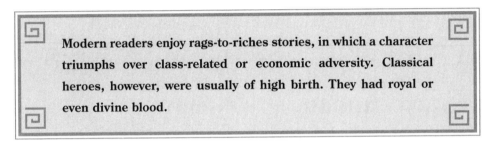

Modern readers enjoy rags-to-riches stories, in which a character triumphs over class-related or economic adversity. Classical heroes, however, were usually of high birth. They had royal or even divine blood.

Beyond confidence, the hero must show loyalty to someone who keeps him grounded, such as a deity or a friend. Even when faced with the most tempting of treacheries, the hero must remain loyal to his allies or his creed. This loyalty might be to the hero's family. Classical mythology is full of adultery, and cheating on one's spouse was often seen as something beyond the hero's control. However, those few heroes who remained faithful were greatly admired.

Heroes also show mastery of a particular skill, sometimes several. It doesn't matter whether that skill was in archery, war strategy, or the art of seduction. What's important is that the hero exhibits unusual skill in some endeavor.

Classical myths also highlighted admirable qualities in women; however, women were less celebrated than their male counterparts. The most important virtue for a woman was loyalty to her family. For example, Penelope remained faithful to her husband, Odysseus, throughout his long absence, tricking the suitors who tried to convince her he was dead. Other common characteristics of a good woman were cleverness, wisdom, and hospitality.

For men and women both, these traits were held in the highest esteem. Understanding what's heroic about a hero's behavior offers insight into the cultural and social values of ancient times.

THE RIGHT TO RULE

Because heroes were of royal or divine blood, myths also justified rulers' claims to power. Roman mythology, in particular, traces the succession of several kings and emperors back to the gods. This divine lineage validated the rulers' claims to power. What people wouldn't want a ruler with divine blood running through his veins? And who would dare to challenge a ruler who had family ties to a deity?

STORYTELLING

Everyone loves a good story, and the ancients were no different. Today, people find stories in books, television, and movies. In antiquity, people listened to the adventures of gods and heroes, told by professional storytellers, or they attended plays. Any discussion of the functions of a myth must include a look at its entertainment value. After all, if myths hadn't been entertaining, they might never have been recorded for you to enjoy today.

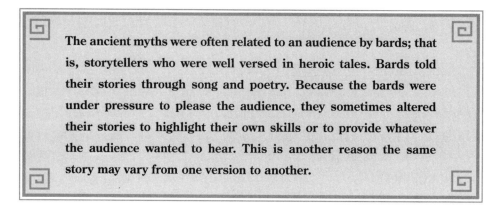

The ancient myths were often related to an audience by bards; that is, storytellers who were well versed in heroic tales. Bards told their stories through song and poetry. Because the bards were under pressure to please the audience, they sometimes altered their stories to highlight their own skills or to provide whatever the audience wanted to hear. This is another reason the same story may vary from one version to another.

THEN AND NOW

In the time they were created, myths offered guidance to living a good life, answers to important questions, and religious information. They also provided entertainment. If the myths hadn't been lively and exciting, they probably wouldn't have been recorded and passed down through the centuries.

Today, mythology is a source of both entertainment and academic study. Modern people do not accept the myths as literal truth or use them for religious purposes. Instead, scholars and others read myths to learn about ancient cultures and human nature—and to enjoy a good story.

BETTER THAN ANY SOAP OPERA

Remember that these myths are, above all else, stories—and what stories they are! Much like Shakespearean plays, mythology presents all the facets of human experience: love, war, passion, jealousy, fear, betrayal, and so much more. There are several types of classical myths.

Adventure stories told of heroic deeds, mortals clashing with gods, rescues, and long journeys and quests. Examples of adventure stories include myths about Heracles (the Greek version of Hercules), Odysseus, and Perseus.

A tragedy is an important type of myth, in which the main character encounters some catastrophe, usually brought about because of an internal flaw such as stubbornness or excessive pride. Even though this kind of story is sad, its audience still received pleasure from it. The Greek philosopher Aristotle believed that audiences enjoy tragedy because it causes them to feel pity and fear for the characters; by feeling these emotions through a story, they experience *catharsis*, a release of emotional tension. Examples of tragedy include the stories of Oedipus, Antigone, and Niobe, all discussed later in this book.

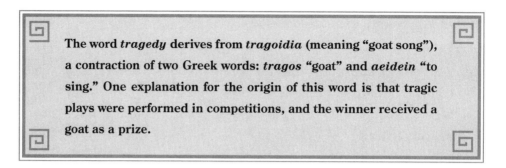

The word *tragedy* derives from *tragoidia* (meaning "goat song"), a contraction of two Greek words: *tragos* "goat" and *aeidein* "to sing." One explanation for the origin of this word is that tragic plays were performed in competitions, and the winner received a goat as a prize.

If you enjoy stories of war and bravery in battle, you'll be glad to know that classical mythology is full of exciting battle scenes. The ancients were fierce warriors, and the myths describe their fights in great detail. The story of the Trojan War, for example, contains many graphic descriptions of fighting.

Horror fans will find a fascinating variety of monsters in classical mythology—including some you never dreamed might be lurking under your bed. From Typhon, who had a hundred serpentine heads, to the Minotaur, who ate children, the monsters of classical mythology will give you chills and might even keep you up at night.

Adventure, tragedy, battles, and monsters are just the beginning. You'll also encounter tales of witchcraft and revenge, murder and mystery, crime and punishment, and passionate love and seduction. Love and sex play a major role in mythology, including stories of scandalous affairs—such as the one between Aphrodite and Ares—and stories of true love—such as the myth of Perseus and Andromeda.

With such a wide variety of tales to choose from, classical mythology is guaranteed to have something for everyone!

CHAPTER 2
CLASSICAL MYTH-MAKERS

ythology doesn't come from a single source. Myths develop as they're told and retold, passed from one storyteller to another, from one generation to the next. This chapter surveys some of the most important myth-makers of the ancient world. These poets, dramatists, and other storytellers were the bestselling authors of their time. Because their works were popular and valued, they were recorded and preserved—and you can read them today.

HOMER: THE BLIND BARD

The name Homer looms large in classical mythology. Homer is regarded as the greatest poet of the ancient world. More than that, he's considered one of the greatest and most influential artists in the history of Western literature. But did Homer actually exist? In other words, was he a living, breathing person, or was he a character created by other poets? Scholars and historians have debated this question for centuries. Everyone agrees, however, that the *Iliad* and the *Odyssey*, epic poems attributed to Homer, are important and fascinating literary works.

HOMER THE MAN

For the moment, assume that Homer did exist and that he was the author of these two great epic poems. Many people, including the ancient Greeks and Romans, believed in his existence. Although no one knows for sure where or when he was born, some historians believe he may have been born around 750 B.C. Homer was a bard, a professional storyteller. The Greeks believed that he was blind, presumably because one of his poems mentions a blind bard.

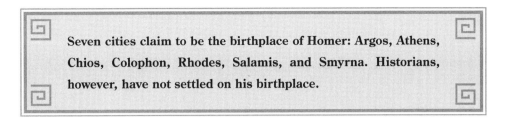

Seven cities claim to be the birthplace of Homer: Argos, Athens, Chios, Colophon, Rhodes, Salamis, and Smyrna. Historians, however, have not settled on his birthplace.

Homer's epic poems, the *Iliad* and the *Odyssey*, each run approximately 12,000 lines. To perform either poem in its entirety would take several evenings. To the ancients, listening to an epic poem was an exciting and entertaining way to spend an evening. These two poems tell of the Trojan War (discussed in Chapter 20) and its aftermath. The Greek victory over Troy was a defining moment for the Greeks and the catalyst for the foundation of Rome. Because the poems center on this pivotal historic event, and because Homer was such a gifted storyteller, these epics became an integral part of Greek culture. In fact, the Greeks were said to have introduced the study of these works into their schools around 400 B.C.

HOMER THE MYTH

Several theories assert that Homer wasn't the single author of all the works attributed to him. Some scholars even doubt that he existed at all. One theory posits that several different people composed these poems, and the result was later attributed to Homer. Other theories suggest that Homer composed the first part of the *Odyssey* and that one or more other bards concluded the poem. Others hold that the man known as Homer never existed and that his name referred to poets in general, a catch-all term for all authors who composed heroic verse. Another theory is that Homer was the name of the scribe who first wrote down these works. By signing his name to the written texts, he got credit for creating them. In the early twentieth century, one scholar shocked his contemporaries by theorizing that the *Odyssey* had been written by a woman.

Why is there this skepticism? The works of Homer have been studied for centuries. Scholars who have compared the *Iliad*, the *Odyssey*, and other poems attributed to Homer have found significant differences. For example, some scholars believe that the subjects and themes of Homer's works are too broad to be the products of a single mind. Others note that Homeric works blend different dialects, even though people typically speak only one dialect. There are strong stylistic similarities between the poems, which may be due to the oral tradition from which they arose.

Although the differences among Homeric works raise questions about who composed them, "Homer" still created the foundation for classical mythology—whether he was a single man or several different authors.

HESIOD: MORALS CAN BE FUN

Hesiod is another important Greek poet. Often called the father of Greek didactic poetry, Hesiod probably lived some time after Homer. Unlike Homer's epic poetry, which typically narrates heroic deeds and important events, didactic poetry tells a story to teach a moral lesson.

HESIOD'S LIFE

Like Homer, Hesiod is shrouded in mystery, but scholars do know a bit more about his life. Most of this information comes directly from his works. The best guess is that he lived sometime around 700 B.C. in the village of Ascra in central Greece. According to his poems, he tended sheep in his youth, becoming a farmer after his father died. Although he was poor, Hesiod wasn't a typical peasant. Yet his works clearly show the perspective of a farmer who lived a difficult life.

While tending his flock one day, the young Hesiod was visited by the Muses, goddesses of literature and the arts. They appeared to him in a mist and gave him a poet's staff and a poet's voice. Then they told him to use these gifts to spread the word about the gods. Hesiod did as he was told, even competing in poetry contests. The results of this mystical visitation were the famous works *Theogony* and *Works and Days*, as well as several lesser-known poems.

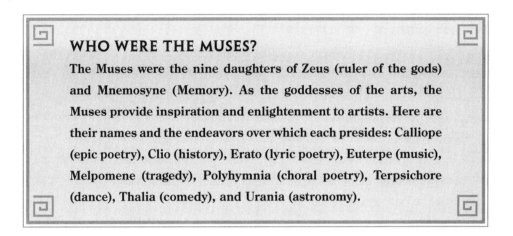

WHO WERE THE MUSES?

The Muses were the nine daughters of Zeus (ruler of the gods) and Mnemosyne (Memory). As the goddesses of the arts, the Muses provide inspiration and enlightenment to artists. Here are their names and the endeavors over which each presides: Calliope (epic poetry), Clio (history), Erato (lyric poetry), Euterpe (music), Melpomene (tragedy), Polyhymnia (choral poetry), Terpsichore (dance), Thalia (comedy), and Urania (astronomy).

Details of Hesiod's death are sketchy. According to legend, Hesiod was murdered by the sons of a family he stayed with during his travels and was buried at Locris. Another legend says that his bones were taken to Orchomenus, where a statue in his honor was built in the marketplace.

THE WORKS

Like Homer, Hesiod was the author of two famous poems that are still studied and enjoyed today. As with Homer, scholars debate whether Hesiod was the sole author of his works. But there is general agreement that Hesiod was an actual person and that he authored most of *Theogony* and *Works and Days*. Only parts of these works are suspected of having been added later by other poets.

Theogony

Theogony fulfilled the Muses' command by telling the history of the gods. Beginning with creation, this poem provides a foundation on which to build the stories of the gods and goddesses. *Theogony* explains the origin of universe, the gods, and the world.

Works and Days

Works and Days, a poem of about 800 lines, is framed as a disagreement between Hesiod and his brother, Perses, over their late father's estate. *Works and Days* is filled with fables and myths as the two brothers debate the issue.

The poem posits that it's the destiny of all men to work, but those who accept their lot and work hard will succeed. Through its stories, the poem prizes honest labor over laziness, injustice, dishonesty, and usury. In fact, Hesiod states that labor is the source of all good things, and that gods and people alike hate idleness.

Works and Days gives Hesiod's version of human history in its Five Ages of Man. The Golden Age, most distant in time, was when people lived among the gods. During the Silver Age, childhood lasted for 100 years, but adulthood was short and full of conflict. The Bronze Age was a difficult era of war. Life got better in the Heroic Age, when heroes walked the earth, but this time passed away and the heroes departed for the Elysian Fields. Hesiod called his own era the Iron Age and saw it as a time of misery and hard work.

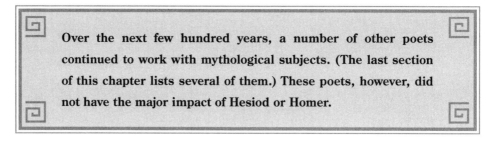

Over the next few hundred years, a number of other poets continued to work with mythological subjects. (The last section of this chapter lists several of them.) These poets, however, did not have the major impact of Hesiod or Homer.

AESCHYLUS: TRAGIC JUSTICE

The next important period for mythology was the fifth century B.C., when Greece experienced a flowering of the theater. During this period, three Greek playwrights rose to fame for their tragic plays. The first of these tragedians was Aeschylus, who wrote more than ninety plays and is sometimes called the father of tragedy.

LIFE

Historians know several facts about Aeschylus. He was born into an aristocratic family near Athens around 525 B.C., served as a soldier in the Persian Wars, and became a celebrated tragedian. He participated numerous times in the Great Dionysia, part of a festival honoring Dionysus, the Greek god of wine. For this festival, three dramatists each created three tragedies and a satyr play (a short play featuring drunkenness, sexuality, and practical jokes), which were performed and judged at the celebration. His first competition is thought to have taken place around 499 B.C., with his first victory in 484 B.C. From then on, Aeschylus won first prize in nearly every competition (although he was bested once by his protégé Sophocles).

Aeschylus died around 455 B.C. in Gela, Sicily, at the age of sixty-nine. The cause of his death is unknown, although a rumor (thought to have been started by a comic writer) claimed that Aeschylus was killed when an eagle dropped a tortoise on his bald head. Regardless of how he died, Aeschylus was honored with a public funeral at which sacrifices and performances were carried out.

WORKS

Aeschylus is thought to have written ninety plays during his lifetime, approximately eighty of which are known from the bits and pieces that have survived. However, only seven of his plays, all tragedies, remain intact today: *The Persians, Seven Against Thebes, The Suppliants, Agamemnon, The Libation Bearers, The Eumenides* (the latter three make up the famous trilogy the *Oresteia*), and *Prometheus Bound*.

A major theme of these tragedies is justice. Aeschylus believed that the gods and goddesses sometimes resented mortals' attempts to attain greatness, which they saw as *hubris* (excessive pride). The deities often pursued justice by tricking a person into causing his own downfall through pride. The unjust were not always punished directly; sometimes, punishment fell upon a culprit's descendants. Zeus, the god of justice, is a central figure in Aeschylus's work.

As was common in his culture, Aeschylus saw revenge as a legitimate form of justice. For example, the three plays of the *Oresteia* show a cause-and-effect chain of violence and revenge, broken only when the goddess Athena intervenes and replaces the old-fashioned blood feud with a new system of trial by jury.

Throughout these plays, gods and goddesses intervene in human affairs. The works of Aeschylus are one of the richest sources of classical mythology that have survived.

SOPHOCLES: THE GREATEST TRAGEDIAN?

Sophocles, a student of Aeschylus, is considered by many to be the most successful of the Greek tragedians. Like Aeschylus, Sophocles lived during a time of many wars, including the Persian Wars (546–479 B.C.) and the Peloponnesian War (431–404 B.C.). Sophocles' work was influenced by this strife.

LIFE

Sophocles came into the world in 496 B.C., in a village outside of Athens. Born into a wealthy family (his father manufactured armor), Sophocles was sent to Athens to receive a good education. He studied military technique, science, mathematics, philosophy, government, law, astronomy, and the arts. It is widely believed that Sophocles studied under Aeschylus.

Sophocles was a talented and popular man who excelled in nearly everything he did. He was handsome and widely respected. He held many public offices and was a patron of the arts. Sophocles also took part in the Great Dionysia, winning his first victory in 468 B.C. at the age of twenty-nine. He went on to win this competition eighteen times (some sources say twenty-four times).

Sophocles died around 409 B.C. at the age of ninety. As with Aeschylus, unlikely rumors circulated about the cause of his death. One rumor humorously claimed he died during an attempt to recite a long sentence from one of his plays without stopping to take a breath; another said he died of happiness after winning the Athens Dionysia competition one last time. A third rumor had him choking on some grapes. However he died, it is certain that Sophocles lived a long, full life and made a significant contribution to Greek literature and our understanding of mythology.

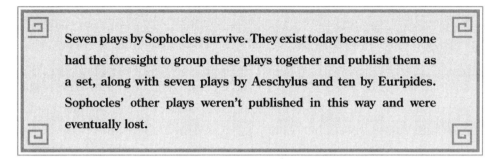

Seven plays by Sophocles survive. They exist today because someone had the foresight to group these plays together and publish them as a set, along with seven plays by Aeschylus and ten by Euripides. Sophocles' other plays weren't published in this way and were eventually lost.

WORKS

During his long life, Sophocles wrote an estimated 123 plays. Today, only seven have survived intact: *Oedipus the King, Oedipus at Colonus, Antigone, Ajax, The Trachiniae, Philoctetes*, and *Electra*. Each of these plays is built on a foundation of mythology.

War and conflict are frequent themes in his plays, and this conflict causes his characters much pain and suffering. The plays suggest that it is through this pain and suffering that people become more human.

Thanks to Sophocles, the character of Oedipus is widely known. Sophocles began with the basic myth of Oedipus and expanded on it, creating three of his most famous tragedies: *Oedipus the King, Oedipus at Colonus*, and *Antigone*. The gods also appear throughout his works. Sophocles saw the gods as higher beings, and humans as subject to their decisions. If the gods felt a man should be punished, for example, he was indeed brought to justice. If the gods felt a man should be rewarded for his pain and suffering, he was aptly rewarded. The gods also took sides in human conflicts.

EURIPIDES: THE DRAMATIST AS PHILOSOPHER

The last of the great Greek tragedians was Euripides, known today for his philosophical plays and strong female characters. Euripides constantly questioned all that the Greeks held sacred. For this reason, he was controversial in his day; in fact, he was openly disliked and criticized during his lifetime.

LIFE

Euripides was born around 480 B.C. on the island of Salamis. Little is known about his background, although he was obviously well educated, which suggests that his family was wealthy. It is likely that he studied the same broad range of subjects as Sophocles, but Euripides developed a strong passion for philosophy. As a philosopher, Euripides questioned cherished assumptions and was openly skeptical of the gods and goddesses.

Euripides started writing plays around the age of eighteen. He, too, competed in the Great Dionysia, beginning in 455 B.C., but he didn't win until he was about forty years old. He is said to have competed twenty-two times, winning only five competitions (one of those after his death). He attributed his losses to the judges' bias against him.

One of the things that gained Euripides renown was his library, believed to be one of the first ever put together by a private individual. Although he lived in Athens for most of his life, he retired to Macedonia, where he died around 406 B.C. at the age of seventy-seven.

WORKS

Euripides is thought to have written ninety-two plays, although only seventeen tragedies have survived. (Notice, however, that this is more than the surviving plays of Aeschylus and Sophocles combined.) The plays of Euripides that you can read today are *Andromache, Hecuba, Iphigenia at Aulis, Bacchae, Alcestis, Medea, The Children of Heracles, Hippolytus, The Suppliants, Electra, The Madness of Heracles, Ion, The Trojan Women, Iphigenia Among the Taurians, The Phoenician Women, Helen,* and *Orestes.* Like the other Greek tragedians, Euripides uses mythology as a foundation for his plays.

As a philosopher, Euripides appreciated realism, and his plays reflect this. His works introduce protagonists—main characters—who are common everyday people. Even the deities function on a common level; people often equal them in importance. Euripides also emphasized strong female characters, making them protagonists who received as much recognition as the traditional war hero. Euripides explored his characters' inner lives and motives in a way no other dramatist had done before.

Euripides saw humans as complex, multifaceted beings. He thought it was essential that people recognized both sides of themselves—body and mind—instead of pretending that people are primarily rational or godlike. For example, in *Bacchae*, the character Pentheus, king of Thebes, suppresses the wild rites of the god Dionysus in the name of law and order. In retaliation, Dionysus punishes Pentheus, and his worshipers tear the king to pieces. Pentheus tries to support rationalism and order; as a result, he is torn apart.

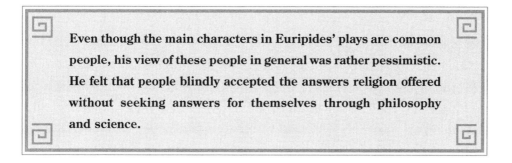

Even though the main characters in Euripides' plays are common people, his view of these people in general was rather pessimistic. He felt that people blindly accepted the answers religion offered without seeking answers for themselves through philosophy and science.

VIRGIL: ROME'S NATIONAL POET

The Greeks weren't the only ones whose culture produced great poets inspired by mythology. During Rome's Augustan Age, two poets, Virgil and Ovid, emerged who are often compared to Homer and Hesiod. Virgil is best known for his epic poem the *Aeneid*, which tells of how the hero Aeneas left Troy to found Rome.

LIFE

Virgil, whose full name was Publius Vergilius Maro, was born on October 15, 70 B.C. in the village of Andes. His father, a wealthy farmer, sent his son to Cremona, Milan, and Rome for his education. Virgil studied both Greek and Roman literature, as well as law, rhetoric, and philosophy. Legend has it that

Virgil's father wanted him to become a lawyer. After arguing his first case, however, Virgil decided that the law wasn't for him and turned his attention to philosophy and poetry.

Virgil was a popular poet who had influential friends, including his patron, the Roman emperor Augustus, and various important political and literary figures. Although Virgil lived for many years in Rome, he never abandoned his love of the countryside, a love that is evident in his poetry.

In 19 B.C., Virgil was traveling to Greece to visit some of the sites described in the *Aeneid* as he revised that poem. En route, he contracted a fever and died on September 21. The dying Virgil asked that his remains be taken to Naples and buried near his villa there. His bones were believed to offer protection to the city of Naples.

WORKS

Virgil is best known for the *Aeneid*. This epic poem, which tells the story of the origins of Rome, follows the Trojan hero Aeneas after the fall of Troy, as he travels and then settles in a new land, where he founds a new race: the Romans. The poem introduces all of the great characters of ancient Roman mythology, mortal and immortal alike, including Dido, Romulus, Jupiter, and Venus, to name just a few. This timeless classic has inspired many authors over the centuries.

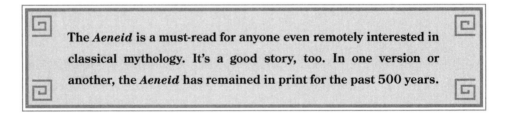

The *Aeneid* is a must-read for anyone even remotely interested in classical mythology. It's a good story, too. In one version or another, the *Aeneid* has remained in print for the past 500 years.

Although the *Aeneid* is Virgil's most famous work, he also wrote other important poems. His earliest work is a collection of ten short pastoral poems entitled *Eclogues*, which show the lives and loves of shepherds in idealized rural settings. Another major work, *Georgics*, reflects Virgil's love of the Italian countryside (and may have served as political propaganda). In this work, Virgil exhorts farmers to go back to the land and preserve the agricultural lifestyle.

Virgil was essentially Rome's national poet. His works are central to the study of Roman history and culture. Thanks to the enduring popularity of Virgil's poems, today's scholars know a great deal about Roman mythology.

OVID: THE MORE THINGS CHANGE . . .

Ovid, another great Roman poet, was a fantastic storyteller. Like Virgil, Ovid was popular in his own day and remains so today. And it's no wonder, his works are full of magic, seduction, love, and transformation. His poetry has been a major influence on European literature for centuries.

LIFE

On March 20, 43 B.C., Publius Ovidius Naso was born in the small town of Sulmo, about ninety miles east of Rome. Ovid came from an affluent, respectable family, and his father sent him and his older brother to Rome for their education. Like Virgil's father, Ovid's father also wanted him to study law, but Ovid was more interested in writing poetry. When his brother died, Ovid left Rome to travel to Athens and Sicily.

Ovid held a minor public office, but he quit to write poetry. This decision turned out to be an excellent career move, because he enjoyed immense popularity as a poet. Ovid's life, however, was not entirely full of glory. By the age of thirty, he'd been married three times and divorced twice. In A.D. 8, he was exiled to Tomis on the Black Sea. His banishment may have been for political reasons or for the subject matter of his poems (some dealt with adultery, which was a crime during that era). One rumor suggested that Ovid was involved an adulterous affair with the emperor's granddaughter. Ovid wrote that his banishment was due to *carmen et error*, "a song and a mistake," suggesting he ran into trouble for something he wrote and for something he did. Ovid died in exile in A.D. 17, still begging to be allowed to return to Rome.

WORKS

Ovid wrote several works, but the most popular by far is his narrative poem *Metamorphoses*, which has been called "the major treasury of classical mythology." Approximately 12,000 lines, this poem is a collection of Roman mythological stories, covering everything from creation to the death of Julius Caesar. *Metamorphoses* is all about transformations, or as Ovid put it, "forms changed into new bodies." For example, the nymph Daphne, fleeing from the god Apollo, is changed into a laurel tree; a woman named Arachne challenges the goddess Minerva to a weaving contest and is turned into a spider for her audacity.

Love is a dominant theme throughout Ovid's work. *Amores*, Ovid's first published poems, describe a love affair, and *Heroides* is a series of imaginary love letters written by mythological characters to their lovers. *Fasti* describes, from one month to the next, the Romans' various religious festivals and their mythological basis. Unfortunately, only the first six books—the first six months—of *Fasti* have survived (or perhaps Ovid never finished this work).

OTHER STORYTELLERS YOU SHOULD KNOW

All of the poets, dramatists, and storytellers described in this chapter contributed greatly to world literature and to our knowledge of classical mythology. Although these men take the spotlight in studies of mythology, others also composed works that have survived and added to our knowledge of mythology.

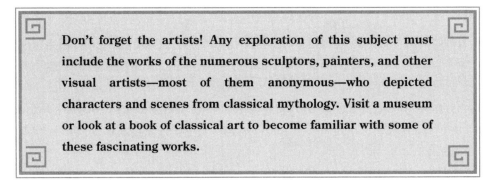

Don't forget the artists! Any exploration of this subject must include the works of the numerous sculptors, painters, and other visual artists—most of them anonymous—who depicted characters and scenes from classical mythology. Visit a museum or look at a book of classical art to become familiar with some of these fascinating works.

GREEK CONTRIBUTORS

These Greek poets, historians, and essayists composed works that drew from mythology and contribute to our understanding of the subject:

- **Apollodorus:** A mythologist and historian whose work *The Library* serves as a guide to classical mythology, covering just about everything you might want to know about the history of the gods.
- **Apollonius Rhodius:** An epic poet who lived in the second century B.C., best known for his poem *Argonautica*, which tells the story of Jason and his quest for the Golden Fleece.
- **Herodotus:** A historian who lived during the fifth century B.C., known as the Father of History; his work *History* is a narration of the Persian Wars (the nine books of which are each named after one of the Muses).
- **Musaeus:** A fifth-century poet best known for his poem about the myth of Hero and Leander.
- **Pausanias:** A second-century writer and traveler whose work *Description of Greece* includes mythology, religious rites, art, and history.
- **Pindar:** A fifth-century poet often called "the greatest of the Greek lyric poets," who wrote a collection of lyric odes celebrating the winners of the Olympic, Pythian, Nemean, and Isthmian games.
- **Plutarch:** A biographer and essayist who wrote biographies of mythological and historical Greeks and Romans.
- **Sappho:** Born between 630 and 612 B.C., Sappho was famous for her love poetry. Sappho's poems were widely admired; Plato, for example, called her the tenth Muse.
- **Stesichorus:** A sixth-century lyric poet whose works tell the stories of Thebes and Troy.

ROMAN CONTRIBUTORS

Although much of Roman mythology was taken from the Greeks—just a few names changed here and there—the Romans had their own mythology as well. The following writers helped make that mythology known to us today:

- **Horace:** A great lyric poet whose works *Odes* and *Epodes* deal with both Greek and Roman mythology.
- **Livy:** A historian whose *History of Rome* relates Roman history and legends.
- **Propertius:** A poet who wrote elegies and mythological poetry.
- **Seneca:** A tragedian who dramatized Greek mythological characters.
- **Statius:** An epic poet who is best known for *Thebaid*, which relates the conflict between Oedipus's sons Polynices and Eteocles as they struggle for control over Thebes.

CHAPTER 3

OUT OF CHAOS: CREATION

 here did humans come from? How was the world created? And what existed before the universe came into being? These are eternal questions that every culture has asked. Classical mythology had its own answers to these questions, creation myths about how the universe came into being, how order rose from disorder. This chapter tells you how it all began, emphasizing similarities and differences among the various creation myths.

IN THE BEGINNING WAS CHAOS

Today, numerous theories, based in religion and science alike, exist about how the universe was created. The ancients also wondered how the universe was created, and their attempts at explaining this creation formed the basis of various myths. One idea was constant, however: The universe emerged from chaos.

It may seem as though nothing good could come from chaos, but it does make sense. Before you can recognize and appreciate order, you have to understand disorder. If chaos preceded creation, then creation is simply a process of imposing order upon disorder.

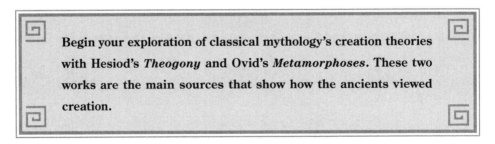

Begin your exploration of classical mythology's creation theories with Hesiod's *Theogony* and Ovid's *Metamorphoses*. These two works are the main sources that show how the ancients viewed creation.

NOTHING BUT CHAOS

Before there was Earth or sky or seas, all of the elements of the universe were one, and this oneness was called Chaos. Chaos was a shapeless void of confusion, but it held the seeds of an organized universe. Contained within Chaos the elements—earth, sky, sea—were jumbled together; no one element had an identity. Earth didn't have its shape, the sky didn't have air, and the sea was not watery.

The elements fought constantly until an unknown force put an end to the disorder. This force is not explicitly identified in the myths. Some consider it to be nature; others speak of it as a divine being or a god. Some myths leave out this force entirely, simply stating that the elements sprang from Chaos on their own. Regardless, the elements were separated—heaven from earth, sea from sky, heat from cold, and so on—and this separation imposed the order needed to create the universe.

OUTLINING THE ELEMENTS

Once separated, the elements still needed shape and definition. According to one popular myth, an unnamed force (some call it the Creator) first gave shape to Earth. The Creator designated water to its appropriate places: marshes, rivers, oceans, brooks, lakes, and seas. He then raised the mountains, smoothed out the plains, and shoveled out the valleys, distributing forests, rocky terrain, and fertile fields.

Next came the sky. The Creator spread out the air like a blank canvas on which to paint a masterpiece. He added clouds, thunder, lightning, and winds. The stars, however, he drew from the confines of darkness.

After setting up the sky and Earth, the Creator added a few more things. This is when the fish came to the seas, the birds to the air, and beasts to land. Not all of the beasts were created at this time—humanity still did not exist. (You'll read more on the creation of people in a later section.)

GIVING PERSONALITY TO NATURE

This account is one of the more popular creation myths, but another version exists in which the elements were born into existence as living beings. The ancients believed that anything that could move and change must be alive. So the elements of the universe were thought to be living—and because they lived, they must also have names and personalities.

BACK TO THE BEGINNING

Again, everything began with Chaos. But from there, this creation myth, taken from Hesiod's *Theogony*, tells a different story. This myth does not posit a Creator; instead, the first elements simply sprang into being on their own.

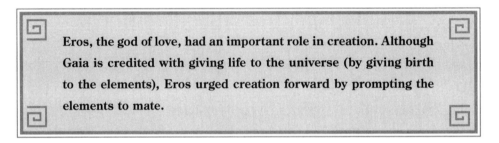

Eros, the god of love, had an important role in creation. Although Gaia is credited with giving life to the universe (by giving birth to the elements), Eros urged creation forward by prompting the elements to mate.

From Chaos came the five elements: Gaia (Earth), Tartarus (the Underworld), Nyx (Night), Erebus (Darkness), and Eros (Love). All on her own (that is, without mating), Gaia gave birth to three children: Uranus (Sky), Pontus (Sea), and Ourea (the Mountains). After these three children were born, creation continued.

THE UNIONS

Uranus, said to have been born to Gaia in her sleep, mated with his mother to create the rest of Earth's elements, such as the waters, forests, and beasts. (Incest is a recurrent theme throughout classical mythology.) Uranus and Gaia also produced other children, including the Titans and Titanesses, the three Cyclopes, and the Hecatoncheires (hundred-armed giants). You'll read about these offspring in Chapter 4.

Nyx mated with Erebus to produce Hemera (Day) and Aether (Air). Nyx also bore several other children, although the myths don't say who fathered them. These children were Thanatos (Death), Hypnos (Sleep), Moros (Doom), Nemesis (Retribution), Oizys (Pain), Momus (Sarcasm), Eris (Strife), the Keres (the female spirits of death), Geras (Old Age), Oneiroi (Dreams), and the Moirai (Fates, although some myths say that Themis [Necessity] gave birth to the Fates on her own or with Zeus as their father).

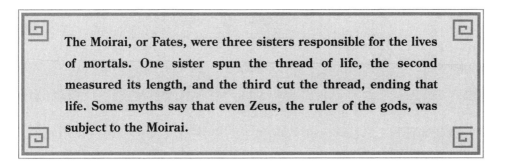

The Moirai, or Fates, were three sisters responsible for the lives of mortals. One sister spun the thread of life, the second measured its length, and the third cut the thread, ending that life. Some myths say that even Zeus, the ruler of the gods, was subject to the Moirai.

In this myth, creation proceeds through a series of generations; those beings created in one generation give birth to the next—and on it goes. With each birth, a little more order and detail is added to the universe.

AND THEN THERE WAS MAN

So far, both myths discussed have set the stage for the creation of humanity. The ancient myths vary on exactly how people were created. This section looks at two of the most popular theories.

One myth, popular with Greeks and Romans alike, states that man simply sprang up from the earth. Remember the seeds of the universe buried in Chaos? This myth contains a similar idea about humanity: The seeds of man were buried in the earth. These seeds produced men, who were considered the children of Gaia.

Another myth held that Prometheus created man. Prometheus was a Titan (Chapter 4 tells more about the Titans) and one of Gaia's many grandchildren. Prometheus and his brother Epimetheus were given the tasks of creating man and giving protection to the other beasts. Epimetheus took it upon himself to present the beasts with gifts of preservation and protection: He gave turtles their shells, leopards their spots, bears their claws, and so on.

Prometheus created man, using clay and water as his materials. He fashioned the form of man in the likeness of the gods. But Prometheus's first attempt would not be recognizable as a human today. Humans went through several prototypes before Prometheus was satisfied with his creation.

PROMETHEUS AND THE GIFT OF FIRE

Epimetheus did such a good job of distributing gifts that by the time he was finished with his task, all the gifts of protection had been given out. But Epimetheus had forgotten humanity. There was nothing left to give man for his protection.

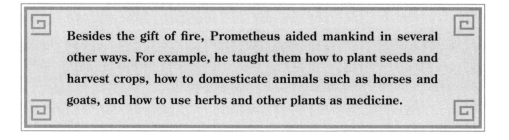

Besides the gift of fire, Prometheus aided mankind in several other ways. For example, he taught them how to plant seeds and harvest crops, how to domesticate animals such as horses and goats, and how to use herbs and other plants as medicine.

Prometheus decided that man also needed a gift of protection, one that went beyond the others—and that gift was fire. But Zeus, ruler of the gods, was angry with humankind and refused to share fire with them. Prometheus was adamant, however, and decided to steal fire from the heavens. According to one account, he stole fire from the forge of Hephaestus, the smith of the gods. Another account states that he stole the fire from the wheels of the chariot of Helios (the sun) and hid it in the stalk of a fennel plant. However he stole it, Prometheus then gave the gift of fire to mankind.

One night, Zeus looked down upon Earth and saw it shining with firelight, and his fury shook the heavens. He ordered his servants to seize Prometheus and chain him to a rock, far from his beloved humans. Zeus then sent an eagle to devour Prometheus's liver. Because Prometheus was immortal, his liver grew back each night, and each day the eagle returned to torment him again. Zeus vowed never to release Prometheus from his punishment.

WELCOMING THE WOMAN

Zeus was unhappy with the strength men had gained from Prometheus's gift of fire. So he devised a scheme to inflict a powerful weakness upon men. Enter the woman. Until this time, according to the myths, mortal women did not exist.

Zeus ordered Hephaestus to fashion a woman from clay and water. The result was the greatest sculpture ever created. Just as man had been molded in the image of the gods, woman was molded in the image of the goddesses. As if this weren't enough, every deity contributed to Hephaestus's creation. Woman was given beauty, along with lust, splendid clothes, lustrous jewelry, and the gifts of music, grace, dexterity, and charm. In addition, woman was given the arts of seduction, deceit, and guile. These traits combined to create a dangerous temptress that man would be unable to resist. Her name was Pandora.

PANDORA'S BOX

As his gift to mankind, Zeus ordered Hermes, the messenger of the gods, to deliver Pandora to Epimetheus. Awestruck by her beauty and charm, Epimetheus accepted Pandora as his bride, even though his brother Prometheus had warned him to not accept gifts from Zeus.

The ancient myths vary in the telling of Pandora's Box. One myth says that the gods gave Pandora a sealed jar and told her it was a gift to man. They did not tell her, however, what the jar held, and it wasn't long before her curiosity got the better of her. Pandora opened the jar and out flew the plagues of mankind: disease, pain, sorrow, insanity, envy, and death. Hastily replacing the lid, Pandora trapped hope, which was all that remained in the jar.

Another myth states that all the evils of the world were kept in a jar or box in the house of Epimetheus (whether this container belonged to Epimetheus or Prometheus is unknown). Overcome by curiosity, Pandora snuck into the room and removed the lid. Again, out poured all the ills of mankind, leaving behind only hope, which did not escape.

Still other versions of Pandora's myth say that the box contained only good things: blessings that were a wedding present from Zeus. In these versions, Pandora's curiosity again overcame her and she opened the box carelessly. All of the blessings escaped and returned to the heavens, except for hope. With the loss of most of the blessings, humanity had to endure all the hardships and evils of the world with only hope as a consolation.

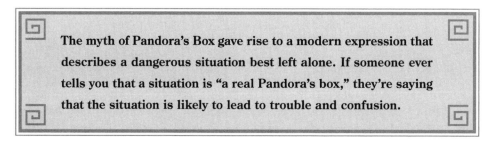

The myth of Pandora's Box gave rise to a modern expression that describes a dangerous situation best left alone. If someone ever tells you that a situation is "a real Pandora's box," they're saying that the situation is likely to lead to trouble and confusion.

Whichever version of her myth you prefer, Pandora's curiosity left humanity virtually defenseless against the difficulties that plague human life—and so Zeus got his revenge.

SUN, MOON, AND DAWN

You may have noticed that certain elements of the universe haven't been accounted for yet. For example, there is day, but no sun; there is night, but no moon. These deities did not appear among the original offspring; they came later, born of the Titans. Chapter 4 discusses the Titans, but the sun, the moon, and the dawn are necessary elements of an ordered universe, so this section explores their myths.

THE SUN

Helios, god of the sun, was considered a lesser god. Even so, the other deities held him in great esteem. Helios was a handsome god who was responsible for giving daylight to Earth by driving his chariot of fire, pulled by four flaming steeds, across the sky from east to west. Night would fall as Helios crossed the western horizon, and it lasted as long as it took him to return to the East. Later myths claim that Helios made his way back to the East in a huge golden cup that floated along the river Oceanus, which encircled the world.

Although Helios was admired, he was also feared. No one, mortal or immortal, could escape his eye during the day. As he crossed the sky, he looked down upon the world and saw everything. To make matters worse, Helios was a something of a gossip; he rarely kept what he saw to himself.

THE MOON

Selene, the moon, was Helios's sister. She also drove a chariot across the sky, though hers was made of silver and pulled by two horses. Selene was responsible for moonlight that shone through the night.

Not much else is known about Selene. The myths state that she was beautiful and famous for her love affairs. It was said that Pan, god of shepherds and flocks, tried to seduce her with either a beautiful fleece or a herd of white oxen—the myths vary. Selene also had an affair with Zeus, bearing him a daughter named Pandia.

Selene's most famous love affair was with Endymion, who may have been a shepherd, a hunter, or even a king. All versions of this myth agree, however, that Endymion was extremely handsome. Selene looked down upon him as he slept and fell instantly in love. She descended from the heavens and made love to him in his dreams. Some myths claim she bore him fifty daughters. At Selene's request, Zeus offered Endymion one wish. He wished for eternal youth—and some say for eternal sleep, as well, so he could continue to experience his amorous dreams—and was granted both sleep and immortality.

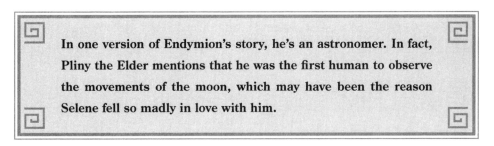

In one version of Endymion's story, he's an astronomer. In fact, Pliny the Elder mentions that he was the first human to observe the movements of the moon, which may have been the reason Selene fell so madly in love with him.

THE DAWN

Eos, the dawn, was Helios's other sister. Every morning, Eos would rise from her golden throne, open the gates of heaven, and announce the coming of the sun. She also accompanied Helios in his journey across the sky. Some myths say she rode alongside him in his chariot of fire; others say she rode in her own chariot in front of Helios, announcing his arrival all day long.

Eos's love life was even more famous than that of her sister, Selene. It would take hours to relate the tales of all her lovers. Eos's many unions resulted in some well-known children. She was the mother of the Winds: Boreas (North), Notus (South), and Zephyrus (West). She also gave birth to Eosphorus (the Morning Star) and all the other stars in the heavens.

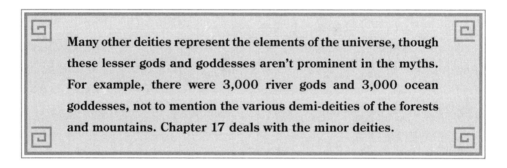

Many other deities represent the elements of the universe, though these lesser gods and goddesses aren't prominent in the myths. For example, there were 3,000 river gods and 3,000 ocean goddesses, not to mention the various demi-deities of the forests and mountains. Chapter 17 deals with the minor deities.

THE WORLD AND HUMANITY'S PLACE IN IT

This chapter began with some fundamental questions about how the world was created and how humans came to inhabit it. The ancients understood creation as a movement from chaos to order, and they saw humanity as a part of creation that could challenge the gods. (Why else would Zeus be so angry with Prometheus and scheme to weaken his creation?)

Every religion has a creation story, and many of these stories have striking similarities from one culture to another. For example, as you were reading the story of Pandora, did the biblical Eve ever cross your mind?

CHAPTER 4

THE CHILDREN
OF MOTHER EARTH

**A**s you learned in Chapter 3, Gaia (Earth) was one of the first beings to emerge from Chaos. Gaia was a powerful goddess. In some myths, she was the original power behind the oracle at Delphi, and an oath sworn to Gaia was absolutely binding. Above all else, though, Gaia was a mother—the original Earth Mother. This chapter tells about the children of Mother Earth and their respective roles in classical mythology.

CHILDREN OF PONTUS

As you recall, Gaia spontaneously gave birth to three children, without mating. One of these was Pontus, the Sea. Gaia mated with Pontus, and their union produced five children: Ceto, Eurybia, Nereus, Phorcys, and Thaumas.

CETO

Ceto was the deity of large marine beasts. The Greeks use her name informally to refer to sea monsters, and in English *cetology* is the study of whales and dolphins. Ceto married her brother, Phorcys. Together they produced several children:

- **The Graeae:** These three daughters were born old and never had a chance to enjoy the freshness of youth. *Graeae* means "old women" or "gray ones." Their individual names were Deino (Dread), Enyo (Horror), and Pemphredo (Alarm). The myths always portrayed these sisters together—and they weren't what most people would call attractive. Between them they had only one eye and one tooth, which they shared in turns. They lived in darkness away from the sunlight (some myths say they lived in a deep cave).

- **The Gorgons:** These three daughters were even less alluring than their sisters. They were monsters with snakes for hair, tusks, bronze claws, wings, and a stare that could turn men to stone. Mortals and immortals alike feared these creatures. Only two of the Gorgons—Euryale and Sthenno—were immortal. The third and most familiar Gorgon, Medusa, was mortal. (Medusa appears in the myth of Perseus in Chapter 19.)

- **The Hesperides:** These daughters were nymphs, female spirits usually associated with a particular place. Their number varies from myth to myth (as do their parents), but most often there are three Hesperides: Aegle, Erythia, and Hesperarethusa. The Hesperides were beautiful and had the gift of song. They lived in the idyllic Garden of the Hesperides, protecting a tree with golden apples that belonged to the goddess Hera.

- **Ladon:** This son was a snakelike dragon (who, according to some myths, had a hundred heads). Ladon lived with his sisters in the Garden of the Hesperides, where he coiled around the apple tree, guarding its golden apples. After his death, Ladon was turned into a great constellation of stars.

- **Echidna:** This daughter had the body and face of a beautiful woman, but instead of legs she had a serpent's tail. She gave birth to some of the most terrifying monsters in classical mythology, including Cerberus, the Sphinx, Chimaera, the Hydra, and the Nemean Lion. (Chapter 18 gives you the gory details about many of these monsters.) Echidna also is said to have lain in wait for people passing through her territory, eager to attack and devour them.

EURYBIA

Mythology doesn't say much about this daughter of Gaia and Pontus. Most myths involving Eurybia simply mention her as the wife of Crius (a Titan) and the mother of three Titan sons: Astraeus, Pallas, and Perses. Astraeus would later father the winds and the stars; Pallas would become the father of Victory, Valor, and Strength; and Perses would father Hecate, a triple goddess you will get to know better in Chapter 17.

NEREUS

Nereus, a marine deity, was sometimes known as the Old Man of the Sea. Although you may think of Poseidon as the Greeks' sea god, Nereus had the title first, before Poseidon was born. Nereus was a shapeshifter—able to take on various forms—and had the gift of prophecy. He is best known as the father of the sea goddesses called the Nereids.

PHORCYS

Like his brother Nereus, Phorcys was a sea deity. In art, he appears as a man with a fish tail, crab claws for legs, and spiky red skin. As mentioned earlier in this chapter, Phorcys had several children with his sister Ceto. Some myths also claim that he was the father of the Sirens, sea deities that were half-woman, half-bird. He is also named as the father of Scylla, the famous sea monster.

THAUMAS

Thaumas, another sea deity, is known only for the children he sired. He married Electra (an ocean deity) and was the father of Iris and the Harpies. Iris, personification of the rainbow, served the Olympian gods and goddesses as a messenger. The Harpies were birdlike women who carried off the souls of the dead. They were also blamed for anything that had gone missing, including children.

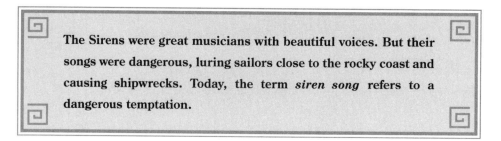

The Sirens were great musicians with beautiful voices. But their songs were dangerous, luring sailors close to the rocky coast and causing shipwrecks. Today, the term *siren song* refers to a dangerous temptation.

THE HUNDRED-HANDED ONES

In her work of creation, Gaia also mated with her other son, Uranus (Sky). The first children born to Gaia and Uranus were the Hecatoncheires, whose name means "hundred-handed ones." There were three Hecatoncheires—named Cottus, Briareus (or Aegaeon), and Gyges (or Gyes)—and each had a hundred arms and fifty heads. These creatures are referred to as giants, although they differ from the giants of later myths.

The Hecatoncheires had incredible strength. For example, they could topple a mountain by bombarding it with boulders. Because of their outrageous strength, these creatures were feared—even by their own father, Uranus, ruler of the universe, who had them imprisoned in Tartarus (the Underworld). You'll read more about the Hecatoncheires later in this chapter.

ONE-EYED WONDERS

Next, Gaia gave birth to three Cyclopes, also sired by Uranus. Like the Hecatoncheires, the Cyclopes also were giants in stature and possessed great strength and dexterity. The Cyclopes were ugly and frightening to look at; each had only one eye, centered in his forehead. You may think of the Cyclopes as fearsome, man-eating monsters, and that is true in later myths. But these first Cyclopes, although bad-tempered, were not like that. Instead, they were known as the first smiths.

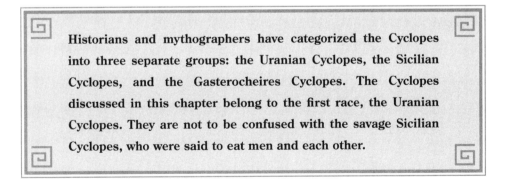

Historians and mythographers have categorized the Cyclopes into three separate groups: the Uranian Cyclopes, the Sicilian Cyclopes, and the Gasterocheires Cyclopes. The Cyclopes discussed in this chapter belong to the first race, the Uranian Cyclopes. They are not to be confused with the savage Sicilian Cyclopes, who were said to eat men and each other.

The three Cyclopes were considered storm deities: Brontes was known as Thunder or Thunderer; Arges was called the Shiner or Thunderbolt; and Steropes (sometimes Asteropes) had the nickname Lightning or Maker of Lightning. Uranus, fearing their strength, threw the Cyclopes into Tartarus, imprisoning them there with their brothers the Hecatoncheires.

TITANIC OFFSPRING

Next came the most famous of Gaia's children—the twelve Titans and Titanesses, six sons and six daughters. Although you have read about numerous deities so far, these beings weren't actually considered "gods" and "goddesses." They held power but as the personification of an element or a division of the universe. The Titans and Titanesses would become the first gods and goddesses. These six sons of Gaia and Uranus were the Titans:

- **Coeus:** Not much is known about Coeus except that he was the father of Leto, who became the mother of Apollo and Artemis.
- **Crius:** He was the father of Astraeus, Pallas, and Perses.
- **Cronus:** The youngest Titan, Cronus overthrew his father—more on this struggle later.
- **Hyperion:** The first god of the sun, Hyperion later sired Helios, who is the god most commonly associated with the sun.
- **Iapetus:** Best known as the father of Prometheus, the champion of mankind, he also sired Epimetheus, Menoetius, and Atlas.
- **Oceanus:** The eldest of the Titans, Oceanus was the god of rivers.

These six daughters were the Titanesses:

- **Mnemosyne:** The personification of memory, she gave birth to the Muses.
- **Phoebe:** The first goddess of the moon, Phoebe was the mother of Leto.

- **Rhea:** A mother deity or earth goddess, Rhea was called the Mother of the Gods because she gave birth to the Olympians (whom you'll read about in Chapter 5).
- **Tethys:** The first goddess of the sea, she gave birth to many children, including 3,000 daughters (yes, you read that right), called the Oceanids.
- **Theia:** This Titaness is best known for giving birth to Helios, Selene, and Eos, discussed in Chapter 3.
- **Themis:** Goddess of necessity, Themis was the mother of Prometheus, the Hours, and (according to some myths) the Fates.

URANUS OVERTHROWN

As you've read, Uranus was afraid of his children, the Hecatoncheires and the Cyclopes, and imprisoned them in Tartarus. His relationship with the Titans was also one of fear and conflict.

Uranus loved ruling the universe and feared anything that threatened his power—and he viewed his children as such threats. Therefore, he also decided to keep the Titans out of the way. Instead of imprisoning the Titans, however, Uranus tried to prevent them from being born by shoving each child back into Gaia's womb. He did this to all twelve of these children. Uranus, pleased with himself, was able to relax because he believed that his power was no longer threatened.

Not surprisingly, Gaia was unhappy with the pain inflicted upon her and with her children's predicament. She decided to take action against Uranus. Gaia made a sharp sickle out of either iron or flint and complained to her children, suggesting they rise up and punish Uranus for his mistreatment of the whole family. Afraid of their father, the Titans and Titanesses refused their mother's request. Gaia, however, did not give up. She kept complaining and cajoling until Cronus, the youngest Titan, agreed to get revenge upon Uranus. Gaia smiled upon this favored son and told him her plan.

Cronus lay in wait that night, armed with the sickle his mother had made. Uranus began to make love to Gaia. Cronus, wasting no time, grabbed his father's genitals and sliced them off with the sickle. He tossed the severed organ from the heavens into the sea.

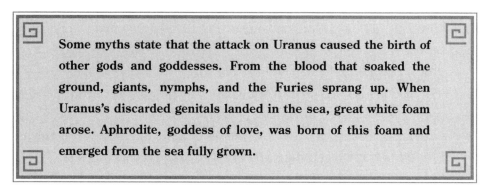

Some myths state that the attack on Uranus caused the birth of other gods and goddesses. From the blood that soaked the ground, giants, nymphs, and the Furies sprang up. When Uranus's discarded genitals landed in the sea, great white foam arose. Aphrodite, goddess of love, was born of this foam and emerged from the sea fully grown.

After this incident, Uranus seems to drop out of the picture. He was no longer worshiped or honored with sacrifice, and he held no power.

CRONUS CROWNED AS RULER

With the defeat of Uranus, the Titans, Titanesses, Cyclopes, and Hecatoncheires were all freed. Cronus took his place as ruler of the universe and married his sister Rhea. Unfortunately, despite the injustice he'd suffered from Uranus, Cronus also fell victim to a lust for power.

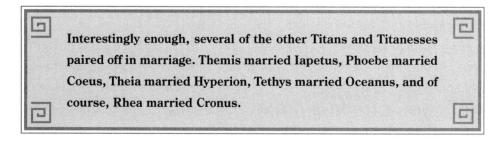

Interestingly enough, several of the other Titans and Titanesses paired off in marriage. Themis married Iapetus, Phoebe married Coeus, Theia married Hyperion, Tethys married Oceanus, and of course, Rhea married Cronus.

No sooner had the Hecatoncheires and the Cyclopes been freed than they were once again imprisoned in Tartarus by Cronus. He feared these giants as his father had. However, he allowed his brothers and sisters, the Titans and Titanesses, to keep their freedom.

LIKE FATHER, LIKE SON

Cronus was every bit as power-hungry as his father had been. As a result, he was not a very good ruler and was a terrible father. Cronus had heard a prophecy that one of his children would overthrow him. So he devised a scheme to prevent his own children from ever challenging him.

Cronus remembered that his mother had planned and initiated the overthrow of Uranus. But he also realized that Gaia probably wouldn't have called for this revenge if she had not been so burdened by the children in her womb. So Cronus decided to remove the threat of his children himself.

Every year for five years, Rhea gave birth to a child. As soon as the child left her womb, it went straight into the mouth of Cronus. Instead of trying to hold the children inside their mother's body, Cronus literally took them into his own, by swallowing them whole.

Rhea was overcome with grief and rage. She couldn't stand to have her children taken away from her so soon after their birth. Cronus had underestimated a mother's love for her children and her natural instinct to protect them. Rhea's maternal feelings became the driving force behind her own scheme of revenge.

When Rhea conceived her sixth child, she asked her mother for help. Gaia sent her to the island of Crete, where she gave birth to Zeus. Rhea returned to Cronus after the child was born but left Zeus behind. She tricked her husband by wrapping a large stone in swaddling cloths and telling Cronus it was Zeus. Cronus swallowed the stone, believing it was his sixth child. Meanwhile, the real Zeus remained unharmed.

ZEUS'S CHILDHOOD

Zeus was left in the care of Gaia. The Curetes (minor gods) and the Nymphs (nature goddesses) helped care for the infant. The Curetes would mimic the rituals of the Cretan youths by performing dances and clashing their weapons together. Their racket hid the cries of the baby Zeus so his father would not discover him.

Like any other baby, Zeus needed nourishment. The nymph Amalthea was responsible for feeding Zeus and suckled him through his infancy. Some myths say that Amalthea was a she-goat and that Zeus was extremely grateful to her. When Amalthea died, Zeus showed his appreciation by turning Amalthea into the constellation known as Capricorn (the goat). He also used her skin to create a shield that he carried into battle.

Zeus was well cared for as he grew into adulthood. A strong, healthy young man, Zeus prepared to fulfill the prophecy and overthrow his father. He left Crete and visited his cousin, Metis, an Oceanid who was the daughter of Tethys and Oceanus. Metis, well known for her wisdom, agreed to help Zeus. She advised him to become a servant of Cronus and, in that position, to place a potion in his drink. Zeus did as he was told. The potion caused Cronus to vomit—and out came Zeus's brothers and sisters, whole and unharmed.

THE BATTLE WITH THE TITANS

With his rescued siblings, Zeus had the beginnings of an army with which to challenge Cronus. However, Cronus had some difficulty in assembling his own forces. Some of the Titans refused to help him in the struggle. None of the Titanesses participated, and Oceanus, Cronus's brother, also refused to fight. Similarly, Helios, son of Hyperion, refused to take part in the war. Prometheus and Epimetheus, sons of Iapetus, blatantly refused to pledge loyalty to Cronus; rather, they eventually sided with Zeus's army. The remaining Titans chose Atlas, another son of Iapetus, to lead them into battle.

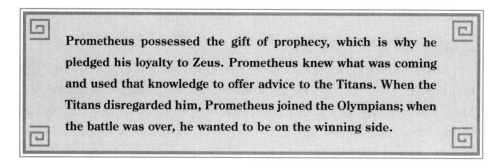

Prometheus possessed the gift of prophecy, which is why he pledged his loyalty to Zeus. Prometheus knew what was coming and used that knowledge to offer advice to the Titans. When the Titans disregarded him, Prometheus joined the Olympians; when the battle was over, he wanted to be on the winning side.

In preparation for war, each side created fortifications. Led by Atlas, the Titans gathered at Mount Othrys; the children of Cronus, under Zeus, gathered at Mount Olympus.

The war was a monumental conflict. The Titans were awesome creatures who possessed considerable strength. The children of Cronus were just as strong and cunning. The two sides met on the battlefield every day for ten long years, each side winning some battles and losing others. After ten years, however, the war was no closer to a decisive victory. So Gaia, who knew a thing or two about overthrowing one's father, interceded and advised Zeus.

Gaia told Zeus that freeing the Cyclopes and Hecatoncheires from Tartarus would gain the Olympians some very powerful allies. Zeus wasted no time. He ventured into the depths of the Underworld and faced Campe, a monster appointed by Cronus to guard the giants. Zeus slew Campe and freed his uncles. As Gaia had predicted, the Hecatoncheires and the Cyclopes were so angry with Cronus for his treatment of them that they joined forces with the Olympians.

With these giants newly recruited to Zeus's army, the tide of the war began to turn. The Cyclopes built impressive weapons, including lightning, thunder, earthquake, a trident, and a helmet of invisibility. The Hecatoncheires threw great boulders at the Titans' fort, weakening it.

Zeus laid siege to Mount Othrys. But strength alone would not win the war, so he devised a plan to force Cronus's army to surrender. Using the helmet of invisibility, one of the Olympians walked into the camp unnoticed and stole all of Cronus's weapons. Another Olympian distracted Cronus with the trident while Zeus shot lightning bolts. Meanwhile, the Cyclopes and Hecatoncheires rained boulders down upon the Titans. Zeus's strategy succeeded, and the war that had nearly destroyed the universe was finally over.

ZEUS TAKES CHARGE

When Zeus became the new ruler, his first task was to dispose of his enemies. The army of Cronus was imprisoned in Tartarus with the Hecatoncheires standing guard to ensure they would not escape.

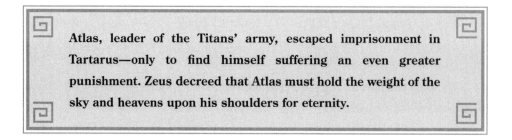

Atlas, leader of the Titans' army, escaped imprisonment in Tartarus—only to find himself suffering an even greater punishment. Zeus decreed that Atlas must hold the weight of the sky and heavens upon his shoulders for eternity.

Zeus was harsh in punishing his enemies and generous in rewarding his allies. The Titanesses, who did not participate in the war, were allowed to retain their power and their positions in the heavens. Zeus also restored the powers of any immortal who had supported him and had been dispossessed by Cronus. And of course, his brothers and sisters received their own rights and powers. In the next chapter, you'll get to know these Olympians.

CHAPTER 5

INTRODUCING
THE OLYMPIANS

he conflict between Zeus and Cronus had shaken the heavens and Earth. Now that the battle was won, a new generation rose to power: the Olympians. These are the familiar gods and goddesses whose exploits run through classical mythology. The reign of the Olympians stabilized the universe, but their rule was anything but boring. These gods and goddesses had strong personalities and were governed by strong emotions. Here, you'll meet the mighty Olympians.

THE ORIGINAL SIX

As you've read, Cronus lost his power after being overthrown by his own children. With the defeat of Cronus, however, this family conflict ended. The children of Cronus united, dividing their realm among them. They agreed, however, that they needed a supreme ruler and unanimously chose Zeus. The following sections introduce the six original Olympian gods and goddesses.

THE BROTHERS

After the fall of Cronus, his three sons—Zeus, Poseidon, and Hades—divided the dominions. To be fair, they drew lots. The three realms up for grabs were the heavens, the seas, and the land of the dead. (Mount Olympus would remain the realm of all the gods, with no one god having control.)

Zeus drew the heavens, which made him the ruler of the gods and the heavens both. Depictions of Zeus often show him as wearing a helmet, wielding one of his thunderbolts, and protected by the aegis (a breastplate or shield). He is also often accompanied by an eagle, an attendant that symbolizes his power.

Poseidon drew the seas as his realm. In the myths, Poseidon often appears as a violent god, associated with savage sea storms and earthquakes. He is depicted as tall with a long, flowing beard, and wielding his trident, which was one of the weapons made by the Cyclopes during the war against Cronus. He may be pictured with seashells or various kinds of sea creatures. Poseidon was also associated with horses; the ancients imagined rearing horses in the mighty waves that crashed into the shore.

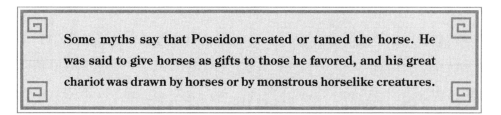

Some myths say that Poseidon created or tamed the horse. He was said to give horses as gifts to those he favored, and his great chariot was drawn by horses or by monstrous horselike creatures.

The third brother, Hades, drew the Underworld, land of the dead. The Greek Underworld is not the same as the Christian concept of hell, nor was Hades considered evil or satanic. In Greek mythology, Hades appears as a loner uninterested in the world of the living. He is often depicted holding a key, signifying his status as the god who keeps the dead locked away from the world of the living. Like Poseidon, Hades was associated with horses; some myths say that Hades, not Poseidon, created the horse.

THE SISTERS

Zeus's sisters did not participate in the drawing of lots, but they had their own powers. The realms governed by Hera, Hestia, and Demeter were essential to an orderly universe.

Hera was the greatest of the Greek goddesses. As Zeus's sister and wife, she was queen of the heavens. Jealous and vindictive, Hera possessed both a quick temper and fearsome passion. She was the protector of wives, defender of marriage, and a goddess of childbirth. Her depictions emphasize her queenly stature: She appears as tall and stately, wielding a scepter. Her bird was the peacock.

Hestia, goddess of hearth and home, does not appear in many surviving myths. Despite this, she is thought to have been held sacred and worshiped in every ancient household. Hestia was closely associated with virginity.

Demeter's name means "Mother Earth." Don't confuse her with Gaia, however. Gaia was Earth itself. Her granddaughter Demeter had dominion over the fruits of the earth, the power of fertility, and agriculture. Demeter loved to be close to the soil. Whereas her sister Hestia never left Mount Olympus, Demeter rarely stayed there, preferring to spend time on Earth. Demeter is often shown seated and may be depicted with a torch or sheaves of grain. Her bird was the crane, her animal the serpent.

A DOZEN DISTINGUISHED DEITIES

These six gods and goddesses were the original Olympians, but they were only half the story. There were twelve great Olympians in all, each playing an important role in the order of the universe. This section introduces the second six.

ARES

Ares, god of war, lived for battle and bloodshed, deriving great pleasure from human warfare. Ares appears in many poems and myths and was worshiped in Sparta, particularly before a battle was to take place.

Depictions of Ares show him wearing armor and a helmet and carrying a spear, sword, and shield. He was associated with the dog and the vulture. Although he was the war god, Ares was not always victorious. In fact, he was defeated in battle several times throughout the myths.

ATHENA

As the goddess of wisdom, Athena was held in high regard by mortal and immortal alike. She was also the goddess of war, crafts, and skills. Unlike Ares, however, Athena was not bloodthirsty. She preferred peace to war. Even so, when she was involved in battle, she proved herself to be an invincible strategist, dominating the field.

Athena usually appears dressed in armor, helmet, and aegis. She wields a spear and a shield. She is associated with the owl (which symbolizes wisdom), and an owl often perches on her shoulder.

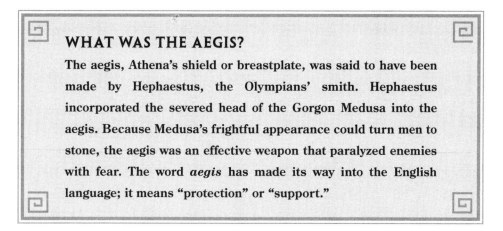

WHAT WAS THE AEGIS?

The aegis, Athena's shield or breastplate, was said to have been made by Hephaestus, the Olympians' smith. Hephaestus incorporated the severed head of the Gorgon Medusa into the aegis. Because Medusa's frightful appearance could turn men to stone, the aegis was an effective weapon that paralyzed enemies with fear. The word *aegis* has made its way into the English language; it means "protection" or "support."

ARTEMIS

As goddess of the hunt, Artemis had little interest in anything besides the thrill of the chase. She roamed the mountains with a band of nymphs, hunting animals (and sometimes men). Although her primary activity was hunting, Artemis was also the protector of children, wild animals, and the weak. Legend has it that her arrows could cause sudden death without pain. You wouldn't want to get on her bad side, though—Artemis could be a vindictive and vengeful goddess.

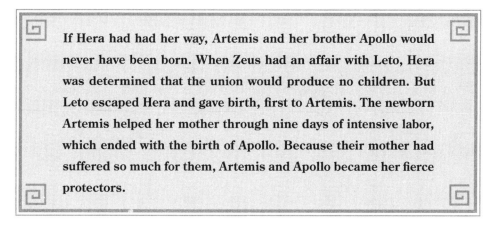

If Hera had had her way, Artemis and her brother Apollo would never have been born. When Zeus had an affair with Leto, Hera was determined that the union would produce no children. But Leto escaped Hera and gave birth, first to Artemis. The newborn Artemis helped her mother through nine days of intensive labor, which ended with the birth of Apollo. Because their mother had suffered so much for them, Artemis and Apollo became her fierce protectors.

Artemis is usually depicted carrying her weapon of choice: a bow and arrows. Some myths describe her as a girl-child—a virgin with eternal youth—who was as wild as the animals she both hunted and protected. As all wild animals were within her domain, she was not associated with one animal in particular, although she often appears with a stag or a hunting dog.

APOLLO

Apollo, Artemis's twin brother, was the god of archery, music, and poetry. While his sister lived only for the hunt, Apollo was a versatile god who enjoyed a great many things. At times, he was a shepherd or a cowherd; at other times he was a great musician. Apollo was also important to prophecy and medicine. He had the ability to inflict illness as well as to cure it.

Because Apollo dabbled in so many arts, there isn't a single typical depiction of him. You might see him playing his lyre, shooting an arrow, or driving a chariot. One constant in all depictions of Apollo, though, is his great beauty, which was considered ideal. Apollo was associated with several different animals—including the wolf, deer, dolphin, crow, vulture, and swan—and he was also associated with the laurel tree (Chapter 13 explains why).

HERMES

Hermes was the god of commerce, travel, and athletics. He brought luck to people, guided travelers and merchants, and protected rogues and thieves. Hermes was an active god, renowned for his agility and athleticism. He was one of the few gods who could enter the Underworld and leave it again without deterrence. He's probably best known, however, as the messenger of the gods.

Hermes is normally shown wearing a winged hat and winged sandals, which symbolize his swiftness (a good trait in a messenger). He is also sometimes shown carrying either a golden herald's wand or a staff with two serpents' heads. Hermes was a trickster who could be mischievous but who also had a kind heart.

APHRODITE

Nearly everyone has heard of Aphrodite—the goddess of love. (You may know her as Venus, which was her Roman name.) Some myths present Aphrodite as a flaky, somewhat ridiculous character; others describe her as a generous and benevolent goddess, due the same reverence as the other Olympians. Regardless of her character, Aphrodite was always passionate.

Aphrodite was a great beauty, with a sweet and seductive smile. Her myths almost always involve love affairs: Either she's having affairs of her own, or she's meddling in those of others. This goddess was associated with the dove, and her plants were the rose and myrtle.

HEPHAESTUS

Hephaestus was Aphrodite's husband. You might assume that the goddess of love would be married to a handsome, charming husband. But that wasn't the case among the Olympians. In fact, Hephaestus, son of Zeus and Hera, was thrown out of heaven at his birth because of his ugliness and deformities. (If you're wondering how this god ended up with the beautiful Aphrodite, see Chapter 15, which tells the story of their marriage.)

As the god of fire, smithing, craftsmanship, and metalworking, Hephaestus erected great palaces for the gods and goddesses and made armor for those he favored. A skilled craftsman, he could build just about anything. Hephaestus is associated with volcanoes, which were thought to be his workshops.

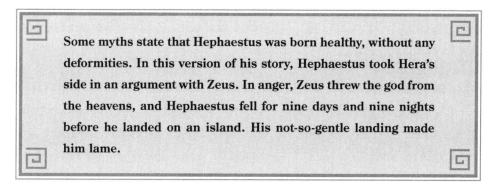

Some myths state that Hephaestus was born healthy, without any deformities. In this version of his story, Hephaestus took Hera's side in an argument with Zeus. In anger, Zeus threw the god from the heavens, and Hephaestus fell for nine days and nine nights before he landed on an island. His not-so-gentle landing made him lame.

DIONYSUS

Dionysus was the god of the vine, wine, and revelry. Whereas most of the Olympians snubbed mortals, Dionysus mingled directly with his mortal followers. His religious festivals often turned into rites of ecstasy.

Dionysus's greatest gift to humanity was the gift of wine, which could provide relief from a person's burdens, if only for a while. However, Dionysus was sometimes cruel—as all gods could be. Those who opposed him felt his wrath, as you'll read in Chapter 16. Dionysus is most often associated with grapevines, dance, music, wine, madness, and sex.

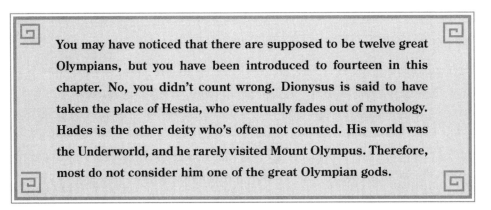

You may have noticed that there are supposed to be twelve great Olympians, but you have been introduced to fourteen in this chapter. No, you didn't count wrong. Dionysus is said to have taken the place of Hestia, who eventually fades out of mythology. Hades is the other deity who's often not counted. His world was the Underworld, and he rarely visited Mount Olympus. Therefore, most do not consider him one of the great Olympian gods.

MOUNT OLYMPUS

Mount Olympus, home to the Olympian gods and goddesses, is described only vaguely in classical mythology. Some myths state that it was a mountain higher than any other on Earth. In these accounts, Mount Olympus has several peaks, each home to a different deity, with Zeus residing on the topmost peak. Other myths refer to Mount Olympus as part of the heavens and not on Earth at all.

Regardless of its exact location, Mount Olympus was a magnificent place, clearly fit for the gods. Beyond the entranceway of clouds were several luxurious palaces and halls, built by Hephaestus, where the Olympians lived and held parties.

For the most part, life on Mount Olympus was easy and peaceful. The gods and goddesses lounged around, feasting on ambrosia and drinking nectar while listening to music and watching graceful dances. Mount Olympus was untouched by the natural disasters and inconveniences that afflicted Earth such as thunderstorms, snow, rough winds, earthquakes, hailstorms, and tornadoes. The atmosphere was one of pleasure and peace, making the inhabitants peaceful (well, most of the time).

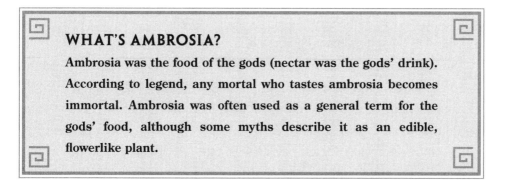

WHAT'S AMBROSIA?

Ambrosia was the food of the gods (nectar was the gods' drink). According to legend, any mortal who tastes ambrosia becomes immortal. Ambrosia was often used as a general term for the gods' food, although some myths describe it as an edible, flowerlike plant.

Mount Olympus was more than the dwelling place of the gods and goddesses. It was also their command center, the place where trials were held, laws were created, and important decisions were made.

LAW AND ORDER, OLYMPIAN STYLE

As ruler of gods and men, Zeus had the duty of bringing ultimate order to the universe. An order of sorts had already been established—the universe had come a long way from the chaos that had preceded it—but Zeus wanted to refine this order further.

Zeus made love to his aunt, Themis, who was the goddess of eternal order. Their union produced numerous daughters, including six who became the personifications of the principles needed to complete the ultimate order he desired. These daughters of Zeus and Themis were:

- **Atropos:** The Fate who was responsible for cutting the thread of life
- **Clotho:** The Fate who was responsible for spinning the thread of life
- **Dike:** The personification of justice
- **Eirene:** The personification of peace
- **Eunomia:** The personification of law and order
- **Lachesis:** The Fate who was responsible for measuring the thread of life

With universal order now established, it became Zeus's job to maintain that order, and he was fully capable of doing so. Zeus was known as a strict but fair ruler who firmly believed in justice.

Zeus did not allow his emotions or biases to affect his rule. If he felt he could not judge a matter impartially, he would either bring it before a council of other deities or find some other way (such as a contest) to determine the final outcome. For example, Zeus's brother Poseidon had a tendency to fight for land and often started battles with other gods and goddesses. Sometimes Zeus thought he could not decide impartially between his brother and, say, his daughter. Who would want to make such a choice? So Zeus would bring the matter before the council or create a contest whose winner could rightfully claim the land. Occasionally Zeus also used compromise to settle a dispute.

In matters of law, Zeus could be very wise. He did have his weaknesses, though—especially women. And some myths say that even though Zeus was supreme ruler, he did not have complete control. Remember his daughters the Fates? All of the gods—even the great Zeus himself—were subject to these three personifications of destiny.

MUTINY ON MOUNT OLYMPUS

You might think that the beauty, tranquility, and splendor of Mount Olympus would be enough to keep the peace. With the ascendancy of the Olympians, law and order were set, justice usually prevailed, and the universe was ruled with intelligence instead of by brute force. Despite this near-utopia, a rebellion was brewing among the gods—one that would threaten the power of Zeus.

A MOB IS ASSEMBLED

The rebellion on Mount Olympus began with three key figures: Athena, Hera, and Poseidon. (Several myths show Hera as the mastermind behind the scheme.) Each of these gods felt that he or she could rule better than Zeus, so they banded together to rally the other gods and goddesses against him. Except for Hestia, all of the other gods joined them.

As Zeus lay sleeping, the group chained him to his bed. They set his weapons out of reach and then congratulated each other on an easy and successful coup. However, their celebration was short-lived. Now that Zeus had been overwhelmed, who would take his place?

The Olympians began to argue, each convinced that he or she would make the best supreme ruler. Not one of the powerful deities was willing to back down. The argument continued for a long time, growing more heated as levels of frustration rose.

While the deities were preoccupied with their claims to power, Thetis, a sea goddess, came to Zeus's rescue. She ventured down to Tartarus and appealed to Briareus (one of the Hecatoncheires) for help; he consented and unchained Zeus. As you might imagine, Zeus was furious at the Olympians' actions. With Zeus free, they quickly backed down, not daring to challenge him face to face. Zeus reclaimed his position as supreme ruler and forced all Olympians to vow that they would never again challenge his power.

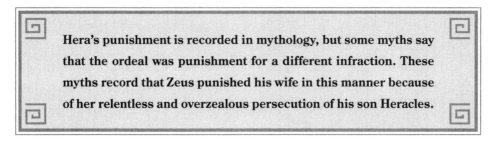

Hera's punishment is recorded in mythology, but some myths say that the ordeal was punishment for a different infraction. These myths record that Zeus punished his wife in this manner because of her relentless and overzealous persecution of his son Heracles.

HERA'S PUNISHMENT

Zeus, as lord of justice (and also out of revenge), decided to punish Hera for her insubordination. He had her suspended from the heavens by attaching chains to her wrists and anvils to her feet to weigh her down. After her eventual release, Hera never incited another rebellion.

WAR WITH THE GIANTS

Hera wasn't the only one who started a rebellion against Zeus. Gaia (Mother Earth) was terribly upset that her children, the Titans, were imprisoned in Tartarus. So she rallied the Giants to avenge them.

The Giants were a very powerful race, with human heads and torsos but legs made of serpents. They were huge and had wild, thick hair and beards, and they terrified everything that crossed their paths.

The Giants represented a serious challenge to the Olympians. Aside from their colossal power and strength, the Giants could not be killed by an immortal alone. Instead, an immortal and a mortal had to work together to slay a Giant. To make matters even more difficult, some myths say that a certain plant could make the Giants immune to mortals' attacks. Zeus caught wind of this and had the plant removed from the earth before the Giants could obtain it.

THE BATTLE BEGINS

The Giants initiated the battle by bombarding the heavens with boulders and flaming trees. Their actions certainly got the Olympians' attention. The gods quickly fought back, but because the Giants could not be killed, the Olympians struggled simply to hold their ground.

An oracle warned them that they needed the help of a mortal to win the war against the Giants. Zeus sent Athena to Earth to recruit Heracles, Zeus's son by a mortal woman. When Heracles entered the war, things started looking up for the Olympians. Athena and Heracles joined forces to bring down Alcyoneus, a leader of the Giants. While Athena attacked, Heracles shot the Giant with a poisoned arrow. Alcyoneus had special protection, however. He was immortal as long as he stood on his native soil. Therefore, Athena advised Heracles to drag the Giant outside of the boundaries of his land. Heracles did as he was told, and Alcyoneus died on the spot.

The next to fall was Alcyoneus's co-leader, Porphyrion. Porphyrion attacked Hera, meaning to kill her. Instead, Zeus filled him with lust for her, turning the Giant's desire to kill into sexual passion. With Hera as the decoy, Zeus hurled a thunderbolt at Porphyrion, while Heracles shot him with an arrow. Porphyrion dropped dead, and Hera remained unharmed.

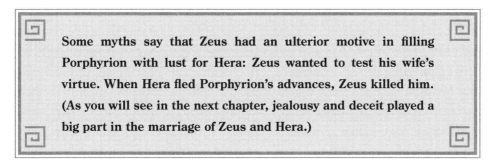

Some myths say that Zeus had an ulterior motive in filling Porphyrion with lust for Hera: Zeus wanted to test his wife's virtue. When Hera fled Porphyrion's advances, Zeus killed him. (As you will see in the next chapter, jealousy and deceit played a big part in the marriage of Zeus and Hera.)

After the Giants' two leaders had fallen, an Olympian victory was assured. But the Giants did not give up easily. The Olympians had to combine their efforts and fight fiercely to win the war.

THE SCARIEST MONSTER OF ALL

News of the Giants' defeat upset Gaia. Her sons were still locked up in Tartarus, and it was beginning to seem they would remain there forever. But Gaia had one last trick up her sleeve. She gave birth to a monster, Typhon. This creature was half-man, half-animal—and 100 percent terrifying.

Typhon had a hundred serpentine heads, each equipped with a flickering tongue and eyes that shot flames. Each head spoke with a different voice: human, god, beast, serpent, evil spirit, and more. Typhon had wings, his body was encircled with snakes, and he was almost incomprehensibly huge. When this creature spread his arms, one arm reached all the way to the west, and the other reached all the way to the east.

AND SO THEY RUN

Typhon advanced toward Mount Olympus. At the sight of him, the gods and goddesses fled, transforming into various animals to disguise themselves. Aphrodite and Ares turned into fish, Apollo transformed into a bird, Hephaestus became an ox, Dionysus turned into a goat, and Hermes changed into an ibis. Only Zeus stood his ground against the fearsome enemy (although some myths claim Athena also retained her own form).

Zeus attacked Typhon with his mightiest weapon: the thunderbolt. By hurling thunderbolts continuously, so many they made the earth quake, Zeus pushed Typhon back a little. Thinking the monster was wounded Zeus grabbed his sickle and left his fort, intending to finish him off. Typhon, however, wasn't as weak as Zeus thought, and a fierce fight ensued. Eventually, Typhon wrestled the sickle away from Zeus and used it to cut the tendons in his foe's arms and legs, leaving Zeus lying helpless on the ground. Typhon placed the tendons under the protection of the dragon Delphyne and carried Zeus off to a cave.

But all was not lost. Hermes and Pan joined forces to trick Delphyne. While the dragon was distracted, they stole the tendons and restored them to Zeus. Regaining his strength, Zeus immediately returned to Olympus, armed himself with thunderbolts, and went in search of Typhon.

NO REST FOR THE WEARY

When Zeus caught up with Typhon, he showed the monster no mercy. Typhon tried to withstand the rain of thunderbolts, but he was no match for them. So he fled in hopes of finding a safe place where he could renew his strength. He encountered the Fates, who advised him he could be healed by eating the food the mortals ate. Typhon did as he was told, but the food of mortals only made him weaker.

Zeus caught up with Typhon and set loose another relentless shower of thunderbolts. Typhon tried hurling mountain peaks at Zeus, but the god used his thunderbolts to deflect them. The bloody battle continued until Typhon fled once more. According to one myth, Zeus picked up an island and flung it at Typhon. The island crushed the monster, trapping him. The myth states that because Typhon was immortal, he remains beneath the island—its volcanic eruptions are his fiery breath.

Another myth says that Zeus set Typhon on fire with the thunderbolts, seized the monster, and flung him into Tartarus, where he remains imprisoned with the Titans. Many say that Typhon is the cause of all dangerous winds—that's where the word *typhoon* came from.

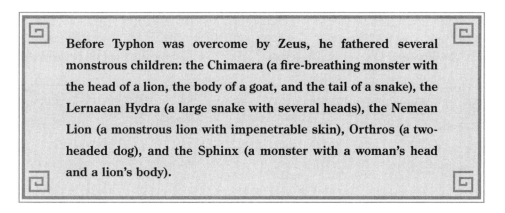

Before Typhon was overcome by Zeus, he fathered several monstrous children: the Chimaera (a fire-breathing monster with the head of a lion, the body of a goat, and the tail of a snake), the Lernaean Hydra (a large snake with several heads), the Nemean Lion (a monstrous lion with impenetrable skin), Orthros (a two-headed dog), and the Sphinx (a monster with a woman's head and a lion's body).

Once again, Zeus was victorious in battle. After Zeus's defeat of Typhon, no one ever again challenged his right to rule gods and men. Thus the Olympians established their rule of the universe until the end of time.

CHAPTER 6

ZEUS AND HERA:
A MARRIAGE MADE IN HEAVEN

ou've no doubt heard the phrase *a match made in heaven,* which refers to a pairing of two perfectly compatible people. In mythology, the marriage between Zeus and Hera was literally a match made in heaven. But these two were not always compatible, and their union was anything but blissful. This chapter travels the rocky road of the marriage of these two great Olympians, a road strewn with betrayal, deceit, jealousy, and revenge.

THE SEVENTH LOVER

Although Hera is the best known of Zeus's wives, she was by no means the first. In fact, Zeus had several other wives and lovers before he married Hera. The ruler of the gods had Olympian-size lusts and passions. He was a god who knew what he wanted—and he took what he wanted with little regard for others.

ZEUS'S FIRST WIFE: METIS

Zeus's first wife was Metis, the wise Oceanid who'd advised him to give his father, Cronus, an emetic so he would vomit up Zeus's brothers and sisters. Most myths say that Metis was initially unwilling to succumb to Zeus. She tried to escape his advances by disguising herself, taking on different forms. In the end, Metis grew tired and gave in to Zeus. She became pregnant with a daughter who would become Athena. Metis did not give birth in the traditional sense, however. If you're curious about Athena's unusual birth, read Chapter 11.

Metis, the personification of wisdom, was her husband's equal. Zeus felt a little intimidated by her—and more than a little intimidated by a prophecy that she would be the mother of extremely powerful children who might pose a threat to his power. Zeus dealt with this threat by swallowing Metis, thereby symbolically taking the quality of wisdom into himself.

THEMIS AND ORDERING THE UNIVERSE

After Metis, Zeus married Themis, one of the original Titanesses and the goddess of necessity and eternal order. Themis worked closely with her husband, acting as his advisor. Together they had several children, including the Moirai (the Fates): Atropus, Clotho, and Lachesis; and the Horae (the Hours): Eunomia (Discipline), Dike (Justice), and Eirene (Peace). The birth of these children completed the order of the universe. Although this marriage also ended, its dissolution wasn't as extreme as Zeus's first divorce; he simply left Themis for another woman.

EURYNOME: MOTHER OF THE GRACES

When Zeus cast his eye upon Eurynome, daughter of Oceanus and Tethys, she was already married to the Titan Ophion. Not only was she married, she was also the sister of Zeus's first wife, Metis. But none of that stopped Zeus. He and Eurynome had three daughters, the Graces: Aglaia (Beauty), Euphrosyne (Joy), and Thalia (Festivity). The Graces brought charm and beauty into the world.

A FELLOW OLYMPIAN: DEMETER

Zeus also had a love affair with his sister Demeter, goddess of agriculture and the harvest. Not much is recorded about their relationship. The myths do record, however, that their union produced a daughter, Persephone. Chapter 8 tells the story of how Persephone became queen of the Underworld.

MNEMOSYNE: MOTHER OF THE MUSES

Zeus's next conquest was Mnemosyne (Memory), a Titaness. Zeus and Mnemosyne made love for nine consecutive nights, leading Mnemosyne to give birth to the nine Muses: Calliope, Clio, Erato, Euterpe, Melpomene, Polyhymnia, Terpsichore, Thalia, and Urania. (Chapter 17 discusses the Muses and their spheres of influence in detail.)

LETO, MOTHER OF OLYMPIANS

Leto, daughter of the Titans Coeus and Phoebe, mated with Zeus and gave birth to the famed twins Apollo and Artemis, who later took their places among the great Olympian gods. (To read about the difficulties of Leto's pregnancy and the birth of these twins, see Chapter 12.)

THY LAWFULLY WEDDED WIFE: HERA

After all of these love affairs, Zeus set his sights on his other sister, Hera. Zeus believed that only this goddess could match him well enough in power to become his permanent wife. Zeus was so used to getting what he wanted that it never occurred to him that he might not be able to have Hera. But Hera, by nature highly jealous, knew about Zeus's past loves and wasn't too keen on his advances. So Zeus had to trick Hera into becoming his wife.

Zeus disguised himself as a cuckoo and created a great rainstorm. In the guise of the cuckoo, he took advantage of Hera's sympathy. Feeling sorry for the poor, drenched bird, Hera picked it up and folded it inside her clothes, clutching it to her body. Zeus transformed back into his own form and violated Hera. Dishonored and shamed, Hera agreed to become his wife.

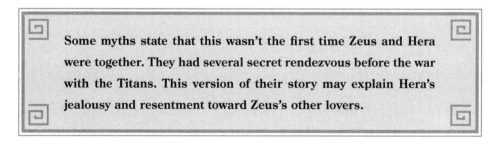

Some myths state that this wasn't the first time Zeus and Hera were together. They had several secret rendezvous before the war with the Titans. This version of their story may explain Hera's jealousy and resentment toward Zeus's other lovers.

A GRAND WEDDING

The marriage ceremony between Zeus and Hera was a grand affair. Different myths give different locations for the divine wedding:

- The *Iliad* places the ceremony on the peak of Mount Ida in Phrygia.
- Other sources say the wedding took place in Euboea, the place where the deities came to rest after returning from the island of Crete.
- Still other sources say that Zeus and Hera were married in the Garden of the Hesperides, located in the westernmost part of the world.

Wherever it took place, the wedding was a magnificent party attended by all of the gods and goddesses. Even Hades left his dark realm to witness the marriage of his brother and sister. The myths say that the tradition of bringing gifts to a newly married couple began with Zeus and Hera. Gaia gave Hera a splendid tree that bore golden apples. This tree was planted in the Garden of the Hesperides and protected by the nymphs.

This divine ceremony became the standard for sacred marriage throughout Greece. Festivals were held to honor the sanctity of marriage and to commemorate the union of Zeus and Hera. In Athens, it became a tradition for brides to receive apples and pomegranates, the favorite fruits of Hera. Throughout Greece, wedding ceremonies were preceded by a procession in which a statue of Hera dressed as a bride was wheeled through the town. Sometimes the statue was wheeled right to the marriage bed. Also, the month attributed to Hera became the traditional time for weddings. (What month was that? Here's a hint: Hera's Roman name is Juno.) Hera became the goddess of marriage, protecting wives and punishing adulterers.

THE CHILDREN OF ZEUS AND HERA

Some myths say that the wedding night of Zeus and Hera lasted for 300 years! Despite their extended honeymoon, the couple had only three children—together, that is.

ARES

According to most myths, Ares was the only son of Zeus and Hera. As Chapter 5 notes, Ares would become the god of war, taking his place among the great gods of Olympus. Chapter 10 gives the details of his life.

EILEITHYIA

Some myths imply that Eileithyia was born out of wedlock. In any case, this daughter of Zeus and Hera was the goddess of childbirth. Hera sometimes took advantage of her daughter's role as the helper of women during labor, and Eileithyia rarely questioned her mother's wishes. For example, jealous Hera wanted to prevent Leto from giving birth to Zeus's children so she tried to prevent Eileithyia from going to Leto's side. Eileithyia wanted to obey her mother, but other goddesses convinced her to help Leto. When Eileithyia arrived there, Artemis was born.

Another example involved the birth of Heracles. Again, Hera's jealousy was intense. She told Eileithyia to sit outside the room where Heracles' mother (Alcmene, a mortal lover of Zeus) was in labor, keeping her own arms, legs, and fingers crossed (or simply clutching her own knees together). This action postponed the birth of Heracles for several days.

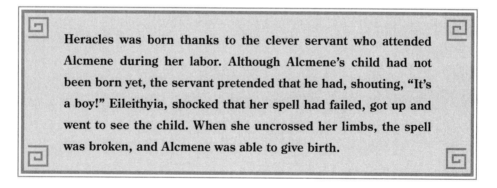

Heracles was born thanks to the clever servant who attended Alcmene during her labor. Although Alcmene's child had not been born yet, the servant pretended that he had, shouting, "It's a boy!" Eileithyia, shocked that her spell had failed, got up and went to see the child. When she uncrossed her limbs, the spell was broken, and Alcmene was able to give birth.

HEBE

Hebe was less prominent than her brother and sister, but she was known for her beauty. The personification of youth, Hebe was forever young and beautiful. She was cupbearer to the Olympians, serving them their divine drink of nectar. Hebe also drew baths, helped Hera into her chariot, and took care of other household chores.

One myth says that Hebe was released from her cupbearing duties when she accidentally tripped and fell at an important festival. As she fell, she indecently exposed herself to the guests and, as a result, lost her job of serving. Later, however, Hebe became the bride of Heracles when he was admitted into the heavens.

HEPHAESTUS: A FOURTH CHILD?

Some myths state that Zeus and Hera had a fourth child together. In those versions, Hephaestus was their second son. But Hesiod tells the story a different way, claiming that Hera conceived Hephaestus without the aid of Zeus or any other man. In this popular version of the myth, Zeus and Hera argue, and afterward Hera gives birth to Hephaestus by an act of sheer will.

If you're wondering what it's like to be the child conceived of only one parent, take a look at Chapter 15, which gives a full account of the life of Hephaestus.

ZEUS'S LOVE AFFAIRS

As you've seen, Zeus had numerous love affairs before he married Hera, but marriage did nothing to end his philandering. This section lists some of Zeus's many adulterous affairs. Hera has a reputation as the most jealous and vengeful Olympian deity. Read on, and you'll see why.

AEGINA

Aegina was the daughter of the river-god Asopus. Zeus took a liking to this young girl and transformed himself into an eagle to steal her away. Asopus, furious, searched all over Greece for his daughter. Zeus, however, put an end to this hunt by striking at Asopus with bolts of lightning. Zeus took Aegina to an isolated island, where she conceived a son, Aeacus. After Aeacus was born, Aegina left the island, but asked Zeus to populate it. He granted her wish, and the island bore her name.

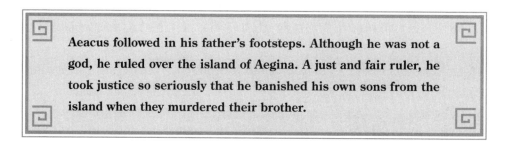

Aeacus followed in his father's footsteps. Although he was not a god, he ruled over the island of Aegina. A just and fair ruler, he took justice so seriously that he banished his own sons from the island when they murdered their brother.

ALCMENE

Alcmene was a mortal woman—and married. But she refused to consummate the marriage until her husband, Amphitryon, completed an act of revenge for her. Zeus disguised himself as her husband, saying he'd returned successfully from his mission of revenge. Alcmene welcomed Zeus into her bed, believing he was her husband. One myth states that Zeus ordered the sun god to take a few days off so that their night of lovemaking would last longer.

The real Amphitryon wasn't happy to return to a wife who claimed she'd already slept with him. But because her lover had been Zeus, there wasn't anything a mortal man could do about it. Alcmene's union with Zeus led to the birth of the famed hero Heracles.

CALLISTO

The myths vary about the identity of Callisto. Some say she was the daughter of the king of Arcadia; others say she was the daughter of the king of Thebes. Still others say she was a wood nymph. All of the myths agree, however, that she was an attendant of Artemis. Callisto took a vow of chastity, as all attendants of Artemis were required to do. However, Zeus fell in love with her—and you know how that goes.

Because Callisto had vowed to remain a virgin, avoiding the company of all men, Zeus had to disguise himself as Artemis to get close to her. The plan worked, and Zeus had his way with her. Callisto was pregnant with her son Arcas when Artemis discovered that her attendant had broken her vow. For this transgression, Artemis transformed Callisto into a bear and (according to some versions of the myth) later killed her.

DANAE

Danae was the daughter of the king of Argos. According to a prophecy, Danae's son would rise up and kill his grandfather. Knowing this, the king decided to keep Danae away from all men, imprisoning her in a tower with bronze doors. Of course, Zeus wasn't a man; he was a god. Zeus transformed himself into a shower of golden rain and visited Danae. As always, Zeus got what he wanted, and the result was Perseus. He became a great hero, and his story appears in Chapter 19.

ELECTRA

Several myths surround Electra, the daughter of Atlas. But none of these myths gives the details of how Zeus seduced her. Even though there isn't a juicy story to narrate their love affair, their union was an important one. Dardanus, son of Zeus and Electra, founded the royal house of Troy.

EUROPA

One day, Zeus looked down from the heavens and saw Europa, daughter of the king of Phoenicia, playing on the beach. He was immediately transfixed by her beauty. Zeus transformed into a glamorous white bull and presented himself to the maiden.

At first, Europa was afraid of the creature, but the bull gently lay down at her feet. Relaxing, Europa petted the creature and then climbed onto his back. Zeus ran off with her, carrying her to the ocean and swimming to the island of Crete. There, he changed back to his true form and made love to Europa beneath a tree. From that time on, the tree was always evergreen. Europa became the first queen of Crete and bore Zeus three sons: Minos, Sarpedon, and Rhadamanthys.

GANYMEDE

No one was safe from the lust of Zeus, not even young men. Ganymede was a prince of the royal Trojan family. Some myths say that he was the most beautiful of all mortals, men and women alike. When Zeus saw Ganymede, it was love at first sight. Zeus sent an eagle (or transformed himself into an eagle) to carry the youth to Mount Olympus. There, Ganymede became a cupbearer for the gods (particularly Zeus), replacing Hebe in this role.

IO

Io, daughter of the river-god Inachus, was a virgin priestess of Hera. That role should have made her off-limits to Zeus, but he lusted after her anyway. Zeus knew he had to avoid Hera's anger, so he lured Io into the woods. He then covered the area with a large, thick cloud, which concealed their lovemaking. Afterward, he turned Io into a white heifer to hide her. But Hera saw through his ruse. You'll read about Hera's revenge later in this chapter.

LEDA

Leda was the daughter of the king of Aetolia and the wife of Tyndareus, king of Sparta. Once again, Zeus transformed himself in order to get close to his target—this time, he changed into a swan. Pretending to be fleeing from an eagle, the swan threw itself into Leda's arms. Zeus seduced Leda, and she became pregnant. Leda didn't give birth in the normal way, however. She laid two eggs, from which hatched Polydeuces and Helen (later known as Helen of Troy). Leda had several children—some with Zeus, and some with her husband. Her children included Helen, Polydeuces, Castor, Clytemnestra, Phoebe, Timandra, and Philonoe.

MAIA

Maia was the oldest and most beautiful daughter of Atlas. It was inevitable that Zeus would notice her. To avoid Hera, Zeus snuck away from his sleeping wife at night to visit Maia. She bore him Hermes, who became one of the great Olympians. Maia was lucky; if Hera took revenge on her, the myths don't record it.

SEMELE

Semele was a mortal woman with whom Zeus fell in love. He came to her disguised as a mortal man, but confided that he was indeed the ruler of the gods. Unlike some of Zeus's other lovers, Semele did not try to escape his advances. They enjoyed a brief love affair, which caused Semele to conceive a son, Dionysus. Zeus promised to give Semele anything she wanted. Taking advantage of this, Semele asked Zeus to show her his true form. But a god's splendor was too much for a mere mortal to bear. When he appeared to Semele in his true form, she burst into flames.

TAYGETE

The nymph Taygete was yet another of Atlas's daughters and a companion of Artemis. When Zeus pursued Taygete, she asked Artemis for help, and Artemis turned her into a doe. Zeus had his way with her anyway, making love to Taygete when she was unconscious. As a result, Taygete gave birth to Lacedaemon.

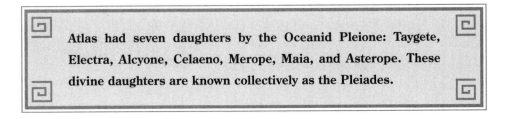

Atlas had seven daughters by the Oceanid Pleione: Taygete, Electra, Alcyone, Celaeno, Merope, Maia, and Asterope. These divine daughters are known collectively as the Pleiades.

AND MANY MORE . . .

As the preceding sections suggest, Zeus had many, many trysts during his marriage to Hera—and that's just scratching the surface. As the ruler of the gods and humanity, Zeus was hard to refuse.

But don't imagine that Hera simply stood by and watched her husband's exploits. Even though she was a goddess, she felt the same emotions mortals do—and she felt jealousy particularly strongly. When she was jealous, Hera demanded revenge. The next section gives you a taste of how Hera punished Zeus's lovers.

THE WRATH OF HERA

Although Zeus's infidelity angered Hera, she tended to take out her feelings on his women instead of him. Granted, most of the women pursued by Zeus tried to escape his advances. But that didn't matter. Hera blamed the women and punished them.

THAT PESKY FLY

One of the best-known stories of Hera's wrath tells of her vengeance upon Io. As you recall, Zeus seduced Io and then transformed her into a white heifer. This stratagem didn't fool Hera. Pretending to believe Zeus's claims that the heifer was an ordinary cow, she asked him to give her the heifer as a gift. Zeus, who didn't dare refuse his wife, consented and gave Io to Hera. Hera placed the heifer under the guard of Argus, a monster with a hundred eyes.

Zeus felt sorry for Io and sent Hermes to release her. Hermes succeeded in slaying Argus and setting Io free. But that wasn't the end of Io's persecution. Hera found out Io had been released and sent a gadfly to torment the heifer. The gadfly followed Io around, continuously stinging her. Io ran farther and farther away in her attempts to avoid this torment. Eventually, after she'd begged Hera for forgiveness, Io was returned to her true form.

PERSECUTION OF MOTHER AND SON

Another famous story of Hera's wrath is the myth of Alcmene and Heracles. As you know, Hera persuaded her daughter Eileithyia to prevent Alcmene from giving birth to Zeus's child. Heracles was born anyway, making Hera even angrier. She transferred her anger to Heracles.

Hera did everything in her power to punish Heracles, attacking him in many different ways throughout his life. She sent serpents to kill him in his crib, made him a slave, and drove him to madness (which caused him to kill his own wife and children). Throughout all of these torments, Heracles behaved like a hero, so Hera never truly got the better of him. (The life of Heracles contained many exciting adventures; Chapter 19 gives you more about this great hero.)

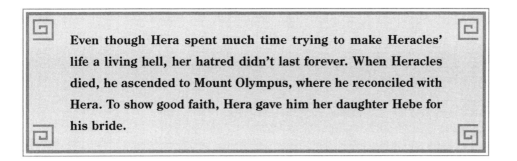

Even though Hera spent much time trying to make Heracles' life a living hell, her hatred didn't last forever. When Heracles died, he ascended to Mount Olympus, where he reconciled with Hera. To show good faith, Hera gave him her daughter Hebe for his bride.

A LOVER'S SPAT

Hera and Zeus once got into a heated debate over who derived the most pleasure from sex: the man or the woman. Zeus claimed that women took greater pleasure in sex, and Hera claimed that men got all the enjoyment. Neither one could convince the other, so they decided to call in Tiresias to settle the dispute.

Tiresias was unusually qualified to judge the matter because he'd lived as both a man and a woman. When he was a child, Tiresias came upon two snakes mating. He took a stick and beat the coupling pair, killing the female. At once, he was transformed into a woman. He lived as a woman for seven years until he chanced upon another pair of mating snakes. This time, he killed the male snake and was transformed back into a man.

When asked his opinion, Tiresias was adamant: Women derive more pleasure from the act of sex. In fact, he said, a woman enjoys lovemaking nine times more than a man does. Hera lost the debate, and she was so furious that she struck Tiresias blind.

CHAPTER 7

POSEIDON:
SOVEREIGN OF THE SEA

ften considered second in command to Zeus, Poseidon was the powerful god of the sea, a god who garnered more fear than respect. Poseidon was like a schoolyard bully, but much more dangerous. He controlled the seas and could create earthquakes. Sailors tried to placate Poseidon, but most of the ancients regarded him as a god best avoided. In this chapter, you will get to know Poseidon and the many myths that surround him.

THE POWER OF POSEIDON

When the Olympian gods divided the domains by drawing lots, Poseidon drew the seas. However, his power extended beyond the sea to include other bodies of water, such as lakes and freshwater springs. Some myths say he also controlled the rivers, although most rivers had their own lesser deities.

Poseidon was often called "Earth-Shaker" because he had the power to create earthquakes. Using his trident, he could generate savage sea storms, force the waves as high as he desired, summon sea monsters, and cause landslides and floods. He answered to no one except Zeus, and even Zeus could not always rein him in before severe damage was done. It is no wonder Poseidon was feared by all, especially seafarers.

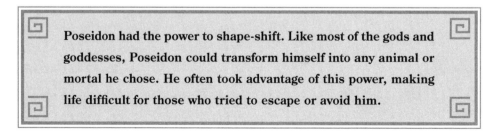

Poseidon had the power to shape-shift. Like most of the gods and goddesses, Poseidon could transform himself into any animal or mortal he chose. He often took advantage of this power, making life difficult for those who tried to escape or avoid him.

But even with the power of the seas at his command, Poseidon was not satisfied with his realm. He wanted more, and his greed led him to challenge Zeus. As you recall, Poseidon was one of the original three Olympians who conspired against Zeus, wanting to take over his role as ruler of the gods. When the attempted mutiny failed, Poseidon was again subordinate to Zeus. The sea god tried to heighten his standing by becoming the patron of more cities than the other gods.

THAT CITY IS MINE!

In the ancient world, each city had a patron god or goddess. The people prayed to various deities, of course, but they usually held one in the highest regard. A temple was often built in that deity's name, and this temple was the town's primary place of worship. Worshipers also erected statues of the deity. Although individuals conducted their own sacrifices, public sacrifice to the patron god or goddess became a major civic event. Poseidon recognized the power afforded by this system and tried to gain the favor of as many cities as possible. This ambition sometimes brought him into conflict with other Olympians.

AT ODDS WITH ATHENA

Poseidon came into conflict with Athena over the city of Athens. Even before this happened, Poseidon bore several grudges against his niece. Poseidon was considered the least clever of the Olympian gods, and Athena was the goddess of wisdom. He was the god of the sea and wanted the ocean reserved for his creatures alone. When Athena taught mortals the art of shipbuilding, she opened up Poseidon's domain to humans. Remember, too, that some myths credit Poseidon with creating the horse, a wild and beautiful beast. Athena gave the bridle to mortals, enabling people to tame Poseidon's creation and use it for their own purposes. So a good deal of animosity already existed between the two deities—and this was heightened when each claimed the city of Athens.

Some myths say that Athens belonged to Poseidon first. In these myths, Poseidon struck his trident into the ground at the Acropolis and created a spring; however, since he was god of the sea, the spring was salty. Later, Athena came along and planted an olive tree, claiming the city as hers. Poseidon, hotheaded as always, challenged Athena to a fight. Zeus interceded but felt he couldn't judge the matter fairly, so he took the argument before others.

One myth states that Zeus allowed the people of Athens to choose their deity by deciding which of the two gifts was more useful. The people judged that the olive tree was more useful than a saltwater spring, so Athena became protector of the city.

Another myth says that Zeus put the dispute before the other Olympians. The gods voted for Poseidon, and the goddesses voted for Athena. Zeus abstained, leaving Poseidon one vote shy of a tie, and Athena claimed the city.

Yet another myth says that Zeus took the matter to Cecrops and Cranaus, early kings of Attica. Cecrops was biased toward Athena and maintained that her claim to the city preceded Poseidon's. Therefore, the arbitrators ruled in Athena's favor.

The myths agree that Athena won the city, and this is where the name *Athens* came from. In retaliation, Poseidon sent water to flood the Attic Plain, the countryside around the city. Eventually, Zeus intervened and reconciled his brother and the people of Athens, who honored Poseidon as second only to Athena.

NEVER GIVE UP

Poseidon didn't give up easily. He continued to challenge the gods and goddesses for the patronage of other cities. Numerous disputes took place, and more often than not Poseidon was the loser. Here are some of the better-known conflicts:

- He challenged Dionysus for the island of Naxos and lost.
- He wanted Delphi but had to go up against Apollo, who won.
- He competed again with Athena for Troezen, and lost.

- He challenged Zeus for Aegina. Zeus, of course, won.
- He challenged Hera for the city of Argos, but the Queen of the Heavens won.

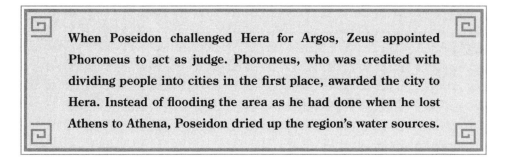

When Poseidon challenged Hera for Argos, Zeus appointed Phoroneus to act as judge. Phoroneus, who was credited with dividing people into cities in the first place, awarded the city to Hera. Instead of flooding the area as he had done when he lost Athens to Athena, Poseidon dried up the region's water sources.

Despite these setbacks, many cities honored Poseidon as their chief god—including Corinth, Helike, and Aegae—and representatives of the twelve cities of the Ionian League met every year at a temple of Poseidon.

WANTED: ONE QUEEN

Amphitrite was the daughter of Nereus (the Old Man of the Sea) and Doris (a daughter of Oceanus). She was part of a circle of deities called the Nereids, who were sea nymphs said to be the personification of the waves. Some myths say there were one hundred Nereids; others claim there were only fifty. Regardless, Amphitrite stood apart from her many sisters in one respect: She was the leader of their chorus.

One day, Amphitrite and her sisters were dancing and singing on the island of Naxos. Poseidon noticed her and fell immediately in love. He carried Amphitrite off to be his bride. Or so one story goes. Other myths argue that Amphitrite did not give in so easily.

HIDE AND SEEK

Although Poseidon ruled the seas, Amphitrite wasn't impressed by her suitor. After all, her father was the Old Man of the Sea, a deity who'd been in power long before Poseidon. But Poseidon claimed to love her, and he was unaccustomed to being refused. Amphitrite wanted nothing to do with Poseidon and tried to escape to the deepest parts of the ocean, but Poseidon always found her. A band of dolphins captured Amphitrite and handed her over to Poseidon. She finally agreed to be his wife.

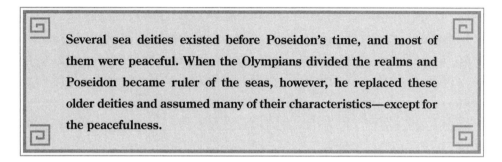

Several sea deities existed before Poseidon's time, and most of them were peaceful. When the Olympians divided the realms and Poseidon became ruler of the seas, however, he replaced these older deities and assumed many of their characteristics—except for the peacefulness.

Another myth says that Amphitrite went to Atlas, asking for protection and a place to hide from Poseidon. But again Poseidon sent his subjects to find her. A dolphin located her and pleaded Poseidon's case, eventually persuading her to go to the sea god. In this myth, Amphitrite marries Poseidon of her own free will. Poseidon was so grateful to the dolphin that he turned the creature into a constellation.

AMPHITRITE'S CHILDREN

Amphitrite bore Poseidon three children: Benthesicyme, Rhode, and Triton. The myths don't say much about Benthesicyme beyond the fact that she was Poseidon's daughter. Rhode is a bit better known. Apollo was in love with her and named the island of Rhodes for her. She became the wife of Helios, however, and bore him seven sons and one daughter. Poseidon's son Triton is the best known of these three children. Triton, half-man and half-fish, was Poseidon's herald. He also possessed the power to calm the seas at will. (To read more about Triton, take a look at Chapter 17.)

POSEIDON'S LOVERS

Much like his brother Zeus, Poseidon had many affairs. Unlike Hera, however, Poseidon's wife was neither jealous nor vindictive. In fact, the myths don't indicate that Amphitrite took much notice of her husband's love affairs. (According to one story, however, Amphitrite did notice Scylla and, in a fit of jealousy, turned her into a monster.)

Poseidon had affairs with mortals and immortals alike, fathering many children. The following sections describe the best known of his many conquests.

AETHRA

Aegeus, ruler of Athens, was unable to have children with his wife, so he went to seek the advice of an oracle. The oracle warned him not to open his wine flask until he reached the highest point in Athens. Aegeus didn't understand the oracle's advice. Disappointed, he went to visit the king of Troezen. The king got Aegeus drunk and sent his daughter, Aethra, to his bedchamber. She and Aegeus made love, but that same night she left his bed to make a sacrifice. Poseidon approached her, and this pair also made love. (Some myths say she was raped by Poseidon and that the whole situation was set up by Athena.)

Aethra conceived a child that night—but no one knew whether the father was Aegeus or Poseidon. Most believed that the child was Poseidon's, although Aegeus claimed the child, a son, as his own. The child, Theseus, became a famous hero. (See Chapter 19 for details about Theseus's life.)

AMYMONE

Amymone was one of the fifty daughters of King Danaus. The king sent Amymone and her sisters to find water in the land of Argos. Poseidon had caused the region to dry up, so locating water seemed an impossible task. After walking for many miles, Amymone became tired and decided to rest. Left alone, she was approached by a satyr. (Another myth states that Amymone, in pursuit of a deer, accidentally hit the satyr with a spear.) The satyr attempted to rape the girl, but Poseidon interceded, using his trident to chase away her attacker.

Poseidon proceeded to court Amymone for himself. After making love to her, Poseidon used his trident to create a spring so Amymone could bring water back to her family. (Some myths tell the story a bit differently, saying that Poseidon did not create the spring intentionally but accidentally struck a rock with his trident while chasing the satyr.) Amymone succeeded in her goal of finding water, and Poseidon succeeded in adding another lover to his list.

Amymone and Poseidon had a son from their union: Nauplius, whose extensive knowledge of the seas and astronomy would make him a hero to seafarers. Nauplius also founded the town of Nauplia, a famous naval port near Argos.

DEMETER

Another of Poseidon's conquests was his sister Demeter. Wishing to escape her brother's advances, Demeter transformed herself into a mare. But Poseidon wasn't to be put off. He transformed himself into a stallion and mated with her in a pasture, both of them in the form of horses.

Together they produced Desponia, a nymph, and Arion, a wild horse. Desponia was worshiped alongside her mother in Arcadia. The people there erected statues of the mother and daughter as women with mares' heads. Arion was a famous winged horse who could speak. Some myths say that his right feet were like a human's.

IPHIMEDIA

Iphimedia was an unhappily married woman. Her husband, Aloeus, a son of Poseidon, was also her uncle. Iphimedia was in love with Poseidon and made a habit of walking along the seashore. She would often sit down and scoop up the water, allowing it to flow over her breasts. Poseidon found this alluring, and his union with Iphimedia produced two sons: the Giants Ephialtes and Otus.

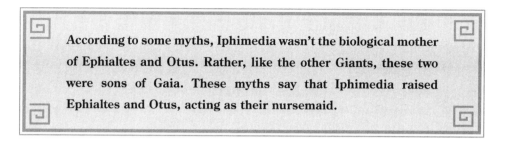

According to some myths, Iphimedia wasn't the biological mother of Ephialtes and Otus. Rather, like the other Giants, these two were sons of Gaia. These myths say that Iphimedia raised Ephialtes and Otus, acting as their nursemaid.

MEDUSA

As you recall from Chapter 4, Medusa was a Gorgon, with snakes for hair and a terrifying appearance that could turn anyone to stone. Some myths say, however, that Medusa wasn't always this fearsome creature. In these myths, she was once a beautiful woman, and her beauty caught Poseidon's eye.

Poseidon approached Medusa as she was visiting one of Athena's temples. They made love in the temple—an act unacceptable to the virgin goddess Athena. As punishment, Athena turned Medusa into the horrifying creature she is known as today. However, this transformation wasn't enough for Athena; she also helped Perseus to slay Medusa.

When Perseus cut off Medusa's head, two children appeared—Chrysaor and Pegasus—the results of her union with Poseidon. Some myths say that Chrysaor was born from Medusa's neck and Pegasus from her blood. Others say that both were born when drops of Medusa's blood landed in the sea.

Chrysaor means "the man with the golden sword"; he was born wielding a golden sword. He would grow to marry Callirrhoe (an Oceanid) and father two children: Geryon (a Giant with three heads) and Echidna.

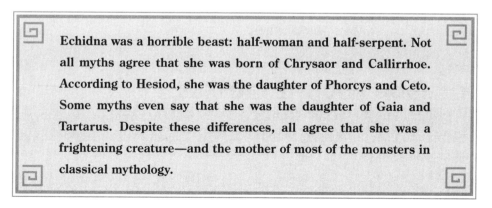

Echidna was a horrible beast: half-woman and half-serpent. Not all myths agree that she was born of Chrysaor and Callirrhoe. According to Hesiod, she was the daughter of Phorcys and Ceto. Some myths even say that she was the daughter of Gaia and Tartarus. Despite these differences, all agree that she was a frightening creature—and the mother of most of the monsters in classical mythology.

The second son, Pegasus, was a winged horse, who would later play a role in several myths. Pegasus was wild and free until tamed by either Athena or the hero Bellerophon (depending on which myth you read). At the end of his days, Pegasus was changed into a constellation.

THEOPHANE

Theophane was a beautiful young woman who had several suitors, including Poseidon. To avoid competition, the sea god abducted Theophane and took her to an island.

Theophane's suitors searched for their missing love. They eventually discovered where she was, but before they could reach her Poseidon turned the island's inhabitants to sheep—including Theophane. At the same time, Poseidon transformed himself into a ram. When the suitors arrived on the island and found nothing but a big flock of sheep, they decided to have a feast. As they prepared to slaughter the animals, Poseidon changed the sheep into wolves that slaughtered the suitors instead.

Poseidon and Theophane mated while in their sheep forms, so their son (whose name is not recorded) was born a ram. But this wasn't just any ram— he had a fleece of gold and was able to speak and fly.

THOOSA

Thoosa was the daughter of Phorcys (a son of Gaia). Her affair with Poseidon is known mostly for its offspring: the Cyclops Polyphemus. Polyphemus was not one of the original race of Cyclopes. Instead, he was a violent, savage, man-eating creature. Chapter 19 tells what happened when the hero Odysseus ran up against Polyphemus.

POSEIDON AND THE TROJANS

You'll read about the Trojan War in Chapter 20, but any overview of Poseidon must mention his relationship with the Trojans, a relationship that's central to understanding this god.

As punishment for their participation in the uprising against Zeus, Poseidon and Apollo were forced to help Laomedon, the king of Troy, build walls around his city. They were to be compensated for this great work, but when it came time to pay, Laomedon refused, angering both gods. After all, the gods had worked hard for an entire year to build the walls. Apollo inflicted a great plague on the city and was satisfied with this revenge. Poseidon sent a sea monster to harass Troy, but his anger continued.

Later, during the Trojan War, Poseidon sided with the Greeks—despite Zeus's order to stay out of the conflict.

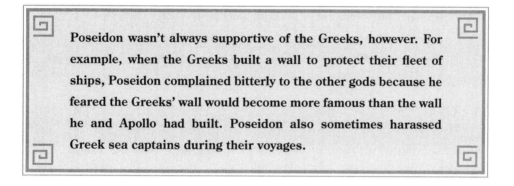

Poseidon wasn't always supportive of the Greeks, however. For example, when the Greeks built a wall to protect their fleet of ships, Poseidon complained bitterly to the other gods because he feared the Greeks' wall would become more famous than the wall he and Apollo had built. Poseidon also sometimes harassed Greek sea captains during their voyages.

Because of his anger and bitterness, Poseidon made life hard for everyone during the Trojan War. He was a god who would hold a grudge for as long as it took to get revenge, and his revenge was often brutal. Selfish and disloyal, Poseidon would switch sides without notice, when it suited him. Like the sea itself, he was powerful, changeable, and treacherous.

POSEIDON COULD BE A NICE GUY, TOO (WELL, SOMETIMES)

You've seen that Poseidon could be a harsh god. He was always ready for a fight, not terribly clever, and untrustworthy. But he also had a kinder, gentler side:

- Poseidon granted the twin brothers Castor and Pollux some of his own power—the ability to calm the seas. He also appointed them protectors of sailors, thus giving away a little of his own glory.
- When Ino and her son Melicertes threw themselves into the sea, Poseidon took pity on them and changed them into sea deities.
- Poseidon also gave his most precious creation—the horse—to those he favored. Many myths attest to this act of kindness.

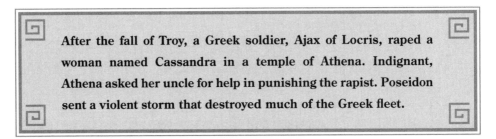

After the fall of Troy, a Greek soldier, Ajax of Locris, raped a woman named Cassandra in a temple of Athena. Indignant, Athena asked her uncle for help in punishing the rapist. Poseidon sent a violent storm that destroyed much of the Greek fleet.

Poseidon was widely worshiped throughout ancient Greece. Sailors offered sacrifices to Poseidon in hopes of calm seas, and he was also connected with fresh water and fertility. Yet he was greatly feared for his ability to whip up storms and cause earthquakes, as well as his unpredictable nature.

CHAPTER 8
THE DARK PRINCE

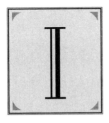I n the ancient world, death was just as complicated as life. The Underworld was the place where all souls (or *shades,* as they were often called) went after death. The Underworld was divided into different regions—some good, some not so good. This chapter takes you on a tour of the realm of the dead, where you'll meet Hades, the fearsome Lord of the Underworld.

A PRIVATE GOD

When the Olympian brothers drew lots for their domains, Hades drew the realm of the dead. This kingdom suited him very well. Hades was a somber, grim god who enjoyed solitude. Although the ancients often described Hades as cold, he was never associated with evil. He was simply the ruler of the dead, and he performed his duties efficiently and with an unrelenting sense of responsibility. Hades never allowed pity—or any emotion, for that matter—to interfere with his work.

As you know, Hades was one of the six original Olympians. But he rarely visited Mount Olympus and didn't socialize with the other gods, so he was effectively kicked out of the top twelve. (This suited Hades just fine, because he had no desire to take part in divine councils.) In his own realm, Hades reigned supreme; most gods stayed away from the Underworld. There, Hades had complete control, and even Zeus usually left him alone.

THE ABDUCTION OF PERSEPHONE

Although Hades rarely left his realm to visit the land of the living, the myths say he visited the mortal world at least once. During this visit, he encountered the beautiful Persephone, daughter of Demeter and Zeus.

Hades noticed Persephone as she gathered flowers on a plain in Sicily, accompanied by some nymphs. He was immediately overwhelmed by her beauty and didn't bother to court her. Instead, he abducted her and took her to the Underworld.

Persephone was a prisoner in Hades' realm. Her mother, Demeter, was frantic at the sudden disappearance of her daughter, and she traveled the world searching for her. (Chapter 9 looks at the travels of Demeter in detail.) Demeter was an earth goddess and as she searched, crops failed, causing people to suffer and go hungry. This was when the first winter came to the world. Because of Demeter's great sorrow and the starving people's cries, Zeus refused to allow a marriage between Hades and Persephone.

Zeus sent Hermes to persuade Hades to release Persephone. Hades couldn't bear the thought of giving up Persephone, but the message brought by Hermes was a direct order from Zeus. Hades had little choice but to let the girl go. Before he did, however, he found a loophole.

Hades pretended to comply with Zeus's orders while he created a plan to keep Persephone. According to a law of the all-powerful Fates, anyone who ate food in the Underworld could never return to the land of the living. Knowing this law, Hades tricked Persephone into eating some pomegranate seeds. (The number of seeds varies according to individual myths: either four, seven, or eight.) Because Persephone ate the seeds, she lawfully belonged in the Underworld.

Even Zeus could not defy the Fates. However, he worked out a compromise. Persephone would live with Hades in the Underworld for four months of the year and spend the remaining eight months with her mother. (Some myths divide the number of months evenly: six and six.) Thus, the myth explains why the seasons change: When Persephone is with her mother, flowers bloom and crops grow and bear fruit, but when she is with her husband in the Underworld, plants wither and die.

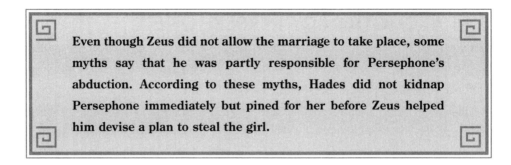

Even though Zeus did not allow the marriage to take place, some myths say that he was partly responsible for Persephone's abduction. According to these myths, Hades did not kidnap Persephone immediately but pined for her before Zeus helped him devise a plan to steal the girl.

Persephone became the wife of Hades and the Queen of the Underworld. Eventually, she accepted her duties as wife and queen. Some myths even claim that eventually she reciprocated Hades' love.

THE HOUSE OF HADES

The Underworld was divided into different regions. One region was for the most exceptional mortals (such as heroes), another region was for the common folk, and a third was for evildoers. But there is more to the Underworld than these three main regions, as you will soon see.

INFERNAL GEOGRAPHY

Some early myths situate the Underworld at the very edge of the land of the living, just past the ocean's shoreline. Later, more common myths situate the Underworld beneath the ground. The Land of the Dead was thought to have many entrances, mostly through caves or lakes.

Several rivers surrounded the Land of the Dead, including:

- **Acheron:** River of Woe
- **Cocytus:** River of Wailing
- **Lethe:** River of Forgetfulness
- **Pyriphlegethon:** River of Fire
- **Styx:** River of Hate

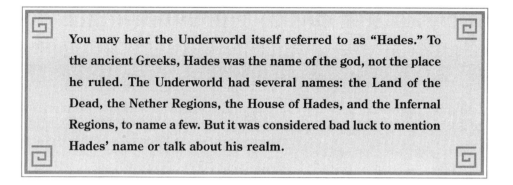

You may hear the Underworld itself referred to as "Hades." To the ancient Greeks, Hades was the name of the god, not the place he ruled. The Underworld had several names: the Land of the Dead, the Nether Regions, the House of Hades, and the Infernal Regions, to name a few. But it was considered bad luck to mention Hades' name or talk about his realm.

ENTERING THE UNDERWORLD

When a person died, Hermes came to collect that person's shade (or soul) and lead him or her to the Underworld. To get to the Underworld required crossing one or more rivers. To cross a river, the shade had to engage the services of Charon, the ferryman of the dead. Charon didn't work for free; he required a coin as payment. If a would-be passenger could not pay Charon's fee, that shade was doomed to wander the shoreline for a hundred years before being allowed passage. Even after they'd paid and boarded the boat, the shades had to do most of the work—they rowed, while the ferryman merely steered.

After crossing one or more rivers, the shade had to pass Cerberus, the watchdog of Hades, before passing through the Underworld's gates. Cerberus wasn't just any dog. Some myths say he had three heads, while others say he had fifty. Regardless, Cerberus loved to eat raw flesh. Cerberus got along fine with shades on their way into the Underworld; his job was to prevent living mortals from entering and shades from escaping.

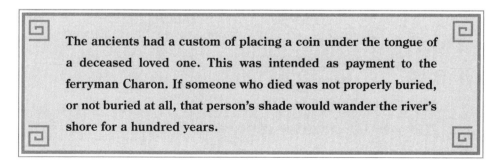

The ancients had a custom of placing a coin under the tongue of a deceased loved one. This was intended as payment to the ferryman Charon. If someone who died was not properly buried, or not buried at all, that person's shade would wander the river's shore for a hundred years.

THE MAIN REGIONS OF THE UNDERWORLD

After passing Cerberus, the shade came to a fork in the road. From this point, three paths led to different regions of the Underworld. At this fork the shade encountered the Judges of the Dead. Usually the Judges determined which path a shade would take, determining that shade's new home for eternity. Sometimes the gods intervened and made the choice instead. (Hades himself never did this, however.)

ELYSIUM

Elysium (sometimes called the Elysian Fields) was the dwelling place of the exceptional. This island was where heroes (and other extraordinary mortals) were sent after death. Elysium was a paradise, where men and women enjoyed a comfortable afterlife. Games were held, music was played, and good times were had by all. The fields were always green and the sun always shone.

ASPHODEL FIELDS

Most shades resided in the Asphodel Fields. This region of the Underworld was a middle ground, neither good nor bad. The final dwelling place for most commoners, the Asphodel Fields held more souls than Elysium and Tartarus combined.

Here, the shades normally mimicked the activities of their former lives. Memories did not exist here, so shades usually acted like machines with no individuality. The Asphodel Fields were monotonous and offered little variety or socialization. Even so, this region of the Underworld was a much better place to be than Tartarus.

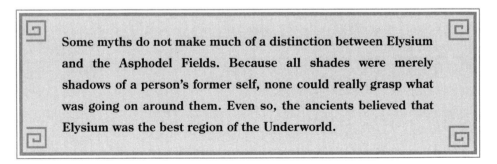

Some myths do not make much of a distinction between Elysium and the Asphodel Fields. Because all shades were merely shadows of a person's former self, none could really grasp what was going on around them. Even so, the ancients believed that Elysium was the best region of the Underworld.

TARTARUS

Tartarus was located beneath the Underworld. It was so far below ground, in fact, that the distance between Tartarus and the surface was said to be the same as the distance between Earth and the heavens. A dark and dismal place, Tartarus was feared by all, even the gods and goddesses. It was here that the very wicked were sent to suffer eternal punishment.

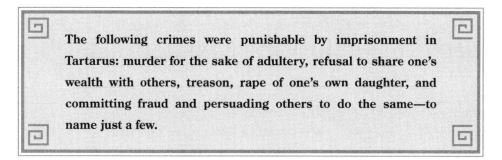

The following crimes were punishable by imprisonment in Tartarus: murder for the sake of adultery, refusal to share one's wealth with others, treason, rape of one's own daughter, and committing fraud and persuading others to do the same—to name just a few.

The Erinyes had the duty of administering severe punishments to the shades assigned to Tartarus. Each Erinye used whips and snakes to torment the evildoers. Sometimes food and drink would be placed before the starving, suffering shadows, and the Erinyes would make sure that the food stayed slightly out of reach.

THE JUDGES AND THE JUDGED

The Judges of the Dead decided the destinies of those who dwelled in the Underworld. Although the Judges were symbolically important to the Underworld, they didn't have much real power. The gods themselves decided whether a person had been wicked enough to send to Tartarus or brave and good enough to spend eternity in Elysium. That meant that the Judges usually sent shades to the Asphodel Fields without much consideration.

AEACUS

Aeacus, son of Zeus and Aegina, was considered to be the most pious of all Greeks. As Chapter 6 describes, Aegina left her son on a deserted island, which Zeus populated to give the boy companions. He grew up to become the ruler of the island, which was called Aegina after his mother.

Aeacus fathered three sons: Peleus, Telamon, and Phocus. When Phocus grew into a great athlete who was adored by all, his two older brothers grew jealous and murdered him. Aeacus discovered what had happened and banished his two remaining sons from the island, leaving him without an heir.

Because Aeacus prized justice over family and lived a pious, upright life, Zeus decided to honor him after his death, and made Aeacus a Judge of the Dead. As an added honor, Aeacus was named the keeper of the keys to the Underworld.

MINOS

Minos was another son of Zeus, born of Europa. He was a king of Crete and, much like his father, ruled with justice and equity. It is said that his laws were so well considered and so well written that they stayed in force for a thousand years.

However, Minos wasn't the ultimate good guy. He fought with Poseidon, had numerous adulterous affairs (some of which resulted in the death of the woman involved), and banished his own brother out of jealousy. Despite some bad personal behavior, he was still renowned for his leadership and dedication to justice. So Minos, too, became a Judge of the Dead after his own death. Among the Judges, he had power to make the final decision.

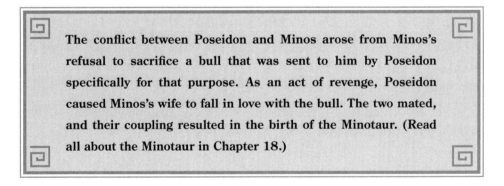

The conflict between Poseidon and Minos arose from Minos's refusal to sacrifice a bull that was sent to him by Poseidon specifically for that purpose. As an act of revenge, Poseidon caused Minos's wife to fall in love with the bull. The two mated, and their coupling resulted in the birth of the Minotaur. (Read all about the Minotaur in Chapter 18.)

RHADAMANTHYS

Yet another son of Zeus, Rhadamanthys was Minos's brother. Some myths say that Rhadamanthys ruled Crete before Minos came to power. As ruler, Rhadamanthys established a code of laws that became so popular it found its way into Sparta. Rhadamanthys lost his position as ruler of Crete when he and Minos got into a dispute over the affections of a young boy. Minos was stronger than his brother and drove Rhadamanthys off the island.

After leaving Crete, Rhadamanthys made his way to the Aegean Islands, where his reputation as a great ruler preceded him. He ruled over these islands until his death.

Rhadamanthys also became one of the Judges of the Dead. Some myths claim that he was responsible for settling disputes among the shades. Other myths say that he ruled Tartarus and participated in punishing the inhabitants.

ESCAPING DEATH

Although most shades were assigned to the Underworld for eternity, a lucky few did manage to escape. Most were living mortals who went down into the Underworld of their own free will—and with a purpose.

HERACLES

Heracles' descent into the realm of the dead was one of the twelve labors given to him by Eurystheus. (Chapter 19 tells you more about the labors of Heracles.) Heracles had to do more than simply visit the Underworld—a difficult and dangerous task in itself—he also had to capture Hades' dog, Cerberus, and return with it to the land of the living.

Guided by Hermes and protected by Athena, Heracles succeeded in reaching the Underworld. He beat Charon until the ferryman agreed to take him across the river. On the other side, Heracles was challenged by Hades. In their fight, Hades was wounded and had to be taken to Mount Olympus to be healed. Heracles captured Cerberus, using no weapons, and left the Underworld with his prize.

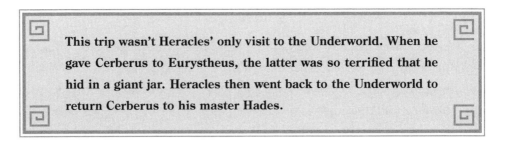

This trip wasn't Heracles' only visit to the Underworld. When he gave Cerberus to Eurystheus, the latter was so terrified that he hid in a giant jar. Heracles then went back to the Underworld to return Cerberus to his master Hades.

ORPHEUS

Orpheus lost his beloved wife, Eurydice, to a fatal snake bite. He tried to live without her, but his grief was so great that he ventured into the Underworld to retrieve her. Orpheus was a gifted musician, and his music allowed him to reach Persephone, the queen of the Underworld. He used his lyre to charm all the monsters, and even Hades himself.

Persephone took pity on Orpheus and allowed him to take Eurydice back to the land of the living. There was one catch, however—Orpheus could not look back as they made their way out of the Underworld. The pair passed through the Underworld unharmed, but just before they reached their destination, Orpheus was overwhelmed by a desire to look behind him to make sure his wife still followed him. When he looked back, Eurydice was pulled back into the Nether Regions. Orpheus had to return to the land of the living alone.

AENEAS

The Trojan hero Aeneas was visited by his father's ghost, who told his son they would soon meet in the Underworld. So Aeneas set out to visit his father's shade there. Knowing he would not succeed in this mission alone, he sought out the prophetess Sibyl, who agreed to help him.

Before he began his journey, Sibyl advised Aeneas to obtain the talismanic Golden Bough from a nearby wood that was sacred to Persephone. Aeneas did as he was told, and Sibyl led him to the River Styx. Here, Charon was at first reluctant to ferry a living mortal across the river, but Sibyl pointed out the Golden Bough; after seeing it, Charon agreed to give Aeneas passage. Sibyl also helped Aeneas by drugging Cerberus so that Aeneas could pass by.

Aeneas passed through several regions of the Underworld and spoke to Dido, the queen of Carthage and his former lover who'd committed suicide when he abandoned her.

Aeneas was able to enter Elysium when he placed the Golden Bough on its threshold as an offering. In the Elysian Fields, he found his father, who showed him the line of their descendants who would found Rome. After visiting with his father, Aeneas was returned to the land of the living.

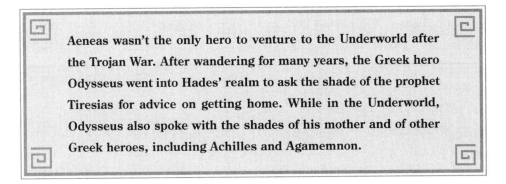

Aeneas wasn't the only hero to venture to the Underworld after the Trojan War. After wandering for many years, the Greek hero Odysseus went into Hades' realm to ask the shade of the prophet Tiresias for advice on getting home. While in the Underworld, Odysseus also spoke with the shades of his mother and of other Greek heroes, including Achilles and Agamemnon.

THESEUS

Theseus's descent into the Underworld wasn't his idea. Unlike the others who journeyed there, Theseus had no great personal mission; rather, he went along to help his friend Pirithous kidnap Persephone. Earlier, Theseus had decided he wanted to marry the famous beauty Helen (who would later become Helen of Troy), so Pirithous had helped him kidnap her. When Pirithous wanted to marry Persephone, Theseus was obliged to return the favor.

The two kings struggled and fought their way through the obstacles of the Underworld and finally reached Hades' palace. Upon arrival, they told Hades that they were going to take Persephone away from him. Hades, greatly amused (and not about to let them succeed), invited them to take a seat. When they did, the men found themselves unable to move. Hades had trapped them in the Chairs of Forgetfulness, where they remained stuck for years. In these chairs, they forgot everything—who they were, where they were, why they were there—and sat motionless, their minds blank.

Later, when Heracles visited the Underworld, he was able to rescue Theseus. Before he could free Pirithous, though, the ground shook violently; Hades was not going to allow the escape of the mortal who'd tried to kidnap his wife. Pirithous remained in the Underworld forever.

SISYPHUS

Sisyphus, king of Corinth, was the cleverest of mortal men—a man who literally outwitted death. During his life, Sisyphus offended the gods, especially Zeus, in many ways. He was greedy, he was a liar, and he often killed guests instead of offering them hospitality. In anger and retaliation, Zeus ordered Hades to imprison Sisyphus in Tartarus, and Hades sent Death (Thanatos) after the mortal.

But Sisyphus fooled Death, chaining up Death with the chains that were intended for Sisyphus. While Death was held prisoner, no mortal could die. Eventually, Ares intervened, because war, his favorite pastime, wasn't much fun for him if no one could die. So Ares freed Death, who turned the tables on Sisyphus.

Before Sisyphus died, though, he made his wife promise that she would deny him proper burial rites, throwing his body into a public square instead of giving him a funeral. She did as he requested, and in the Underworld Sisyphus could not pay the fee to cross the river Styx. He pleaded with Persephone to let him return to the land of the living for three days so that he could punish his wife for her "neglect." The queen of the Underworld granted his request.

Not surprisingly, Sisyphus broke his promise to Persephone and did not return to the Underworld. (He didn't punish his wife, either.) He lived to a ripe old age in complete defiance of the gods. However, since he was a mortal, he eventually returned to the Underworld (some myths say that Hermes dragged him back by force), where he was immediately sent to Tartarus to suffer eternal punishment.

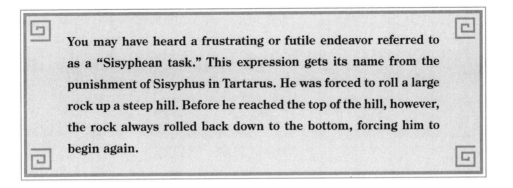

You may have heard a frustrating or futile endeavor referred to as a "Sisyphean task." This expression gets its name from the punishment of Sisyphus in Tartarus. He was forced to roll a large rock up a steep hill. Before he reached the top of the hill, however, the rock always rolled back down to the bottom, forcing him to begin again.

CHASING THE SECRETS OF THE UNDERWORLD

Unless you were favored by the gods and sent to Elysium, the afterlife did not hold much promise for mortals. Ordinary people didn't have much to look forward to in death—and evildoers had much to fear.

Religious rites and cults were created to address the bleakness of the afterlife. For example, several cults concentrated on individual deities (such as Demeter or Dionysus). Worshipers hoped that these deities would share the secrets of the Underworld—including a map of the Underworld that warned of its dangerous places—so that they could gain entry to Elysium. For example, the Eleusinian Mysteries, secret rites celebrated every year in honor of Demeter and Persephone, promised participants union with the gods and rewards after death. You'll read more about the Eleusinian Mysteries in Chapter 9.

DEMETER AND HESTIA:
HOME IS WHERE THE HEART IS

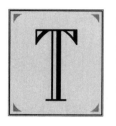

he last two of the original Olympians are Demeter, the goddess of the harvest and fertility, and Hestia, the goddess of the hearth. Taken together, these two goddesses represent the things that sustain and protect life: food and shelter. They were widely honored by the ancients for their importance to people's most basic needs, and they were more directly involved in the daily lives of mortals than the other Olympians.

DEMETER

Demeter was the goddess of fertility, grain, and the harvest. As an earth goddess, she preferred to be near the soil, so she didn't spend much time on Mount Olympus. Unlike Hades, however, who stayed within his realm in the Underworld, Demeter participated in the Olympians' councils or tribunals. Her presence, however, was felt most strongly on Earth. More than any other Olympian deity, Demeter could claim to rule Earth because it was her home.

Generally perceived as a kind and generous goddess, she was popular throughout ancient Greece, perhaps because she was thought to spend more time among the people than the other Olympians did or perhaps because her blessing was so important. Her status as the goddess of the harvest and grain meant that the ancients relied on her to provide them with the food they needed to survive. In addition, Demeter held the powers of destruction and creation, so the people wanted to keep her happy.

DEMETER'S WRATH

Although Demeter's basic nature was kind, she felt emotions just as humans did—and her kindness could change to cruelty when she became angry or upset. For example, when Persephone disappeared, Demeter's grief created hardship for humans as well. Another example of Demeter's cruelty is seen in the story of Erysichthon, a foolish young man who felt her wrath.

Erysichthon was the son of the king of Dotion. He decided to build a great hall in which to hold feasts, but he needed timber. Having no respect for the gods, he entered an oak grove that was sacred to Demeter and planned to cut down enough trees to build his banquet hall. As Erysichthon began chopping, blood flowed from the trees' wounds. A passerby warned him not to proceed, but Erysichthon beheaded the man for his meddling. As he continued his attack on the grove, the tree spirits cried out in despair to Demeter.

Demeter disguised herself as a priestess and approached Erysichthon. She begged him to stop destroying the grove, but he ignored her. Next, Demeter ordered him to leave the place. Laughing at the audacity of a mere priestess, Erysichthon threatened her with his ax. Demeter left, telling him to carry on because he was going to need his dining hall.

Demeter was appalled by Erysichthon's blatant act of sacrilege. She called upon Peina (Hunger) to help her punish him. Peina, glad to be of assistance, immediately went in search of the impious young man.

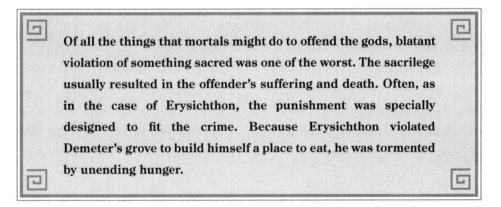

Of all the things that mortals might do to offend the gods, blatant violation of something sacred was one of the worst. The sacrilege usually resulted in the offender's suffering and death. Often, as in the case of Erysichthon, the punishment was specially designed to fit the crime. Because Erysichthon violated Demeter's grove to build himself a place to eat, he was tormented by unending hunger.

When she found him, Peina plagued Erysichthon with constant hunger, no matter how much he ate. Within a few days, he'd spent his entire fortune on food—and still was not sated. Everything was gone but his daughter, who sold herself into slavery to buy her father food. Erysichthon was left with absolutely nothing at all. Still tormented by hunger, he began to eat his own legs. Eventually, he killed himself by devouring his own flesh.

As this myth shows, it was never wise for mortals to challenge the gods. Even Demeter, normally a benevolent goddess, could be cruel when crossed.

DEMETER'S LOVE AFFAIRS

Demeter never married, but she wasn't a virgin goddess like her sister Hestia (whom you'll read about later in this chapter). The myths tell that Demeter had several lovers.

ZEUS

Demeter's first lover was her lustful brother Zeus. Their union produced a daughter, Persephone, and a son, Iacchus. As you read in Chapter 8, Persephone became queen of the Underworld. Iacchus was a minor deity who was involved in the Eleusinian Mysteries (more on those in a moment).

IASION

Another of Demeter's love affairs began when she attended a wedding. There she met the bride's brother Iasion and instantly fell in love. She called him away from the festivities, and the two made love in a fallow field. When they returned to the wedding, Zeus saw mud on Demeter's back and figured out what they'd done. As punishment, he struck the mortal Iasion with a thunderbolt. Some myths say this attack killed him on the spot; others say it crippled him for life.

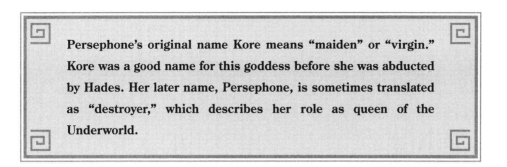

Persephone's original name Kore means "maiden" or "virgin." Kore was a good name for this goddess before she was abducted by Hades. Her later name, Persephone, is sometimes translated as "destroyer," which describes her role as queen of the Underworld.

During this tryst in the field, Demeter conceived two sons: Plutus and Philomelus. Plutus, meaning "wealth," became the protector of the harvest's abundance. Some myths say that Zeus blinded Plutus to ensure that he would not distribute wealth unevenly among the people. Philomelus was a farmer, content simply to work the land with no desire for riches. The myths say that Philomelus invented the wagon (or the plough, according to some), which was pulled by his two oxen. After his death, Philomelus was turned into the constellation of the Ploughman.

MACRIS

Demeter was also said to be smitten by a young nymph, Macris, nursemaid of the infant Dionysus. Together, Macris and her father nurtured and raised the young god, hiding him from Hera. But Hera eventually found out about the child, whose father was Zeus, and in a fit of jealousy drove Macris from her homeland. Macris took refuge in a cave on a small island.

Demeter came forward to help the persecuted nymph. She taught the people on the island how to plant and harvest corn. The myths never say directly that Demeter and Macris had a love affair, but they suggest that Demeter was quite taken with the nymph.

WANDERING THE COUNTRYSIDE

The best-known myth involving Demeter is the story she shares with her daughter Persephone. As you recall from Chapter 8, Hades abducted Persephone and carried her off to the Underworld. Persephone's screams reached her mother's ears, and Demeter immediately rushed to help her daughter. When she arrived at the site of Persephone's abduction, however, she couldn't find her daughter anywhere. Embarking on a frantic search, Demeter wandered the entire earth for nine days and nine nights, carrying a great torch. As she searched, she did not eat, drink, bathe, or sleep.

On the tenth day, she came across Hecate (a minor goddess) who'd heard about the abduction but did not know who had taken Persephone. Hecate led Demeter to Helios, the sun god. As he crossed the sky each day, Helios saw everything that happened in the world below, and he had witnessed Persephone's kidnapping. Helios told Demeter what had happened and tried to reassure her that Hades would take good care of her daughter.

Demeter could not be consoled; she was beside herself with fury, pain, and grief. She abandoned Mount Olympus and her duties as a goddess. Without Demeter's attention, the world was plagued by drought and famine. Plants withered and died, and no new crops would grow.

DEMETER'S TRAVELS

In her grief, Demeter wandered the countryside. Sometimes she encountered hospitality; other times she met with ridicule. For example, a woman named Misme received Demeter in her home and offered her a drink, as was the custom of hospitality. Thirsty, Demeter consumed her drink quickly, and the son of Misme made fun of her, saying she should drink from a tub, not a cup. Angry with his rudeness, Demeter threw the dregs of her drink on the boy, turning him into a lizard.

In Eleusis, Demeter transformed herself into an old woman and stopped to rest beside a well. A daughter of King Celeus invited her to take refreshment in her father's house. Demeter, pleased with the girl's kindness, agreed and followed her home.

At the king's house, Demeter was met with great hospitality from the king's daughter and the queen. Although Demeter sat in silence and would not taste food or drink for a long time, eventually a servant, Iambe, made her laugh with her jokes.

Demeter became a servant in the house of Celeus along with Iambe. The queen trusted Demeter and asked her to nurse her infant son Demophon. In caring for this baby, Demeter found comfort only a child could give her and decided to give the boy the gift of immortality. To do this, Demeter fed him ambrosia during the day and, at night, placed him in the fire to burn away his mortality. But the queen saw the child in the fire and screamed in horror and alarm. Angry at the interruption, Demeter snatched the child from the flames and threw him on the floor.

Demeter changed back into her true form and explained that she would have made the boy immortal, but now he'd be subject to death like other humans. Then, she ordered the royal house to build her a temple and taught them the proper religious rites to perform in her honor. These rites became known as the Eleusinian Mysteries.

A NECESSARY COMPROMISE

When Demeter had neglected her duties for nearly an entire year, Zeus realized that he'd have to intervene or the human race would starve. So Zeus went looking for his sister.

When he found her, however, she would not listen to reason. Instead, she demanded that her daughter be restored to her. Demeter refused to relent, and Zeus knew that his only choice was to appease his sister. He ordered Hades to return Persephone. Hades agreed, but he tried to keep Persephone in the Underworld by tricking her into eating some pomegranate seeds.

The gods reached a compromise: Persephone would spend part of the year with her mother on Earth and part of the year with Hades in the Underworld. Her time in each place corresponded with the seasons. While Persephone was in the Underworld, Earth underwent autumn and winter: Crops withered, it grew cold, and nothing would grow. While Persephone was with her mother, however, Demeter's happiness caused plants to grow and ripen.

STILL A MYSTERY: ELEUSINIAN RITES

The Eleusinian Mysteries, religious rites held in honor of Demeter and Persephone, were the most sacred ritual celebrations in ancient Greece. Eleusis was the city where Demeter stayed while she was in mourning for her daughter. The people built a temple in her honor, where the Eleusinian Mysteries were observed.

The cult was a secret cult, and so it was considered a mystery religion, in which only initiates may participate in rituals and are sworn to secrecy about what happens during those rituals. At Eleusis, stipulations existed about who could be initiated. For example, any person who had ever shed blood could not join the cult. Women and slaves, however, were allowed to participate, even though other sects excluded these groups.

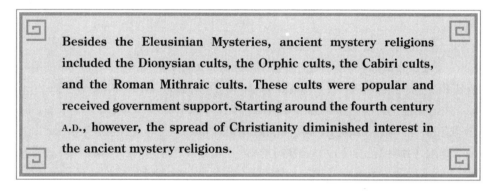

Besides the Eleusinian Mysteries, ancient mystery religions included the Dionysian cults, the Orphic cults, the Cabiri cults, and the Roman Mithraic cults. These cults were popular and received government support. Starting around the fourth century A.D., however, the spread of Christianity diminished interest in the ancient mystery religions.

The Eleusinian initiates took their pledge of secrecy seriously and were careful to honor it. In fact, they did such a good job of maintaining silence that today's scholars do not know what happened in the Eleusinian rites, although there are many theories. There were two sets of rites: the Lesser Mysteries (which corresponded with the harvest) and the Greater Mysteries (which corresponded with the planting season and took ten days to complete).

HESTIA HONORED

Hestia, the eldest of the original Olympian deities, was considered the most compassionate, virtuous, and generous. Her worshipers regarded her as pure goodness.

As the goddess of the hearth, Hestia was a family goddess, and every household worshiped her. Hestia protected the home and all family members, and she kept an eye on everything that happened around the house.

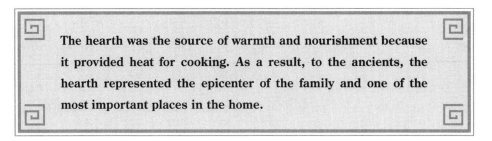

The hearth was the source of warmth and nourishment because it provided heat for cooking. As a result, to the ancients, the hearth represented the epicenter of the family and one of the most important places in the home.

Although Hestia's primary focus was the home, she was also the protector of communities. In effect, her powers expanded outward from the home to include city halls, civic gatherings, and communal properties. In this sense, she was the goddess of places where people gathered.

Because she was worshiped in the home, Hestia had few temples built specifically in her honor (aside from those of the Vestal Virgins, which you'll read about in a moment). In her role as protector of a community, public hearths were sacred to her.

Hestia's role as goddess of the hearth also extended to the home of the gods and goddesses. In her devotion to her own home, Hestia spent all of her time on Mount Olympus; unlike her siblings, she did not leave it to traipse about Earth. Even Hades left his home more often than Hestia did.

This reluctance to leave her home may be the reason Hestia doesn't have a myth of her own. Myths rarely mention her, although this silence may be due to the fact that she was a chaste goddess and it was sacrilegious to gossip about her. Or it could be that the exploits of the other gods—filled with love affairs, jealousy, rivalries, and revenge—simply made more entertaining stories.

HESTIA'S UNSUITABLE SUITORS

Like her niece Athena, Hestia loved peace. While Athena would participate in war if necessary, Hestia refused to get involved in any dispute, no matter the cause or the consequences. This strong belief in peace was one reason that Hestia, though essentially goddess of the home and family, did not marry and have a family of her own. Even so, she did have suitors.

Her brother Poseidon and her nephew Apollo, the god of music, both courted her—or at least they wanted to. Rivalry sparked between the two gods, creating a heated argument that had the potential to turn into a larger battle. Hestia, not wanting to be a catalyst for war, refused them both and appealed to Zeus to intervene.

Zeus granted Hestia permission to remain a virgin and offered her his protection. With Zeus on her side, Hestia swore an oath to remain eternally chaste. Her vow of chastity was the reason that she required the Vestal Virgins to be chaste while they served her.

But not everyone respected Hestia's vow of chastity. During a Dionysiac festival, Priapus, son of Aphrodite and Dionysus, saw Hestia and lusted after her. That same night, as Hestia lay sleeping, Priapus attempted to violate her. He nearly succeeded, but a donkey brayed loudly and awoke the goddess. Seeing Priapus, Hestia screamed, and he ran away. From that time forward, the feast of Hestia included adorning donkeys with flowers.

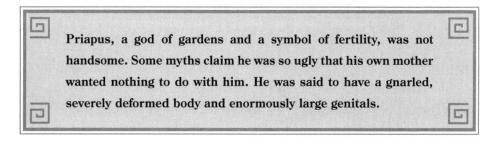

Priapus, a god of gardens and a symbol of fertility, was not handsome. Some myths claim he was so ugly that his own mother wanted nothing to do with him. He was said to have a gnarled, severely deformed body and enormously large genitals.

THE VESTAL VIRGINS

Although most people worshiped Hestia in their homes, one of the most famous temples of the ancient world was erected in her honor: the Temple of Vesta. Located in Rome (Vesta was Hestia's Latin name), this temple was attended by priestesses known as the Vestal Virgins.

In the Temple of Vesta, six priestesses served the goddess. Chosen from the best families of Rome, the priestesses were required to be good-looking, with no physical deformities. They were also required to have two living parents at the time of their appointment. Priestesses of Vesta began their training between the ages of six and ten. The Vestal Virgins were a very important part of Roman culture, and for a child to be chosen was a great honor for the girl and for her family.

BECOMING A VESTAL VIRGIN

A young girl who was in training to become a priestess of Vesta was required to take a vow of chastity and to promise to serve the temple for thirty years. Her initiation included a ceremony in which she was escorted to the temple and met by other Vestal Virgins. They dressed her in white clothing and cut her hair. The training took ten years. After that, the new priestess went into active service for another ten years. During this time, her responsibilities included maintaining the Vestal Fire and sprinkling it with holy water each day. After her active service ended, the priestess spent another ten years training new initiates.

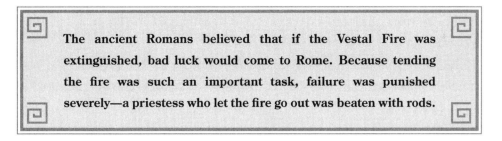

The ancient Romans believed that if the Vestal Fire was extinguished, bad luck would come to Rome. Because tending the fire was such an important task, failure was punished severely—a priestess who let the fire go out was beaten with rods.

After thirty years of service to the temple, the priestess could become a private citizen, able to marry and bear children if she desired. However, most Vestal Virgins chose to continue serving the goddess for the rest of their lives. Service to Vesta was, after all, the only life they had ever known.

The Vestal Virgins were treated differently from the common women of Rome. Because they were not under the power of any man, they had some of the same rights men enjoyed. For example, priestesses of Vesta could participate in court trials and create wills to bequeath their belongings to whomever they chose.

BREAKING THE VOW OF CHASTITY

The greatest crime a Vestal Virgin could commit was to break her vow of chastity. Doing so was a betrayal of the goddess, but it was also a betrayal of the city of Rome, because Romans believed that the city's well-being depended on the Vestal Virgins' faithfulness. Any priestess caught breaking her vow of chastity was buried alive.

This burial was part of an elaborate ceremony. The disgraced priestess was wrapped in a burial shroud: thin strips of cloth covered with thick linens. This shroud immobilized her and stifled any cries or pleas. Then, she was placed on a stretcher used to carry the dead and conveyed through town in a procession. A priest intoned prayers at the burial site, and the heavy linens were stripped from the woman.

The woman was lowered into the vault, which had been prepared earlier, and placed on a bed. The vault held a single day's worth of water, food, and light. The vault was shut and the grave was filled in. Those participating in the execution were careful to smooth the earth so that no one could tell it was a gravesite.

Because she was buried without the customary burial rituals, it was thought that a disgraced priestess of Vesta would never reach the Land of the Dead. Her sacrifice was meant to appease the deities and prevent any harm from befalling Rome.

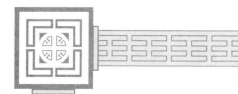

CHAPTER 10

ARES AND THE ART OF WAR

ncient battlefields were places of confusion, bravery, violence, brutality, and bloodlust. They were also where Ares, god of war, felt most at home. Ares loved nothing more than a good fight; he represented the violence and chaos of war. As you'll read in this chapter, Ares would rather use his weapons than his brain; this god was all about muscle and brute force.

A DETESTABLE DEITY

As the son of Zeus and Hera, Ares deserved respect. As this divine child grew older, however, he developed a repugnant personality. Even though he was one of the twelve great Olympians, not many could bring themselves to like Ares—not even his parents.

Ares cared for nothing but battle and bloodshed. He had no interest in ideals of justice or the strategic challenges of war. Instead, he strove to heighten war's terror and destruction. Most myths associate him with the spirit of war itself and show him without morality, principles, or decency.

Ares certainly looked the part of a fearless, brutal warrior. A tall, muscle-bound god who towered over mortals, Ares always wore armor and a helmet and carried a shield and either a sword or a spear (sometimes both). Ares was known for his terrible war cry, which he would loose before or during a battle, striking fear into the hearts of his enemies.

Despite his fearsomeness, Ares lacked cleverness and wisdom. A god of action, Ares lived for the excitement of battle and bloodshed, but he avoided strategizing. Since he was unwilling to think things through, he was easily outwitted.

LIVING AMONG THE WILD

Ares lived in Thrace, a land beyond the borders of Greece located north of the Aegean Sea. The Thracians didn't speak Greek, but their language appealed to Ares even more: They spoke the language of war.

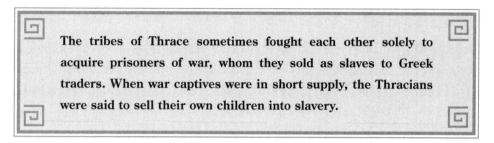

The tribes of Thrace sometimes fought each other solely to acquire prisoners of war, whom they sold as slaves to Greek traders. When war captives were in short supply, the Thracians were said to sell their own children into slavery.

The Thracians were divided into tribes, and each tribe had a warlord. The Greeks saw the Thracians as a rowdy race, known for becoming intoxicated and picking fights. The Thracians were skilled, savage warriors who wielded heavy swords and were ferocious in battle. This is why the Greeks regarded Thrace as the ideal dwelling place for Ares—he could live there among bloodthirsty, war-loving bullies.

ON THE WARPATH

Although Ares was unpopular among gods and mortals alike, he wasn't a complete loner. The myths often describe him in the company of one or more of these attendants:

- **Deimos:** Personification of fear
- **Enyo:** Goddess of battle
- **Eris:** Personification of discord
- **Phobos:** Personification of terror

These four beings often helped Ares prepare for battle. As Ares created a fog of fury that filled warriors on both sides with the desire for battle, his four companions would work to spread terror and discord among them. The work of Ares' attendants made the battle even more bloody and desperate.

THE GOD OF WAR IN LOVE

Although Ares was generally hated and feared (as war itself is), he still had several love affairs. In particular, the goddess Aphrodite was one of the few who truly loved him. Ares also had a few other conquests on the field of love.

LOVING APHRODITE

The best known of Ares' love affairs was with Aphrodite, goddess of love, a case of "opposites attracting." Aphrodite was the only Olympian deity who cared for Ares. Their love affair was passionate and rather scandalous. (Chapter 15 gives all the details.) Together they had four children, although some myths put the total at five.

Deimos and Phobos, sons of Aphrodite and Ares and the personifications of fear and terror, delighted in accompanying their father to battles. Anteros, another son, grew up to become the god of passion and was sometimes also called the god of tenderness. Harmonia, a daughter, was later given in marriage to Cadmus, king of Thebes.

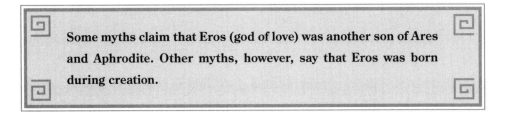

Some myths claim that Eros (god of love) was another son of Ares and Aphrodite. Other myths, however, say that Eros was born during creation.

AEROPE

Ares fell in love with a young mortal woman named Aerope. The myths don't record much about their love affair aside from the fact that they had a son together. Sadly, giving birth to a god's son was too much for this young woman and she died in childbirth. The child survived, however; Ares made sure the baby was able to suckle from his dead mother's breasts.

AGLAURUS

Aglaurus was a name shared by a mother and her daughter. Ares fell in love with the daughter. Her father was Cecrops, a king of Athens. The union of

Aglaurus and Ares produced a daughter, Alcippe. Later, the son of Poseidon raped Alcippe, an act that eventually led to Ares' trial for murder.

CHRYSE

The union of Ares and Chryse led to a son, Phlegyas. One myth says that Phlegyas's daughter was violated by Apollo. When Phlegyas learned of the rape, he set fire to Apollo's temple at Delphi. Apollo, appalled by this act of sacrilege, killed Phlegyas with his arrows. Then Apollo sent Phlegyas to the Underworld, where the mortal suffered the eternal torment of being beneath a huge boulder that could fall and crush him at any moment.

CYRENE

Cyrene, a nymph, was the daughter of the king of Lapithae. Her affair with Ares produced a son named Diomedes, who would become the king of the Bistones in Thrace. He was best known for his four savage mares, which he fed human flesh each day. Diomedes shows up later in a myth of Heracles (see Chapter 19).

DEMONICE

By Demonice, Ares had four sons: Evenus, Molus, Pylus, and Thestius. Evenus became the king of Aetolia and had a river named after him. Molus met an untimely death when he tried to rape a nymph and was beheaded. Pylus was not well known, and Thestius became a king in Aetolia.

HARPINNA

Harpinna was the daughter of Asopus, a river god. The union of Ares and Harpinna produced a son, Oenomaus, who grew up to become king of Pisa. He also founded a city, which he named after his mother. (Some myths claim that Sterope, one of the Pleiades, and not Harpinna was the mother of Oeno-maus, but in these myths Ares is still his father.)

OTRERE

Otrere was queen of the Amazons. She gave birth to Ares' daughter Penthesilea, who later took her mother's place as the Amazons' queen. During the Trojan War, Penthesilea was slain in battle by Achilles. After Achilles had stripped the dead queen of her armor, he fell in love with her beauty and was saddened by her loss.

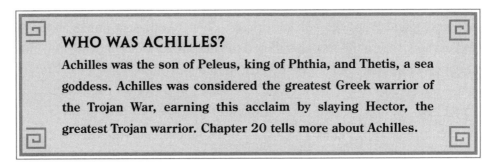

WHO WAS ACHILLES?
Achilles was the son of Peleus, king of Phthia, and Thetis, a sea goddess. Achilles was considered the greatest Greek warrior of the Trojan War, earning this acclaim by slaying Hector, the greatest Trojan warrior. Chapter 20 tells more about Achilles.

PROTOGENIA

Protogenia was the daughter of Calydon and Aeolia. Calydon, a great hero, was held in such high regard that a city in Aetolia was named after him. Aeolia herself was a famous heroine. You'd think that Protogenia's bloodline, combined with an Olympian's, would add another hero to the family, but she and Ares produced Oxylus, a rather ordinary child.

PYRENE

The union of Ares and Pyrene produced a son, Cycnus, who inherited his father's bloodlust. Cycnus murdered pilgrims as they traveled to Delphi and used his victims' skulls to build a temple to his father. Cycnus is most famous for battling Heracles. Ares' son didn't stand long against the hero, who was aided by Athena. Angered by the death of his son, Ares tried to take revenge on Heracles, but Zeus intervened, using his thunderbolts. The death of Cycnus was never avenged.

AMAZON WARRIORS

You read earlier that Ares mated with an Amazon queen and their union produced another Amazon queen. Ares was an important god to the entire Amazon race, not just those who were looking for help in battle. The myths surrounding these women were popular in ancient times.

The Amazons were a mythological nation of female warriors. They were thought to have their own laws, their own means of providing food and shelter, and their own government ruled by a queen. Different myths place the Amazons' realm in different locations, including Thrace, Scythia, the Caucasus Mountains, and the areas occupied by modern-day Turkey or Libya.

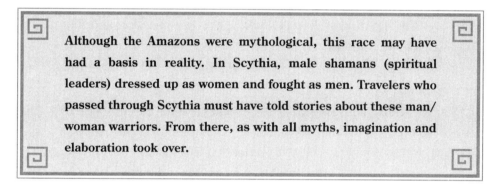

Although the Amazons were mythological, this race may have had a basis in reality. In Scythia, male shamans (spiritual leaders) dressed up as women and fought as men. Travelers who passed through Scythia must have told stories about these man/woman warriors. From there, as with all myths, imagination and elaboration took over.

THE MEN AND CHILDREN

According to the myths, Amazon women could not bear to be in the presence of a man. (The only exceptions were male servants who performed menial tasks.) Of course, the Amazons also needed men to propagate their race. So Amazon women mated with strangers, normally travelers or foreigners, with the intention of getting pregnant. These women wanted nothing more to do with the biological fathers of their children. There was no such thing as a father in Amazon culture.

When a male child was born, the Amazons disposed of the baby. Some stories say the Amazons sent male children to live with their fathers. Others paint the Amazons as cruel, injuring the child in some way (perhaps by blinding) and then leaving him to die. (Occasionally, a kind passerby took pity on the wounded child.) Yet others say the male babies were killed at birth. A few male children, however, were allowed to live and were raised as slaves of the tribe.

Girl children were valued. Yet because the girls were destined to become warriors, they were raised with that outcome in mind. Since the right breast could interfere with a woman's skill in archery, the girls were fed mare's milk to prevent them from developing breasts, according to some myths. Other myths say that the Amazons cut off or burned the girls' right breasts to ensure their skill. Classical writers have also traced the word *Amazon* to *a-mazos*, which meant "without a breast."

WARRIOR PRINCESSES

Like Ares, the Amazons revered war. War was their passion and their talent. They worshiped Ares, whom they considered the father of their tribe, and his half-sister Artemis, a virgin goddess who represented female strength and shunned men.

Several Greek heroes—such as Heracles, Bellerophon, and Theseus—appear in myths with the Amazons (see Chapter 19). The Amazons were also featured in the Trojan War (Chapter 20). They fought on the side of the Trojans, and their queen, Penthesilea, was killed by Achilles.

SUPERWOMEN

In art, Amazon women were depicted like the male warriors of the time. Normally seen on horseback, the Amazons wore armor made of animal skins and carried either a bow or spear. An Amazon warrior possessed the strength of a man and was as savage as a wild animal, but she was especially dangerous because she had reason and cunning.

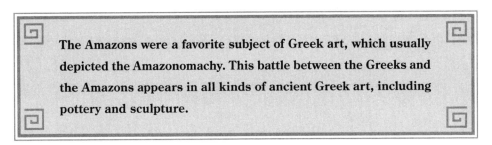

The Amazons were a favorite subject of Greek art, which usually depicted the Amazonomachy. This battle between the Greeks and the Amazons appears in all kinds of ancient Greek art, including pottery and sculpture.

The myths about the Amazons entertained men and women alike, but in different ways. Ancient Greece was essentially a man's world in which women had few rights, so the Amazons, a symbol of freedom and strength, were admired by many housewives of the time. (These women probably enjoyed the stories about the Amazons having male servants to do household chores.) The men, on the other hand, were in awe of the Amazons. The idea that a woman did not need men, that she could possess the same strength as a man (or perhaps even greater), must have been a bit frightening. For the ancients, the figure of the Amazon held both horror and fascination.

SIBLING RIVALRY: ARES VERSUS ATHENA

Ares was the god of war and his half-sister Athena was the goddess of war. How could two deities enjoy dominion over the same realm? The answer lies in the different aspects of war that appealed to each. Ares loved the bloodshed and destruction that war brought. Although Athena was a skilled fighter, she preferred peace; she stood for justice and the ideals for which battles were fought. Athena enjoyed the intellectual side of war, the strategy and planning, whereas Ares preferred the chaos and physical exertion of an actual battle. Because of their different approaches to war, these two deities often found themselves in conflict.

One example of their animosity appears in accounts of the Trojan War. Ares joined the Trojan forces, while Athena fought with the Greeks. During a battle, Ares was fighting beside Hector (the best Trojan warrior) when he came face to face with Diomedes (not his son but the king of Aetolia). This Diomedes was held in high regard by the Greeks as a magnificent warrior.

Ares and Diomedes met in combat. Their fight caught Athena's attention. Athena used Hades' helmet of invisibility to intervene and set Ares' spear off-course. This allowed Diomedes to strike, and his blow wounded Ares severely. The injury forced Ares to leave the battlefield and return to Mount Olympus, where Zeus healed him.

At another point in the war, Ares attacked Athena with his spear. But the spear hit Athena's protective magical aegis. The spear didn't hurt Athena, but it did make her angry. She picked up a boulder and hurled it at Ares. Stunned by the blow, Ares collapsed. Aphrodite saw him fall and tried to help him escape. But Athena, still angry, attacked Aphrodite and struck her the old-fashioned way—using her bare fist.

TRIED FOR MURDER

It probably comes as no surprise that Ares, in light of his hunger for blood and destruction, was once put on trial for the murder of Alirrothios, the son of Poseidon and Euryte, a nymph.

One day, Alirrothios came across Ares' daughter Alcippe near a spring. His lust for her culminated in rape. Ares was livid when he learned of this crime against his daughter. (According to some accounts, he witnessed the violation.) Ares killed Alirrothios to avenge Alcippe. Because Ares had killed his son, Poseidon took Ares to court for murder.

The trial was held on the hill overlooking the spot where the killing had occurred. The gods gathered in a tribunal and listened to both sides of the case. After deliberating, the tribunal acquitted Ares of murder.

The site of Ares' trial became known as the Areopagus, or "hill of Ares." The Areopagus was the meeting place of the council that governed Athens. During the era of Athenian democracy, the Areopagus was also the site of a court that tried cases of murder and other serious crimes. The court had approximately 250 members, and its decisions were final.

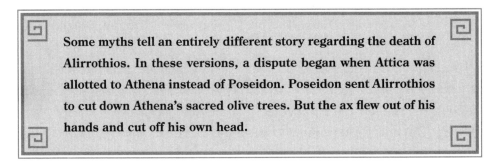

Some myths tell an entirely different story regarding the death of Alirrothios. In these versions, a dispute began when Attica was allotted to Athena instead of Poseidon. Poseidon sent Alirrothios to cut down Athena's sacred olive trees. But the ax flew out of his hands and cut off his own head.

ARES IMPRISONED

As you read in Chapter 7, Poseidon had two sons who were Giants, Otus and Ephialtes, known for wreaking havoc among the gods and goddesses. One of their exploits involved the capture and imprisonment of Ares. The story of Ares' imprisonment begins with the death of Adonis, a beautiful young man for whom Aphrodite felt great love. Some myths say her love was romantic and passionate; others say her love for the youth was that of a mother for her son. Regardless, Ares was unhappy with the attention his lover paid to Adonis. So while Adonis was hunting on Mount Lebanon, Ares transformed himself into a wild boar and gored Adonis to death.

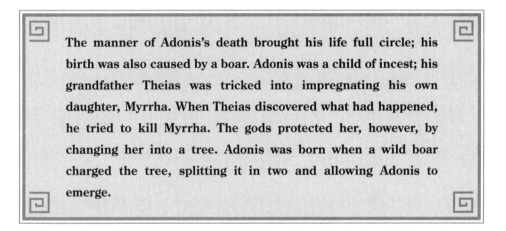

The manner of Adonis's death brought his life full circle; his birth was also caused by a boar. Adonis was a child of incest; his grandfather Theias was tricked into impregnating his own daughter, Myrrha. When Theias discovered what had happened, he tried to kill Myrrha. The gods protected her, however, by changing her into a tree. Adonis was born when a wild boar charged the tree, splitting it in two and allowing Adonis to emerge.

Some myths say that Otus and Ephialtes were upset by the death of Adonis because he'd been entrusted to their care by Aphrodite. Or perhaps they simply admired the beautiful youth, as most did. Whatever the reason, the two Giants set out to punish Ares for killing Adonis.

They captured Ares and bound him with chains. Then, they imprisoned him in a bronze cauldron (or jar) and left him there. Ares suffered in this prison for thirteen long months. The Giants' stepmother, Eriboea, eventually told Hermes where Ares was. The clever Hermes was able to slip past the two Giants and release Ares.

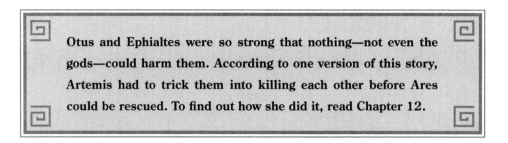

Otus and Ephialtes were so strong that nothing—not even the gods—could harm them. According to one version of this story, Artemis had to trick them into killing each other before Ares could be rescued. To find out how she did it, read Chapter 12.

Although his long imprisonment nearly caused Ares to lose his appetite for war, he soon recovered and returned to his bloodthirsty ways.

CHAPTER 11
ATHENA:
THE PEACEFUL WARRIOR

his chapter introduces Athena, goddess of war and wisdom. Unlike her bellicose half-brother Ares, Athena preferred peace to war. She preferred settling disputes through reason and intelligence. When war was inevitable, however, Athena was a goddess you'd want on your side. Skilled in strategy and warfare, Athena was both a master tactician and a fierce warrior. She was also a prolific inventor and skilled craftswoman.

THE BIRTH OF ATHENA

Athena was the daughter of Zeus and Metis. But Athena wasn't born in the way babies usually come into the world. Her unique birth made her special even among the gods.

When Metis became pregnant with Zeus's child, Gaia warned Zeus that if Metis gave birth to a daughter, a son would then follow. That son would grow to surpass Zeus in strength and would depose his father. Zeus, like his own father and grandfather, feared being overthrown. So he decided to make sure that this fearsome son would never be born. Zeus tricked Metis into transforming herself into a tiny fly. Then, he swallowed her.

Even though Zeus had swallowed Metis, she was still pregnant. One day, Zeus was incapacitated by a massive headache. Crying out in pain, Zeus ordered Hephaestus to use his ax to split open his pounding head. Hephaestus did as he was told. (Other versions of the myth say it was Prometheus, Hermes, or Palaemon who did the deed.) As soon as the ax split Zeus's skull, his daughter Athena emerged from his head, fully grown and dressed in armor. Instead of a baby's wail, Athena met the world with a battle cry.

In her youth, Athena had a friend Pallas, whose name meant "maiden." Pallas was the beautiful daughter of Triton, a sea god. The two girls often practiced warfare together. One day, they quarreled over some small matter, and Pallas tried to hit Athena. Zeus, playing the part of overprotective father, interfered and deflected the blow. Athena retaliated, striking at Pallas, but Pallas was frightened of Zeus and didn't defend herself. Athena's blow killed her young friend.

Athena was deeply sorry for her death and erected a statue in her friend's honor. The statue took its place next to Zeus on Mount Olympus, but later it fell to Earth in the region that would become the city of Troy. Athena also took Pallas's name and was often referred to as Pallas Athena.

ALMIGHTY ATHENA

Athena inherited her mother's wisdom and her father's sense of justice. These two features made for a brilliant and merciful goddess. She excelled equally in activities traditionally associated with either women or men, such as weaving and warfare. People in need of aid, especially heroes and soldiers, called upon Athena's protection. Under her care, heroes such as Heracles and Odysseus successfully completed their difficult missions.

But Athena's realm of protection extended beyond individuals. She was also the protector of several cities (including Athens and Argos), and she created a system of justice based on law and order (replacing the old system of blood feuds and revenge). A wise and just goddess, Athena sat on many councils and took part in many tribunals.

A GODDESS WHO HAD IT ALL

Athena's influence extended beyond wisdom and war to encompass other spheres. For example, she was a patron goddess of the arts, including literature, poetry, music, and philosophy. Several poets were inspired to praise her gray eyes and her stately presence. Athena was also the patron of spinners and weavers; she was credited with the invention of weaving and other domestic crafts.

Thanks to her cleverness and her willingness to work hard, she also became the patron goddess of metalworkers, carpenters, and other skilled workers. Athena was universally admired: by men and women, by warriors and craftsmen, by heroes and commoners.

WELL, WHO ALMOST HAD IT ALL

There was one area of human experience, however, that Athena could neither understand nor relate to: sexuality and motherhood. Athena was born without a mother, and she herself had no children, so the idea of motherhood did not interest her. She was similarly uninterested in passionate love and all that went with it. As a virgin goddess, Athena never allowed physical love to interfere with her sound judgment—unlike so many other gods and goddesses. Athena did enjoy the company of men, but as comrades, not lovers.

ATHENIAN CULTS

Nearly everyone had a reason to worship Athena, and numerous shrines and temples were built in her honor. Because she protected several cities, those cities built elaborate temples and dedicated them solely to Athena. Two of the best-known of Athena's temples are the Parthenon and the Erechtheum, both of which were located atop the acropolis in Athens.

THE PARTHENON

The Parthenon is one of the most famous temples of ancient Greece. Part of the reason for its fame is that it remains standing today. The Parthenon is a popular destination for tourists and students of architecture.

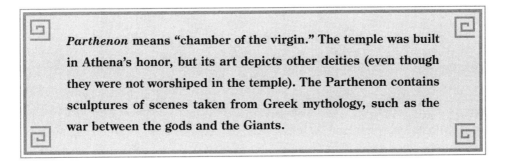

Parthenon means "chamber of the virgin." The temple was built in Athena's honor, but its art depicts other deities (even though they were not worshiped in the temple). The Parthenon contains sculptures of scenes taken from Greek mythology, such as the war between the gods and the Giants.

Built in the fifth century B.C. to house a thirty-five-foot-high ivory-and-gold statue of Athena, the immense temple both honored Athena and glorified the city of Athens. Looking at the expensive and elaborate Parthenon, no one could doubt the grandeur and wealth of Athens. Although it was a magnificent showplace, the Parthenon did not serve the practical purposes that other temples did. The massive statue of Athena was not associated with any known cult. In fact, the traditional rituals and sacrifices were performed for an older cult statue of Athena, which was housed in the Erechtheum.

THE ERECHTHEUM

The Erechtheum, located near the Parthenon and not nearly as grand, served a more practical purpose. It was home to the olivewood statue of Athena that was central to the Panathenaea festivals. The ancient Athenians believed that this statue had fallen from the heavens themselves.

At midsummer, the traditional time of Athena's birth, those who wished to pay tribute to the goddess gathered. Athletic and musical competitions took place, but the main event was the dressing of the wooden statue. Every year, a select group of women made a new woolen gown for the statue. During the festival, a procession carried this gown through the city and draped it over the statue in the Erechtheum. Another festival involving this statue took place every four years and was called the Great Panathenaea. During this celebration, the statue was carried to the sea, where it was washed.

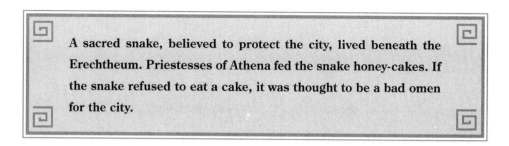

A sacred snake, believed to protect the city, lived beneath the Erechtheum. Priestesses of Athena fed the snake honey-cakes. If the snake refused to eat a cake, it was thought to be a bad omen for the city.

ATHENA THE INVENTOR

Athena was credited with several inventions that advanced civilization and made life easier for people. The long list of Athena's inventions illustrates her versatility. Various myths claim that she invented the plow, the yoke, and the bridle. Other inventions included the war chariot, the flute, the trumpet, and the science of mathematics. On a culinary note, she introduced olive oil.

Athena is also said to have overseen the building of the first ship, the *Argo*, which carried Jason and the Argonauts on the quest for the Golden Fleece. Although some myths deny that this was the first ship ever built, all agree that it was the largest ship ever made.

A HERO'S BEST FRIEND

Athena often appears in myths that feature a great hero or adventurer trying to succeed in a challenging trial. With her intelligence, versatility, and skill, Athena was the natural choice to help a hero aspiring to great achievements. This section details some of the adventures in which Athena stepped in to help a hero.

DIOMEDES

Diomedes was a famous hero of the Trojan War. His successes, however, were largely due to Athena. As one of the lucky men under her protection, Diomedes made a name for himself as a great warrior.

During the Trojan War, Diomedes fought on the side of the Greeks. He wounded Ares in battle, driving him from the field. Aphrodite was also wounded while trying to help Ares from the field. (Some myths say that Diomedes wounded her, but others say it was Athena.) On the same day, Diomedes also wounded Aeneas (son of the Trojan prince Anchises and an excellent fighter) and killed the Trojan prince Pandarus—a war's worth of work accomplished in one day. Even a great warrior like Diomedes could not have achieved these victories without Athena's aid; he probably would have been killed by Ares if Athena had not stepped in to protect him.

Athena's assistance was not restricted to the battlefield. After the war ended, Athena offered her protection to Diomedes to ensure his safe and speedy voyage home.

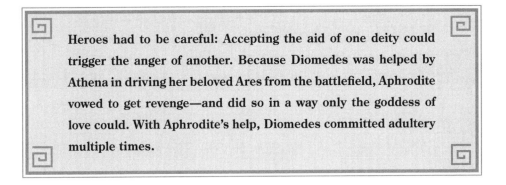

Heroes had to be careful: Accepting the aid of one deity could trigger the anger of another. Because Diomedes was helped by Athena in driving her beloved Ares from the battlefield, Aphrodite vowed to get revenge—and did so in a way only the goddess of love could. With Aphrodite's help, Diomedes committed adultery multiple times.

HERACLES

The hero Heracles undertook the Twelve Labors (see Chapter 19). These labors were seemingly impossible tasks—and indeed, no mortal man would have been able to accomplish a single one without the help of an immortal. Luckily for Heracles, he had two advantages: He was the son of Zeus, and he was assisted by Athena. On the other hand, the wrathful Hera, furious at Zeus's affair with Heracles' mother, opposed his every move. The story of Heracles is more than the story of a hero; it's the story of the gods in strife with each other.

Athena proclaimed herself the protector of Heracles throughout his ordeals. She came to his aid several times, offering guidance and always keeping him one step ahead of the game. Heracles' success would have been impossible without the help of the goddess of wisdom.

JASON

Jason gained fame through his quest for the Golden Fleece, a quest under-taken to reclaim a throne that was rightfully his. The Golden Fleece belonged to a great flying ram, son of Poseidon and Theophane. The task was intended to be impossible, preventing Jason from claiming his birthright.

As if his near-impossible quest weren't enough, Jason had to overcome several other challenges along the way. This was where Athena came in, giving Jason the bravery and spirit to take on these obstacles. To read about the challenges of Jason's quest and how he rose to meet them, flip ahead to Chapter 19.

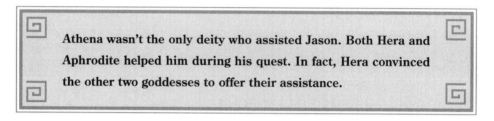

Athena wasn't the only deity who assisted Jason. Both Hera and Aphrodite helped him during his quest. In fact, Hera convinced the other two goddesses to offer their assistance.

PERSEUS

Perseus, another great hero described in Chapter 19, accepted a mission from King Polydectes to retrieve the head of the Gorgon Medusa, a terrifying creature with hair of snakes and a stare that could turn mortals and immortals alike to stone. Obtaining Medusa's head seemed an impossible task, but Perseus knew that with the goddess Athena on his side he would be victorious.

Athena had her own reasons for wanting Perseus to succeed. To put it simply, she hated Medusa. Athena gave Perseus a polished bronze shield and offered him guidance, and Perseus readily accepted.

When Perseus reached Medusa's lair, Athena told him what to do. Instead of looking at the sleeping Medusa directly—which would turn him to stone—Perseus watched her reflection in his bronze shield. Keeping his eyes on the reflection, rather than looking at Medusa herself, Perseus beheaded the monster.

Perseus knew that he never would have succeeded without Athena, so he showed his appreciation by mounting Medusa's head on Athena's shield. A Gorgon's head was a great aid in battle, because it had the power to paralyze one's enemies. This shield became a symbol of the goddess, and rarely was she depicted without it.

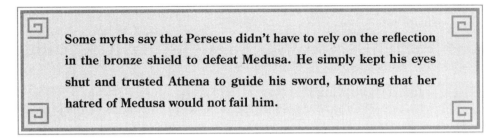

Some myths say that Perseus didn't have to rely on the reflection in the bronze shield to defeat Medusa. He simply kept his eyes shut and trusted Athena to guide his sword, knowing that her hatred of Medusa would not fail him.

ODYSSEUS

The great hero Odysseus was another favorite of Athena's. In fact, she had a respect for him that most deities never felt for mere mortals. Odysseus possessed intelligence, cunning, and a sense of justice that reminded Athena of herself. She showed her appreciation by aiding him throughout the Trojan War and his journey home—quite a task, considering that the war lasted ten years and the journey took another ten years.

The ten-year journey was full of obstacles, but Odysseus remained pious and Athena remained his protector. You may be wondering why such a powerful goddess did not see Odysseus quickly and safely home as she did Diomedes. Unfortunately, Odysseus had managed to get himself on Poseidon's bad side, and earning the enmity of the god of the seas was a problem when he had to cross those seas to get home. (To read about Odysseus's journey, see Chapter 19.)

ATHENA'S OTHER STORIES

As the goddess of wisdom, war, and skill, Athena played a role in many myths. Sometimes she starred as a main character; other times she played a supporting role. Athena was a popular deity among the ancients, and one way the storytellers showed their respect—and benefited from her popularity—was to feature her in their stories. Here are some of the many myths in which Athena plays a role:

- Athena worked with Hermes to purify the Danaides of the murders of their husbands.
- She struck Marsyas for playing a double flute that she had cursed and thrown away.
- Athena competed in a beauty contest, judged by the Trojan Paris, with Hera and Aphrodite. (Aphrodite won.)
- When Ajax violated Cassandra, who'd sought sanctuary in Troy's temple of Athena, the goddess made sure Ajax didn't survive his journey home.
- Athena cast the deciding vote at Orestes' trial for the murder of his mother, Clytemnestra.
- Athena planned to make one of her favored mortals, Tydeus, immortal, but changed her mind when she witnessed him eating the brains of his enemy.

It isn't difficult to find myths that involve Athena. With her intelligence and interest in the affairs of mortals, Athena is a character who doesn't disappoint.

CHAPTER 12

ARTEMIS:
THE THRILL OF THE HUNT

Daughter of Zeus, Artemis took her place among the twelve great Olympians as the goddess of archery and hunting. She was the elder twin sister of Apollo, and brother and sister were devoted to each other. A virgin goddess, Artemis valued her own chastity and demanded chastity of her followers. She was usually depicted as a young, untamed, independent woman, roaming the forests and mountainsides and forever on the hunt.

LADY OF THE WILD

As the daughter of Zeus and Leto, Artemis was one of many who suffered Hera's jealous fury. During Leto's pregnancy, Hera sent Python, a great snake, to chase Leto. Leto managed to escape, but when it was time to give birth, she had a difficult time finding someone to shelter her because all were afraid of Hera's wrath. Eventually, Leto found refuge with her sister Asteria on the island of Ortygia, where she gave birth to Artemis. As soon as Artemis was born, the girl was strong enough to help her mother cross the sea to the island of Delos and assist her in giving birth to her brother Apollo. Apollo later strangled Python (or shot her with arrows) to punish the snake for pursuing his mother.

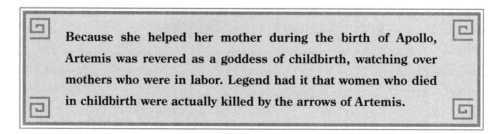

Because she helped her mother during the birth of Apollo, Artemis was revered as a goddess of childbirth, watching over mothers who were in labor. Legend had it that women who died in childbirth were actually killed by the arrows of Artemis.

Zeus favored his young daughter and told her to ask for anything she wanted. At the age of three, Artemis asked for three things: a bow and arrows, all the mountains on Earth as her home, and eternal virginity. Zeus granted all she asked. Along with these gifts, he also granted her thirty cities.

Hera, of course, was jealous of the attention Zeus paid to a child he'd had with another woman. So she tormented the young girl by insulting her, spilling her arrows, and striking her. Perhaps it was due to Hera's ill treatment that Artemis grew into a strong-willed woman who was quick to punish those who crossed her.

Aside from Hera's torment, Artemis had a happy existence. She roamed the mountainsides in the company of her nymphs, hunting, and occasionally punishing those who offended her.

It may seem ironic that the goddess of the hunt was also the protector of all wild animals. Although she hunted and killed animals, she did not want to see them suffer. Her arrows were said to provide a clean and painless death (when she wanted them to). But Artemis also enjoyed the challenge of the hunt. The mountains were her playground and hunting her favorite game. Homer called her the "Lady of Wild Animals."

AN OVERPROTECTIVE DAUGHTER

Artemis could be harsh and even cruel, but one of her greatest qualities was her complete and unreserved devotion to her mother. Both she and Apollo recognized the difficulty their mother had had in bringing them into the world, and they respected no one more than her. Throughout the myths Artemis and Apollo joined forces to protect their mother or to seek revenge on those who bothered her.

TORTURING TITYUS

Filled with jealousy and recognizing that she could not prevent the birth of the divine twins, Hera still wanted to punish Leto. While the twins were away from their mother, Hera filled the Giant Tityus with lust for Leto. Acting on his desires, Tityus tried to rape Leto, but Leto cried out to her children, who rushed to her aid. The two shot their arrows at Tityus and killed him before he could violate their mother. (Some myths say that Apollo wasn't present and that Artemis killed Tityus.)

After his death, Tityus was sent to Tartarus. This Giant was so huge that, when he was secured to the ground, his body covered several acres (between two and nine, depending on the myth). Every day, a pair of vultures tore out his liver and ate it, but it grew back every night.

NIOBE SPEAKS HASTILY

Niobe was the wife of Amphion, a son of Zeus. She bore him six daughters and six sons. (Some myths disagree about the number: Some say seven daughters and seven sons or even ten daughters and ten sons.) Niobe was a proud mother, and she made the mistake of bragging about her many children on Leto's feast day. Niobe said that her children were better than the twins of Leto, and that she was superior to Leto because she had twelve children, whereas Leto had only two.

Offended by the audacity of this woman, Leto called upon her children to take revenge. Happy to oblige their mother, the twins killed all of Niobe's children with poisoned arrows. Artemis killed the six daughters, and Apollo killed the six sons. (Some myths say that not all the children were killed; two were spared, one girl and one boy.)

According to the *Iliad,* the children remained unburied for ten days. Finally, on the eleventh day, the gods buried the slain children. The grief-stricken Niobe wept without ceasing. She fled to Mount Sipylus but found no refuge there. The gods took pity on her and turned her to stone. Even after her transformation, Niobe could not stop crying. On Mount Sipylus, there is a limestone rock formation that resembles a human face; after a rain, water seeps out of the porous rock. This is said to be Niobe, still weeping for her lost children.

ARTEMIS TAKES OFFENSE

Artemis was not one to take insults and perceived slights lightly. She could be merciless in punishing those who offended her in any way.

ACTAEON

Actaeon was the grandson of Apollo. He was a great hunter, trained either by his father or by the centaur Chiron. One day, Actaeon accidentally came across Artemis while she was bathing in a spring. Though he tried not to disturb her, Artemis was furious that he'd seen her naked. Artemis turned Actaeon into a stag, and he was torn apart by his own hunting dogs.

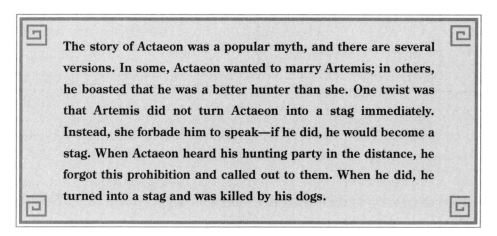

The story of Actaeon was a popular myth, and there are several versions. In some, Actaeon wanted to marry Artemis; in others, he boasted that he was a better hunter than she. One twist was that Artemis did not turn Actaeon into a stag immediately. Instead, she forbade him to speak—if he did, he would become a stag. When Actaeon heard his hunting party in the distance, he forgot this prohibition and called out to them. When he did, he turned into a stag and was killed by his dogs.

Actaeon's hounds did not realize whom they had just killed. They went howling through the forest in search of their master. Eventually, Chiron created a statue in the image of Actaeon. The statue was so lifelike that the dogs believed they'd found their master at last.

ADMETUS

Admetus was the king of Pheres. He fell in love with Alcestis, the daughter of the king of Iolcos. However, the king would not consent to their marriage. The king sent a proclamation out that no man could marry his daughter unless that man had a chariot that was drawn by a wild boar and a lion yoked together. Luckily for Admetus, he was favored by Apollo, who provided his friend with the chariot.

Admetus won the hand of Alcestis. However, he forgot to offer a sacrifice to Artemis on their wedding day, as was the custom. Insulted by this neglect, Artemis wanted revenge. On their wedding night, Admetus and Alcestis found their bridal chamber seething with snakes. Again, Apollo came to his friend's aid. He soothed his sister's anger and advised Admetus to offer Artemis the sacrifice she was due. After he did, Artemis removed the snakes.

ADONIS

Chapter 10 tells a version of the death of Adonis, a beautiful young man loved by Aphrodite, in which Ares takes the form of a boar and gores him to death. Other myths make Artemis responsible for Adonis's death. In one, Artemis punished Adonis's boast that he was a better hunter than she by sending a wild boar to kill him. In another, Aphrodite caused the death of Hippolytus, a hunter who'd scorned her to serve Artemis instead. Artemis then killed Adonis in retaliation for the death of Hippolytus.

AGAMEMNON

Agamemnon, commander of the Greek forces during the Trojan War, was already disliked by Artemis because of his family's history. (His father, Atreus, had promised to sacrifice his best lamb to Artemis but broke that promise when he found and hid a golden lamb, keeping it for himself.)

Before sailing for Troy, Agamemnon went hunting and killed a deer in a grove sacred to Artemis. Impressed with his own accomplishment, Agamemnon boasted that his skill as a hunter was equal to—or even better than—that of Artemis. The goddess, offended by both his act and his boast, decided to punish Agamemnon.

Artemis prevented the winds from blowing, so Agamemnon's fleet could not sail to Troy. She refused to relent unless Agamemnon made a sacrifice to her, but she didn't want just any sacrifice. Artemis demanded that he sacrifice his eldest daughter, Iphigenia.

Agamemnon sent for his daughter. The myths differ on what happened next. Some say that Agamemnon did indeed sacrifice his daughter to Artemis so the winds would blow again. Others say that Artemis took Iphigenia to Tauris (where she became a priestess in Artemis's temple) and left a deer or goat in her place to serve as the sacrifice.

OENEUS

Oeneus, king of Calydon, learned how to make wine from Dionysus and taught this skill to his people. Oeneus was normally a pious man who took care to honor the gods. One year, however, he neglected to honor Artemis in the sacrifices to celebrate the harvest.

Artemis sent a monstrous boar to ravage the area around Calydon. The boar did massive damage, trampling vineyards and destroying crops, and forced the Calydonians to shut themselves up inside their city, where they were in danger of starving. A group of the best hunters in Greece went after the boar, and several were killed before Atalanta, a young huntress raised by Artemis herself, wounded it with an arrow. Oeneus's son Meleager then killed the boar. During a dispute over who should claim the boar's hide (Meleager thought it belonged to Atalanta, who'd first injured the beast), Meleager was killed—and Artemis had her revenge against his father.

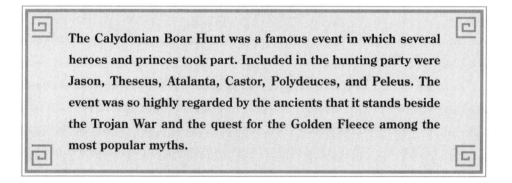

The Calydonian Boar Hunt was a famous event in which several heroes and princes took part. Included in the hunting party were Jason, Theseus, Atalanta, Castor, Polydeuces, and Peleus. The event was so highly regarded by the ancients that it stands beside the Trojan War and the quest for the Golden Fleece among the most popular myths.

THE ETERNAL VIRGIN

Artemis was the third of the virgin goddesses, the other two being Hestia and Athena. As you know, Zeus had granted Artemis the right to remain a virgin forever. Keeping her virginity, however, wasn't as simple as taking a vow of chastity. Artemis sometimes had to fight off would-be suitors.

As you read in Chapter 10, the Giants Otus and Ephialtes were so strong that not even the gods could hurt them. These brothers successfully kidnapped Ares and then decided they should rule the universe. So they built a mountain as tall as Mount Olympus and demanded that the gods surrender to them. They also demanded two goddesses for their wives: Ephialtes claimed Hera, and Otus claimed Artemis. The gods could not defeat these Giants in battle, so Artemis decided to trick them.

When the brothers were out hunting, Artemis transformed herself into a deer and ran between them. Each Giant threw his spear at the deer, but Artemis leaped out of the way. The spears hit the Giants instead, and in this way the brothers killed each other.

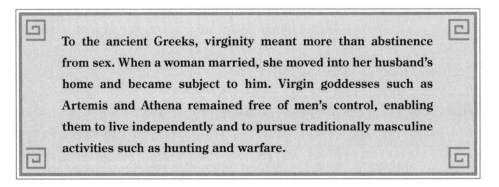

To the ancient Greeks, virginity meant more than abstinence from sex. When a woman married, she moved into her husband's home and became subject to him. Virgin goddesses such as Artemis and Athena remained free of men's control, enabling them to live independently and to pursue traditionally masculine activities such as hunting and warfare.

Artemis valued her own virginity so highly that she required her attendants to be chaste as well. When a woman associated with Artemis broke her vow, she was punished severely—even if she'd broken that vow unwillingly.

Callisto, one of Artemis's attendants, had vowed to remain chaste throughout her life. One myth states that Callisto was so committed to Artemis that she shunned all contact with men. However, Zeus lusted after her, and when Zeus wanted a woman he usually got his way. But Callisto's avoidance of men made this conquest a challenge.

To approach Callisto, Zeus disguised himself as Artemis. Callisto, of course, allowed Artemis into her presence and was shocked to find herself face to face with Zeus. Zeus raped Callisto and then left her.

Unfortunately, Callisto became pregnant from the rape. One day, when Artemis and her attendants were bathing in a spring, Callisto had to undress and join them. When she saw Callisto naked, Artemis realized that her attendant was pregnant. In her anger, she transformed Callisto into a bear. Artemis then shot and killed the bear (although she may have been persuaded to do so by the ever-jealous Hera). Zeus, knowing Callisto's death was his fault, felt remorse and changed her into the constellation of the Great Bear (Ursa Major).

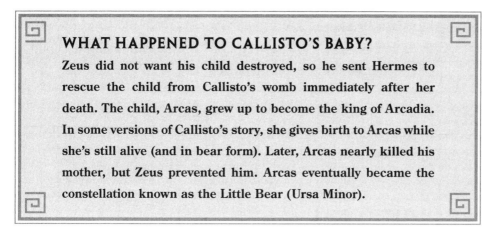

WHAT HAPPENED TO CALLISTO'S BABY?

Zeus did not want his child destroyed, so he sent Hermes to rescue the child from Callisto's womb immediately after her death. The child, Arcas, grew up to become the king of Arcadia. In some versions of Callisto's story, she gives birth to Arcas while she's still alive (and in bear form). Later, Arcas nearly killed his mother, but Zeus prevented him. Arcas eventually became the constellation known as the Little Bear (Ursa Minor).

THE MANY DEATHS OF ORION

Artemis didn't care for the company of men, but there were a couple of exceptions, usually hunters. Hippolytus was one; Orion was another. Like Hippolytus, Orion was an excellent hunter, and Artemis considered him a friend. The two were said to have gone on several hunting expeditions together in Crete. But the friendship didn't last. Numerous myths concern the death of Orion. But in all accounts, Artemis plays a major role:

- **Myth 1:** Orion fell in love with Artemis and tried to rape her. Artemis summoned a giant scorpion, which stung Orion over and over, killing him.
- **Myth 2:** Orion boasted that he would kill all the animals on Earth. Artemis, protector of wild animals, killed him with her arrows.
- **Myth 3:** Artemis was so taken with Orion that she actually considered marrying him. Apollo became jealous; while hunting with his sister in Crete, he saw Orion swimming far out at sea. Apollo challenged

Artemis to an archery contest, shooting at a tiny speck of a target in the ocean. Artemis accepted the challenge and shot her arrow at the target, not realizing it was Orion's head. Artemis never missed, and so she killed her beloved.

- **Myth 4:** Orion tried to rape Opis, one of Artemis's attendants. Artemis shot and killed him.
- **Myth 5:** Orion was in love with Eos (Dawn) and made her his mistress. Again, Artemis shot and killed him.

Although these myths give different accounts of Orion's death, all agree that he was turned into a constellation. Orion, also known as the Hunter, is a prominent constellation in the night sky.

WILD BUT LOYAL

Artemis was a complex character, a goddess who inspired admiration and fear in mortals. She exhibited loyalty (as to her mother) and harshness (punishing anyone who offended her or wronged those she loved). She was quick to take offense and could be fierce in her revenge. Although Artemis was a hunter, she felt great love and respect for the animals she hunted, protecting them from mistreatment.

As a virgin goddess, Artemis was independent; she knew what she wanted and went after it. She was free spirited and closely bound to nature. Her depictions in ancient art suited her well: a young woman dressed in a short tunic, carrying a bow and arrows and as wild as the countryside she roamed.

In Chapter 13, you will meet Artemis's twin brother, Apollo. Like real-life twins, these two shared many similarities but also exhibited some differences. One constant, however, was the devotion they felt for each other. You have already seen how loyal these siblings were to their mother; they had the same loyalty to each other.

For example, Apollo fell in love with Coronis, a mortal woman. The two shared a passionate love affair, and Coronis became pregnant with Apollo's child. During her pregnancy, however, she married Ischys, another mortal. Apollo was devastated by her betrayal. Artemis, taking vengeance on her brother's behalf, shot and killed Coronis. Apollo's child was removed from his mother's body and raised by the centaur Chiron.

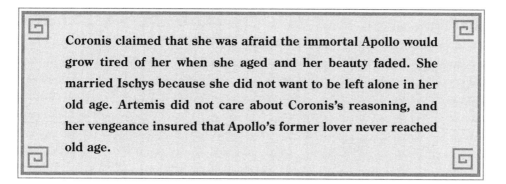

Coronis claimed that she was afraid the immortal Apollo would grow tired of her when she aged and her beauty faded. She married Ischys because she did not want to be left alone in her old age. Artemis did not care about Coronis's reasoning, and her vengeance insured that Apollo's former lover never reached old age.

Apollo was similarly devoted to his sister. These divine twins often appeared together throughout classical mythology, whether they were fighting side by side or enjoying a challenging hunt.

CHAPTER 13

APOLLO:
A (MOSTLY) CIVILIZED GOD

**Y**ou've met the sister; now it's time to meet the brother. If Artemis was the wild child of nature, the accomplished and cultivated Apollo represented some of the best aspects of civilization. This god took great pleasure in a wide variety of activities, including archery, music, healing, and prophecy. His mastery of many skills made him the embodiment of the highest ideals of the ancient Greek world.

TALL, DARK, AND HANDSOME

Apollo was smart, good-hearted, and a mighty Olympian—but even better, he was tall, dark, and handsome. The ancients usually depicted Apollo as an ideal of masculine beauty: He was tall and muscular, with the charm of youth and long, slightly curling hair. Even though he was physically attractive, the young god was often unlucky in love and suffered numerous rejections. Never fear, though, he had his share of amorous successes as well.

Apollo was highly skilled in many fields of endeavor. He was the god of archery, fine arts, music, religious purity, prophecy, medicine, and eloquence. Although his sister was associated with all wild animals, Apollo had a few select animals as his companions. Most often he was linked with the wolf, even though he was a shepherd and the protector of shepherds and their flocks. He was also connected with deer and with several species of birds, including crows, vultures, swans, and kites.

Apollo was an admirable deity, one to be respected and appreciated. Yet, like his sister (and all of the gods), he could also be harsh. As related in Chapter 12, Apollo did not hesitate to commit murder to defend his mother's honor.

He also sent plagues to cities that defied him (as the god of medicine, he could inflict illness as well as cure it). Although he wasn't as quick to take revenge as his sister was, Apollo suffered no insults.

GOD OF MUSIC

Several myths highlight Apollo's artistic gifts, particularly in his role as the god of music. The Olympians themselves recognized Apollo's musical virtuosity and loved to lounge around Mount Olympus listening to Apollo play his lyre.

One myth that tells of Apollo's musical genius is the story of Marsyas, a satyr from Phrygia. When Marsyas found a double flute that Athena had thrown away, he began to play it. He thought that the flute produced the loveliest sound he had ever heard—and he was willing to bet that its music was even sweeter than Apollo's. So he challenged Apollo to a musical contest.

Apollo accepted Marsyas's audacious challenge. They set some ground rules, selected the Muses as judges, and agreed that the winner could do as he chose with the loser. Apollo would play his lyre, and Marsyas would play his flute.

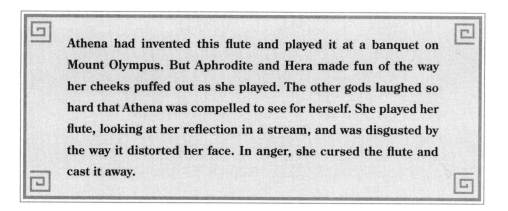

Athena had invented this flute and played it at a banquet on Mount Olympus. But Aphrodite and Hera made fun of the way her cheeks puffed out as she played. The other gods laughed so hard that Athena was compelled to see for herself. She played her flute, looking at her reflection in a stream, and was disgusted by the way it distorted her face. In anger, she cursed the flute and cast it away.

During the first phase of the competition, both played equally well. The Muses declared a draw, which spurred Apollo to tilt things in his own favor.

Apollo challenged Marsyas to play his instrument upside down. It is possible to play a lyre this way, but not a flute. Marsyas lost the round.

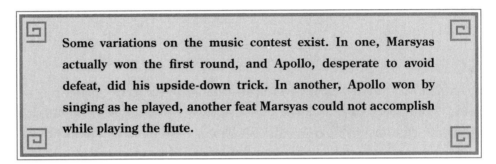

Some variations on the music contest exist. In one, Marsyas actually won the first round, and Apollo, desperate to avoid defeat, did his upside-down trick. In another, Apollo won by singing as he played, another feat Marsyas could not accomplish while playing the flute.

Apollo chose a severe punishment. He hung Marsyas from a pine tree and skinned him alive. Some myths say that the satyr's blood and tears (or possibly the tears of his friends) formed the river Marsyas. Other myths say that Apollo later regretted the harsh way he'd treated his defeated opponent, so he broke his own lyre and turned the satyr into a river.

THE PLAYBOY

Apollo never married, but like most of the other Olympians he had numerous affairs, producing several children. Here are some of Apollo's most famous amorous successes:

- Apollo had a love affair with Coronis, whom Artemis killed for marrying a mortal man. Coronis's son by Apollo was Asclepius, who became a god of healing and medicine.
- Chione was visited by both Hermes and Apollo in the same night. She had a son from each union. With Apollo, she had Philammon, who became a great musician.
- Cyrene was watching her father's flocks when a lion attacked. She wrestled the lion; Apollo saw this act of courage and fell in love. Together they produced two sons: Aristaeus and Idmon. Aristaeus was the inventor of bookkeeping, and Idmon became a famous prophet.

- Apollo had a tryst with Hecuba, the wife of King Priam. Their love affair produced a son, Troilus. A prophecy predicted that Troy would never fall if Troilus lived to the age of twenty, but he was killed by Achilles during the Trojan War.
- Manto, daughter of the seer Tiresias, was given to Apollo as a war prize. She perfected her prophetic abilities at Delphi and gave Apollo a son, Mopsus, who grew up to become a famous prophet as well.
- Apollo's lover Phthia bore him three sons: Dorus, Laodocus, and Polypoetes. All three were killed by Aetolus to gain control of the country they ruled, which then became known as Aetolia.
- When Rhoeo's father discovered she was pregnant, he assumed that her lover was mortal and punished her by putting her in a chest and setting her adrift in the ocean. But the child was Apollo's, and she landed safely on Delos, Apollo's own birthplace and an island sacred to him. There, she gave birth to Anius, a prophet who became one of Apollo's priests.
- Apollo was closely associated with the arts, so it's no surprise that one of his lovers was a Muse, Thalia, who ruled comedy and idyllic poetry. Their children were the Corybantes, male followers of the nature goddess Cybele.
- Another Muse, Urania, also had an affair with Apollo. Urania was the Muse of astrology and astronomy, and her union with Apollo produced two sons: Linus and Orpheus. Both grew up to be famous musicians.

Although this is only a partial list, you can see that Apollo favored Muses, nymphs, and mortal women as lovers. But he wasn't always successful in his amorous pursuits.

UNLUCKY IN LOVE

The romantic relationships in the previous section were mostly mere flings. Sadly, when Apollo went in search of love, he almost always came up empty-handed. Not everyone was impressed by the playboy's courtship, and Apollo was often left heartbroken and angry. This section tells the stories of some who refused Apollo's love.

CASSANDRA

Cassandra was the daughter of Priam and Hecuba, king and queen of Troy. She was the most beautiful of all of the king's children, and many men admired her beauty and wished to court her. Apollo was one of her suitors. As a god, he could offer gifts no mortal man could.

Cassandra, however, wasn't interested. Unlike other gods who'd simply take what they wanted, Apollo agreed to bargain with her. He promised to teach Cassandra the art of prophecy if she would agree to become his lover. Their deal was made.

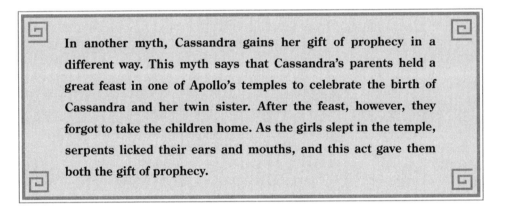

In another myth, Cassandra gains her gift of prophecy in a different way. This myth says that Cassandra's parents held a great feast in one of Apollo's temples to celebrate the birth of Cassandra and her twin sister. After the feast, however, they forgot to take the children home. As the girls slept in the temple, serpents licked their ears and mouths, and this act gave them both the gift of prophecy.

Apollo kept his side of the bargain, giving Cassandra the gift of prophecy and teaching her how to foretell the future. But when she'd learned these things, Cassandra reneged on her promise. Furious, Apollo spat in her mouth and condemned her to this fate: although she possessed the gift of prophecy, no one would ever believe her predictions. Later, during and after the Trojan War, Cassandra tried to warn others of their impending fates, but her warnings went unheeded.

DAPHNE

The beautiful mountain nymph Daphne was perhaps the most famous of the women who refused Apollo. Two myths tell the story of Apollo's great, unrequited love for Daphne—and in both, she suffers the same fate.

In one version, Daphne was loved both by Apollo and by Leucippus, the son of King Oenomaus. Daphne was not interested in either of her suitors. In order to get close to her, Leucippus disguised himself as a girl. This worked for a little while, until Apollo caught on.

To get rid of the competition, Apollo persuaded Daphne's attending nymphs to take off their clothes to bathe. When Leucippus refused to participate, the nymphs became suspicious. They stripped him naked, and when they discovered he was a man, they killed him on the spot.

Even with Leucippus out of the picture, Apollo had no luck with Daphne, who fled from him. As the love-struck god pursued her, Daphne cried out for help and was transformed into a laurel tree.

In the other version, Eros caused Apollo to fall in love with Daphne. Apollo had boasted that his own bow and arrows were superior to those of the god of love. To teach Apollo a lesson, Eros shot the Olympian with one of his gold-tipped arrows, causing Apollo to fall hopelessly in love with Daphne. Then Eros shot Daphne with one of his lead-tipped arrows, making her resistant to love.

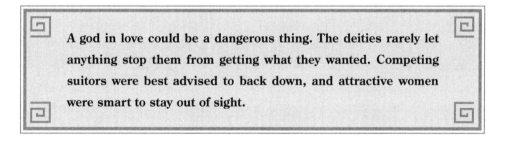

A god in love could be a dangerous thing. The deities rarely let anything stop them from getting what they wanted. Competing suitors were best advised to back down, and attractive women were smart to stay out of sight.

Apollo chased his love fervently. Daphne tried to avoid him, but to no avail. He pursued her through the forests, until the exhausted Daphne called out to her father, a river god named Peneus, for help. Peneus came to the rescue and changed her into a laurel tree. Daphne's skin became the tree's bark, her hair became its leaves, her arms its branches, and her feet its roots. All that was left of the original nymph, the myth says, was her beauty.

Both versions of this myth end with Apollo choosing the laurel as his sacred tree. Laurel branches became a symbol of honor and were used to crown the winners of the Pythian Games at Delphi (more on those later in this chapter).

MARPESSA

Marpessa, daughter of the river-god Evenus and granddaughter of Ares, caught Apollo's eye. Although Apollo fell in love with this "fair-ankled" girl (as Homer calls her), she was already engaged to Idas, a mortal son of Poseidon. That didn't stop Apollo. He abducted Marpessa and carried her away from her betrothed.

Devoted to his love, Idas pursued the god and challenged him. The two came to blows, and Zeus had to intervene. Separating the fighters, he held them apart and asked Marpessa to choose one. Marpessa picked Idas, explaining (like Coronis) that she desired a mortal husband because she was afraid Apollo would grow tired of her as she aged. So Idas had the distinction of being one of the few mortals to challenge a deity and survive.

SINOPE

Sinope was another nymph whom Apollo adored. Several myths say that Sinope was also desired by Zeus. Both gods were persistent in their advances, and Sinope realized that running and hiding would do her no good.

She also realized that a god in amorous pursuit wasn't always as clever as usual. So she decided to trick each of her divine suitors in the same way. She stopped running, pretending to have given up, and surrendered herself. However, in exchange for her surrender, she asked the god to grant her a wish. Overcome with love, each god fell for the trap and promised the young nymph anything she desired. Her wish? To be granted eternal virginity.

TRAGIC LOVE

Apollo certainly loved the ladies and was loved by some of them in return. But he did not limit himself to love affairs with women; he also was attracted to young men. The two most famous stories of Apollo's male loves both ended in tragedy.

CYPARISSUS

Cyparissus was the son of Telephus (and Heracles' grandson) and lived on the island of Ceos. He was a beautiful young man, and Apollo loved him. Cyparissus spent most of his time with a sacred stag that had been tamed by nymphs (or, in some accounts, by Cyparissus himself). Every day, Cyparissus led the stag to graze and kept it company.

He was content with this peaceful existence, until one fateful summer's day. The stag was napping in the shade to escape the hot midday sun. To amuse himself, Cyparissus practiced throwing his spear. Without intending to, he hit and killed the sleeping stag.

Cyparissus was so upset that he wanted die. Apollo tried to comfort him, but nothing could soothe Cyparissus's grief. He asked Apollo to let him weep forever. Taking pity on the youth, Apollo changed him into a cypress tree. The sap of the cypress looks like tears flowing along its trunk, so the tree is associated with sadness and mourning.

HYACINTHUS

Hyacinthus was another beautiful young man who was loved by many. Apollo and Thamyris, a musician, both declared their love for him at the same time. Hyacinthus chose Apollo as his companion.

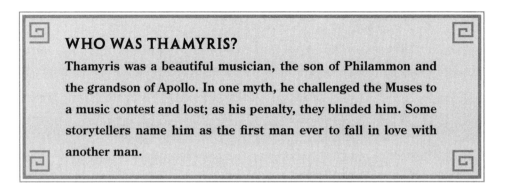

WHO WAS THAMYRIS?

Thamyris was a beautiful musician, the son of Philammon and the grandson of Apollo. In one myth, he challenged the Muses to a music contest and lost; as his penalty, they blinded him. Some storytellers name him as the first man ever to fall in love with another man.

One day, Apollo and Hyacinthus were throwing a discus and tragedy intervened. Naturally, different myths give different accounts. In some, the discus hit a rock and rebounded, striking Hyacinthus in the head. In another, Hyacinthus was struck as he ran to catch the discus after Apollo threw it. In yet another, Zephyrus (the West Wind) was also in love with Hyacinthus and jealous of his relationship with Apollo. Zephyrus caused the discus to change direction in midair, blowing it toward Hyacinthus so that it hit him in the head.

Regardless of how Hyacinthus was struck, the outcome was the same: Young, beautiful Hyacinthus was killed instantly. Apollo failed to revive him. Terribly saddened, Apollo transformed the blood from the deadly wound into a flower, which he named *hyacinth* to immortalize his friend.

A MORTAL'S SLAVE

As the ruler of the Olympians, Zeus sometimes had to dispense justice. Twice, he punished Apollo for misdeeds. In both cases, Apollo was sentenced to serve mortal men as a slave.

APOLLO THE BRICKLAYER

Not long after the Olympians established their dominance, a mutiny arose against Zeus (see Chapter 5). This rebellion was headed by Hera, and all of the gods and goddesses except Hestia took part. Zeus punished the conspirators in various ways. For Apollo and Poseidon, the sentence was to work for King Laomedon, building a great wall around the city of Troy.

For one long year, the two gods lived as mortals, doing the hard labor of stone masons. Laomedon promised to pay them well for their work. At the end of a year, they'd completed the wall, an impressive defensive structure. The two gods approached Laomedon and requested their wages, but the king laughed and refused to pay. Laomedon cut off their ears with a knife and threatened to bind Apollo's hands and feet and sell him into slavery. The furious gods left, planning their revenge. They punished not just the king but the entire city: Poseidon sent a great sea monster to attack Troy and Apollo sent a deadly plague.

Buffeted by the gods' revenge, Laomedon tried to sacrifice his own daughter in hopes of appeasing Poseidon. He chained her to a rock as an offering to the sea monster. But the hero Heracles offered to save the girl and kill the monster in return for the king's mares. Laomedon agreed. Heracles did as he'd promised, rescuing the girl and saving the city, but again the king reneged on his promise, refusing to give Heracles the horses. Heracles led an army against Troy and eventually killed Laomedon and most of his sons.

APOLLO THE HERDSMAN

Apollo also got in trouble for murder. Apollo's son Asclepius was a famous healer (in fact, he was known as the god of healing). Asclepius was so adept at his art that he could bring the dead back to life. This interfered with Hades' domain, so he complained to Zeus. Zeus sided with Hades and struck Asclepius with a thunderbolt, killing him.

Outraged by the death of his son but unable to challenge Zeus directly, Apollo turned his anger toward the Cyclopes, the beings who created thunderbolts and gave them to Zeus for weapons. Apollo killed the Cyclopes, and Zeus was determined to punish him. At first, Zeus intended to throw Apollo into Tartarus, but Leto interceded on her son's behalf. So instead, Zeus sentenced Apollo to a year in servitude to a mortal master, King Admetus of Pheres. (Some myths say that the sentence lasted for nine years.) Apollo went to the king in mortal form and served him as a cowherd.

Apollo's punishment was nowhere near as severe as Zeus intended. For one thing, Apollo enjoyed herding the cattle; he was, after all, the protector of herdsmen. Unlike Laomedon, King Admetus was kind to his servant.

Apollo repaid Admetus for his generosity several times over. He made all the cows give birth to twins. He helped the king win the hand of the woman he loved. When Artemis was angry with Admetus for neglecting her rites, Apollo smoothed things over. He even tricked the Fates into extending the king's life. When it was time for Admetus to die, Apollo got the Fates drunk and convinced them to delay the king's death if he could find someone else to die in his place. (When neither of his elderly parents volunteered, his wife Alcestis stepped forward to take his place in the Underworld.) Instead of being a humiliating punishment, Apollo's time with Admetus gained him a friend.

DELPHI: PYTHIAN GAMES AND A TRICKY ORACLE

Apollo was famously associated with Delphi, one of the best-known and most influential shrines of ancient Greece.

As you recall from Chapter 12, Hera had sent a snake named Python to chase Leto while she was pregnant with Artemis and Apollo. The young Apollo pursued Python to Delphi and killed her. But Gaia, the mother of Python, demanded retribution. To appease Gaia, Apollo founded musical and theatrical festivals at Delphi, naming them the Pythian Games in honor of Python. (He also went to the Vale of Tempe to undergo ritual purification and be cleansed of Python's murder.)

In Delphi, Apollo learned the art of prophecy from Themis, a Titaness who controlled the oracle. (Some myths disagree and say that Pan taught prophecy to Apollo.) Apollo then took charge of the oracle, granting the power of prophecy to a priestess known as the Pythia. At Delphi then, people could receive communication from the gods and learn about their fates.

Apollo's prophecies were delivered by the Pythia, who would go into a trance and allow Apollo to speak through her and answer the supplicants' questions. The oracle was so busy that often the services of three Pythia at a time were required.

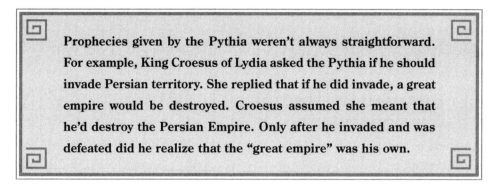

Prophecies given by the Pythia weren't always straightforward. For example, King Croesus of Lydia asked the Pythia if he should invade Persian territory. She replied that if he did invade, a great empire would be destroyed. Croesus assumed she meant that he'd destroy the Persian Empire. Only after he invaded and was defeated did he realize that the "great empire" was his own.

Pilgrims traveled from all over to consult the oracle. However, the divination only took place on nine days during the year: the seventh day of each month, except for three months when Apollo was not present in the sanctuary. Because the demand far exceeded the oracle's ability to answer every question, the pilgrims had to draw lots. Those who were chosen would undergo a purification ritual and then ask their questions. The Pythia would mutter something unintelligible, and a male priest would interpret her words for the supplicant.

The oracle at Delphi remained popular for many years. It began to lose its importance in the first century A.D., as Christianity emerged. In the late fourth century, Emperor Theodosius I banned the old pagan religions, and the oracle was no more.

CHAPTER 14
HERMES:
SWIFT AS THE WIND

W. ROBERTS SC. N.Y.

ermes, the messenger of the gods, was charming and likable—if not always well behaved. Mischievous and roguish, Hermes often played tricks to demonstrate his cunning, yet the gods still trusted him with many important missions. A versatile god of many talents, he created inventions that advanced civilization, from numbers to musical instruments, and he was the patron god of diverse groups, including travelers, inventors, liars, thieves, and athletes.

A CHILD'S FIRST PRANK

As Chapter 6 describes, Zeus was enamored with Maia, one of the Pleiades. In order to spend time with her, Zeus had to sneak away from his sleeping wife. One of these meetings led to the birth of Hermes. As Zeus's son, this was no ordinary baby.

Hermes was born at dawn in a cave on Mount Cyllene. By noon, he had developed enough to explore his surroundings and sneak out of the cave. In his explorations, Hermes found a tortoise shell. He used this shell, along with an animal skin and sheep-gut strings, to devise the first lyre. He then taught himself to play the instrument he'd invented—all on the first afternoon of his life.

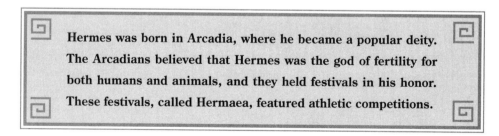

Hermes was born in Arcadia, where he became a popular deity. The Arcadians believed that Hermes was the god of fertility for both humans and animals, and they held festivals in his honor. These festivals, called Hermaea, featured athletic competitions.

Hermes' first day wasn't over yet. He continued to explore, wandering through the countryside, and came across the cattle of Apollo. Since Apollo was nowhere to be seen, little Hermes stole fifty cattle. He tied brushwood to his feet to obscure his footprints, and he drove the cattle backward so their tracks faced the opposite direction from where they'd actually gone.

An old man named Battus had witnessed Hermes' theft. Hermes made Battus promise not to tell anyone what he'd seen. The old shepherd agreed, but Hermes didn't trust him. After leaving, Hermes doubled back and disguised himself. He approached Battus as a stranger and asked about the missing cattle, offering a hefty reward. Battus did not hesitate—he told everything he'd seen. Angry with the man for breaking his promise, Hermes turned Battus into a stone.

Hermes hid the cattle in a cave in Pylos. At a nearby river, he sacrificed two of the cows to the Olympian deities, and then he burned the hooves and heads to get rid of the evidence. He also threw his brushwood sandals into the river. Satisfied that the cattle were safely hidden, Hermes crept back to his mother's cave by dusk. He dressed himself in the swaddling clothes he'd shed earlier and lay down to sleep, looking like an innocent child.

When Apollo returned to his herd and discovered that fifty cows were missing, he searched for them all over the world. Finally, he had to rely on his powers of divination, which led him to Hermes. Of course, Hermes proclaimed his innocence. How could a newborn child even know what a cow was? Furious, Apollo searched the cave where Hermes and Maia dwelled, but he found nothing. He was unwilling, however, to let the matter drop. Convinced of the young boy's guilt, he took Hermes before Zeus and accused him of stealing.

Again, Hermes feigned innocence, but he couldn't fool Zeus. In fact, during his hearing before Zeus, Hermes stole a bow and arrows from Apollo. Amused by these displays of his new son's cunning, Zeus ordered Hermes to lead Apollo to the cattle. Hermes complied willingly with a direct order from Zeus.

When Hermes and Apollo reached the cave on Pylos, Apollo asked why two of the herd were missing. Hermes admitted that he'd sacrificed two cows to the Olympian deities, dividing the meat into twelve equal portions. At this time, there were only eleven Olympian gods. Apollo wanted to know who Hermes thought the twelfth was. Hermes stated matter-of-factly that he was the twelfth god.

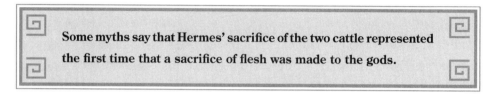

Some myths say that Hermes' sacrifice of the two cattle represented the first time that a sacrifice of flesh was made to the gods.

As Apollo gathered the herd, Hermes sat down and played his lyre. At once the god of music was enchanted. He wanted to know all about this new instrument and how it could make such beautiful sounds. Hermes took advantage of Apollo's interest and offered to trade his lyre for Apollo's entire herd. Craving the beautiful music, Apollo readily agreed. To cement the peace between them, Hermes returned Apollo's stolen bow and arrows. Apollo was amused by Hermes' skill, because he hadn't even realized they were gone. The two became good friends.

After giving Apollo his lyre, Hermes decided to create another musical instrument. This time, he made a reed-pipe. Hermes positioned himself where Apollo could hear him and began playing. Of course, Apollo was immediately interested in this new instrument and followed its sound. Apollo asked Hermes what he would take in trade for his reed-pipe. The two settled on Apollo's golden staff, which included the rights due to the god of shepherds, as a fair trade for the reed-pipe.

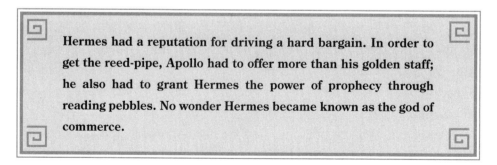

Hermes had a reputation for driving a hard bargain. In order to get the reed-pipe, Apollo had to offer more than his golden staff; he also had to grant Hermes the power of prophecy through reading pebbles. No wonder Hermes became known as the god of commerce.

TAKE A MESSAGE

Although Hermes had resolved his dispute with Apollo, he was still in trouble for his mischief. He was called before his father to be reprimanded. Hermes, however, charmed Zeus and convinced him that he would never again tell a lie. However, the cunning Hermes wanted something in return for his promise: to become Zeus's messenger.

Zeus agreed and gave his son a pair of winged golden sandals, which allowed him to travel with the speed of the wind. He also gave Hermes a wide-brimmed hat and a herald's staff, which became the symbol of his position as messenger of the gods.

As a messenger, Hermes undertook missions on behalf of the other gods and was often entrusted with their secrets and even their welfare. Using his skill and cunning, Hermes usually succeeded in his missions. He even managed to keep his promise to Zeus that he wouldn't lie.

Here are some of Hermes' best-known adventures (but there were many others):

- During Zeus's battle with Typhon, Zeus was left helpless when the monster stole his tendons. Hermes stole the tendons back and replaced them in Zeus's body. This gave Zeus the strength to overcome Typhon.
- After the fifty Danaides (daughters of King Danaus) murdered their husbands, Zeus ordered that they be purified of the murders. Hermes and Athena were responsible for the purifications.
- When Io, Zeus's lover, was changed into a heifer, Hera sent Argus (a hundred-eyed monster) to stand guard over her. To free Io, Zeus sent Hermes to kill Argus. Hermes killed the monster and helped Io to escape.
- Zeus showed Ixion, king of Thessaly, great hospitality and allowed him to sit at the table of the gods on Mount Olympus. But Ixion responded by trying to seduce Hera. This breach of the rules of hospitality was unacceptable, and Zeus ordered Hermes to chain Ixion to an eternally revolving wheel of fire (some myths locate the wheel in the night sky; others put it in Tartarus).

- When Otus and Ephialtes captured Ares and imprisoned him in a bronze jar, it was Hermes who eventually rescued the god of war.
- After the Trojan War, Odysseus's journey home was interrupted by the sea nymph Calypso, who detained him on an island for several years. Calypso wanted Odysseus to become immortal and remain with her forever. Odysseus, however, wanted to go home. Zeus sent Hermes to convince Calypso to let Odysseus leave (which she did, although it broke her heart).
- Upon Zeus's orders, Hermes led Aphrodite, Hera, and Athena to the Trojan prince Paris, who was being raised by a shepherd. The goddesses wanted Paris to settle their dispute about which was the most beautiful.
- Zeus wanted to test mankind and asked Hermes to accompany him to Earth. The two gods wandered the world disguised as travelers. No one offered them hospitality except for one couple, Baucis and Philemon. The gods rewarded these two for their kindness.
- When Dionysus was born, Zeus had to hide him from Hera's wrath. He entrusted his son to Hermes' care.
- Zeus sent Hermes to the Underworld to retrieve Persephone from Hades.

Hermes often came to the aid of the other gods. Although he had a reputation for mischief, the Olympians respected and trusted him, enough to carry their important messages.

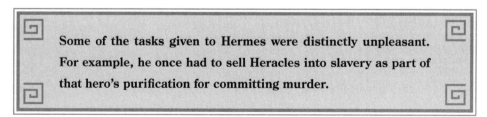

Some of the tasks given to Hermes were distinctly unpleasant. For example, he once had to sell Heracles into slavery as part of that hero's purification for committing murder.

RECONCILING WITH HERA

Hera's wrath often fell upon the illegitimate children of Zeus; her relentless persecution of Heracles (Chapter 19) is a prime example. Hermes was the son of Zeus but not of Hera, so he was in a similarly dangerous position. To make matters worse, as Zeus's messenger, Hermes was often charged with protecting Zeus's various mistresses and illegitimate children. This made the young god doubly irritating to Hera. But Hermes was blessed with cleverness and cunning—and he used these qualities to his advantage.

Hermes knew that he needed to protect himself from Zeus's wrathful, jealous wife, so he dressed himself in an infant's swaddling clothes. (He could get away with this because he was still very young.) Passing himself off as Ares, Hera's son, he sat on Hera's lap and demanded to be fed. Fooled, Hera suckled the child. When Hermes had finished his meal, he revealed his true identity. Because Hera had suckled him, she was now considered his foster mother—and she was forced to treat Hermes as her own son. Through his cleverness, Hermes escaped the harsh punishments that Hera normally inflicted upon Zeus's illegitimate children.

MORE THAN A MESSENGER

Hermes' duties went beyond being the deities' messenger. As the protector of travelers, for example, Hermes was said to remove stones from the roads. These stones were often collected and piled around pillars that lined the roads, becoming mini-shrines dedicated to Hermes. In time, these shrines became more elaborate and resembled phalluses, because Hermes was also a fertility god. In fact, several ancient Greek pillars contain carvings that show only the god's face and genitals.

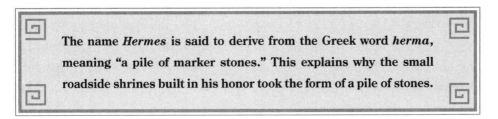

The name *Hermes* is said to derive from the Greek word *herma*, meaning "a pile of marker stones." This explains why the small roadside shrines built in his honor took the form of a pile of stones.

An athletic god, Hermes was associated with athletes and games. He is credited with the invention of boxing, wrestling, and gymnastics. Games were held in Hermes' honor at Pheneus. Gymnasiums were built in his name and displayed his statues. All of the gymnasiums and athletes of Greece were under his protection.

In addition to sports and musical instruments, Hermes took credit for several other inventions. For example, he was said to have worked with the Fates to create the Greek alphabet. The myths also say that he invented astronomy, weights and measures, and the musical scale, and some even say he invented numbers.

Hermes was responsible for guiding the shades of the dead to the Underworld. This important task had previously been undertaken by Hades. Hermes escorted the shades from the upper world to the lower regions as far as the Styx, where Charon ferried them across the river. Hermes was the god who retrieved Persephone from the Underworld. He also escorted Eurydice back into the Underworld when she had almost gained—and then lost—her freedom.

Hermes was the god of eloquence and speech, crops, mining, and buried treasure. He was also the god of prudence, cunning, sleep, fraud, perjury, and theft.

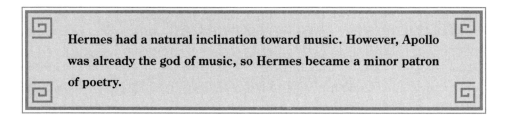

Hermes had a natural inclination toward music. However, Apollo was already the god of music, so Hermes became a minor patron of poetry.

A jack-of-all-trades, Hermes resembled his half-brother Apollo in his diverse talents. He also resembled Apollo in physique: Most depictions show Hermes as a handsome, muscular man, usually wearing the winged sandals and hat given to him by Zeus and dressed as a traveler or herald. Many representations show him carrying his herald's staff or accompanied by a lamb or a ram.

BAD-BOY ATTRACTION

Although many myths show Hermes as a mischievous little boy, this god did grow up to have several adult love affairs. As an adult, Hermes retained his youthful, fun-loving high spirits. This made him popular with the ladies—for flings, at least. Hermes never married, but he did love a challenge, and many of the myths about his love life show his ability to trick a goddess or a woman into becoming his lover.

APHRODITE AND HERMES

Aphrodite was one of Hermes' favorite lovers. But even the goddess of love initially posed a challenge. Hermes let Aphrodite know he desired her, but she refused to return his affection. Her rejection made him want her even more. So he came up with a plan to win her love—or at least her consent.

Hermes asked Zeus for help in winning Aphrodite. Zeus listened to Hermes' pleas and felt sorry for him. He sent an eagle to steal one of Aphrodite's sandals as she bathed. The eagle brought the sandal to Hermes, who offered to return it to Aphrodite if she would become his lover.

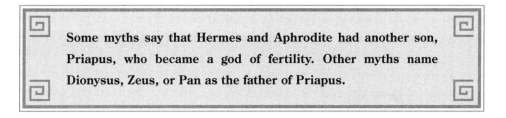

Some myths say that Hermes and Aphrodite had another son, Priapus, who became a god of fertility. Other myths name Dionysus, Zeus, or Pan as the father of Priapus.

Although she was annoyed by this manipulation, Aphrodite agreed. Her union with Hermes produced Hermaphroditus, an incredibly handsome son whose name blended the names of his parents. Later, Hermaphroditus blended more than just masculine and feminine names: He physically merged with the nymph Salmacis and became androgynous, possessing the sexual characteristics of both a man and a woman.

THE CHALLENGES OF LOVE

Although Hermes' relationship with Aphrodite was his best-known love affair, he had several other affairs. One was with Herse, a daughter of Cecrops. This time, the obstacle was not his beloved, but her sister: Herse's sister Aglaurus refused to let the god enter Herse's bedroom. This didn't stop Hermes, however. He simply turned Aglaurus to stone and walked right past her. Together, Herse and Hermes produced a son named Cephalus.

Another love was Apemosyne, the daughter of Catreus, king of Crete. Apemosyne did not want to have an affair with Hermes and tried to outrun him, but Hermes didn't give up easily. As Apemosyne fled, he threw animal hides in her path, causing her to slip. She fell, and Hermes caught and violated her. Apemosyne went to her brother for help, saying Hermes had raped her and she was pregnant as a result. Her brother grew so furious that he kicked Apemosyne to death.

Chione, a beautiful young woman whose name meant "snow white," had many admirers and counted Apollo and Hermes among her suitors. Chione wasn't interested in either god, but she could not dissuade them. Both gods visited her at different times on the same night. That night, Chione conceived twins: one child with Apollo, the other with Hermes. Autolycus, her son with Hermes, inherited his father's thieving abilities and became one of the most famous thieves of ancient Greece.

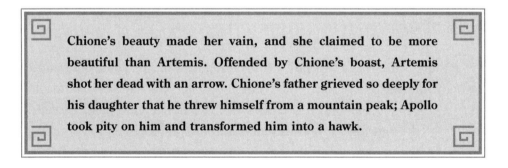

Chione's beauty made her vain, and she claimed to be more beautiful than Artemis. Offended by Chione's boast, Artemis shot her dead with an arrow. Chione's father grieved so deeply for his daughter that he threw himself from a mountain peak; Apollo took pity on him and transformed him into a hawk.

Other famous offspring resulted from Hermes' love affairs, including Pan, Myrtilus, and Echion. All of these sons inherited at least one of Hermes' characteristics. Pan was a god of shepherds and fertility and was renowned for his musical abilities. Myrtilus was a famous charioteer, known for his swiftness. Echion, one of the Argonauts, was the *Argo*'s herald.

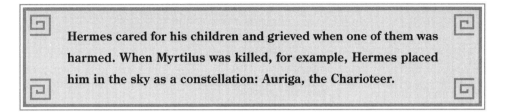

Hermes cared for his children and grieved when one of them was harmed. When Myrtilus was killed, for example, Hermes placed him in the sky as a constellation: Auriga, the Charioteer.

A GOD OF MANY MYTHS

Hermes appears in more classical myths than any other deity, often as a supporting character. Because Hermes was so multifaceted, storytellers could easily fit him into their tales: He could be a good guy or a bad guy, a helper or a troublemaker—audiences knew what to expect of him in all of these roles. Hermes could be a messenger, a lover, a helper whose cleverness got the other gods out of fixes, or a mischievous boy who liked to play tricks. Sometimes, his tricks involved stealing from the other gods. Remember, he stole some of Apollo's cattle and later his bow and arrows. Hermes also stole Poseidon's trident, Zeus's scepter, Aphrodite's girdle, and some of Hephaestus's tools. In each case, however, he used his boyish charm to get himself out of trouble. That boyish charm was what made him so popular.

Hermes' personality added a playful touch to Mount Olympus. He was well liked by everyone, mortal and immortal. Often childlike, Hermes could also be responsible and trustworthy when necessary. He performed his duties as a god, but he also had fun. No wonder he appears in so many myths.

CHAPTER 15

EROTIC APHRODITE AND
HARD-WORKING HEPHAESTUS

his chapter introduces Aphrodite, the goddess of love. Aphrodite emphasized passion and desire over the more spiritual forms of love, and her myths offer some of the juiciest reading of the ancient world. Here you'll also meet her husband, Hephaestus. You'd think the goddess of carnal love would be married to a sexy, attractive man. Not so. Hephaestus was a master craftsman, but he was ugly and walked with a limp. They were the original odd couple.

THE QUEEN OF HEARTS

The myths give different versions of Aphrodite's birth. Some myths say she was the daughter of Zeus and Dione, an Oceanid. But the best-known version says that Aphrodite preceded the other twelve Olympians. This makes sense, because physical love is one of the oldest and strongest forces of human experience.

As you read in Chapter 4, Gaia, mother of Cronus, persuaded her son to overthrow his father, Uranus. One night, Cronus attacked Uranus, cut off his genitals, and tossed them into the sea. When they hit the water, foam gathered. From this foam emerged Aphrodite, beautiful and fully grown. She made her way to land, where her steps created a trail of flowers.

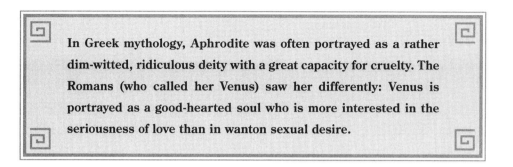

In Greek mythology, Aphrodite was often portrayed as a rather dim-witted, ridiculous deity with a great capacity for cruelty. The Romans (who called her Venus) saw her differently: Venus is portrayed as a good-hearted soul who is more interested in the seriousness of love than in wanton sexual desire.

Regardless of her origin, Aphrodite was the undisputed goddess of love. As you've seen in previous chapters, some of the Olympian deities had multiple duties, but Aphrodite's only job was to make love. She approached this duty with gusto. Because the Greeks associated several other qualities with physical love, Aphrodite was also the goddess of beauty, desire, and sex.

A powerful goddess, Aphrodite held sway over mortals and immortals alike. She could make anyone desire anyone else (except for Athena, Hestia, and Artemis, because the virginity of these goddesses was protected). Aphrodite took great pleasure in helping young mortals obtain their beloved. She also enjoyed making the immortals squirm by causing them to fall in love with each other or with a mortal. Of course, Aphrodite herself was also subject to love. This goddess loved many beings, both mortal and immortal, although she had a particular fancy for mortal men.

Zeus's greatest weapon was the thunderbolt. Poseidon's greatest weapon was the trident. Aphrodite's greatest weapon, however, was a girdle. This wasn't the kind of undergarment some women wear to look slimmer; rather, it was a sash or belt—a magical one. Any woman who wore this magic girdle became irresistible to all who saw her. In moments of generosity, Aphrodite lent her girdle to others. For example, she sometimes let Hera borrow the girdle to seduce Zeus or to reconcile quarreling spouses.

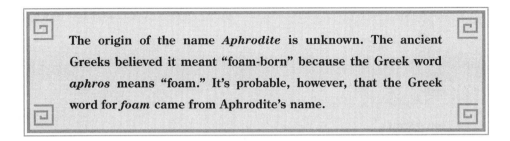

The origin of the name *Aphrodite* is unknown. The ancient Greeks believed it meant "foam-born" because the Greek word *aphros* means "foam." It's probable, however, that the Greek word for *foam* came from Aphrodite's name.

Although Aphrodite was the goddess of sensual love and desire, which often occur outside marriage in the myths, she was also a wife. She and her husband, Hephaestus, were opposites in many ways: She was beautiful, graceful, fickle, and spent her time making love; he was ugly, lame, stable, and spent his time working. Even though it's often said that opposites attract, these two didn't get along.

A MASTER CRAFTSMAN

Hephaestus was the son of Hera. In some myths, Zeus is named as his father; in others, Hephaestus was fatherless. In either case, Hera wasn't a very good mother; when she saw her newborn son, she was so disgusted by his ugliness that she threw him out of the heavens. Hephaestus fell for nine days and nine nights before he splashed into the ocean, where he was saved by the Oceanids Thetis and Eurynome. For nine years, they hid him in an underwater cave. It was in this cave that Hephaestus learned his craft.

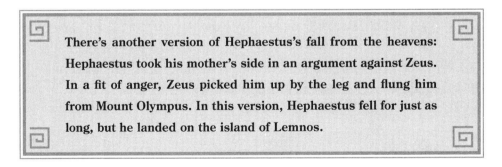

There's another version of Hephaestus's fall from the heavens: Hephaestus took his mother's side in an argument against Zeus. In a fit of anger, Zeus picked him up by the leg and flung him from Mount Olympus. In this version, Hephaestus fell for just as long, but he landed on the island of Lemnos.

Hephaestus was the god of fire, the smithery, metalworking, and general craftsmanship. He could build just about anything. He never forgot his mother's cruel treatment, and when he was grown, he used his skill to create a beautiful golden throne as a gift to Hera. Dazzled by the magnificent gift, Hera readily accepted it. The moment she sat down, however, the throne trapped her so she couldn't get up again. None of the other deities could figure out how to make the throne release her.

When the gods asked Hephaestus to free his mother, he replied that he had no mother. Eventually, Dionysus got Hephaestus drunk and loaded the smith onto a mule. A procession of Dionysian revelers accompanied the two gods back to Mount Olympus, and Hephaestus told Dionysus how to release Hera.

After this episode, the animosity between Hephaestus and the other Olympians subsided. They accepted him as one of their own, although they still made fun of him from time to time. Hephaestus was ugly and, thanks to his fall from the heavens, also lame. But no one surpassed Hephaestus as a master craftsman, and he built gorgeous halls and palaces on Mount Olympus.

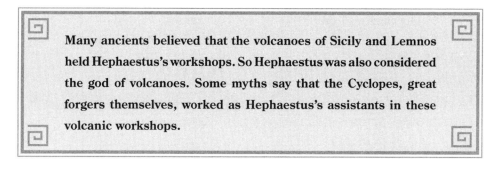

Many ancients believed that the volcanoes of Sicily and Lemnos held Hephaestus's workshops. So Hephaestus was also considered the god of volcanoes. Some myths say that the Cyclopes, great forgers themselves, worked as Hephaestus's assistants in these volcanic workshops.

If something could be imagined, Hephaestus could create it. The myths say that he fashioned the first woman from clay. He created the unbreakable chains that bound Prometheus to the mountainside. He made the arrows for Artemis and Apollo, and he also made suits of armor that the other deities gave as gifts to those they favored.

Smart, skilled, and generous, Hephaestus's downfall was his unattractive appearance. Despite his impressive talents as a master craftsman, Hephaestus is best known as Aphrodite's husband—and when the myths mention their marriage, they usually point out Aphrodite's infidelity.

BEAUTY AND THE BEAST

They made an unlikely couple: the goddess of beauty and the ugliest of the gods. Yet these two were husband and wife, although their marriage wasn't a "happily ever after" fairy tale.

After Hephaestus was welcomed to Mount Olympus and accepted as one of the twelve great Olympians, he reconciled with his mother. When Hephaestus saw the beautiful and irresistible goddess of love, he implored his mother to make Aphrodite his wife. Both Hera and Zeus agreed to his request—and they didn't give Aphrodite a choice in the matter. The wedding took place, but the marriage wasn't happy.

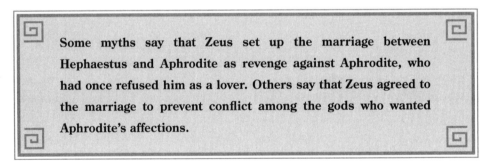

Some myths say that Zeus set up the marriage between Hephaestus and Aphrodite as revenge against Aphrodite, who had once refused him as a lover. Others say that Zeus agreed to the marriage to prevent conflict among the gods who wanted Aphrodite's affections.

As the goddess of love, Aphrodite's nature made her generous in her affections. So it isn't surprising that Aphrodite had numerous affairs outside her marriage. The best-known was with Hephaestus's half-brother, Ares.

Aphrodite loved the one god that everyone else abhorred. They had a passionate love affair, which they kept secret for a time. Eventually, however, their meetings became less discreet. All-seeing Helios discovered their love affair and took the news directly to Hephaestus. Angry and betrayed, Hephaestus decided to get revenge.

He built a great bronze net that only he could handle. He attached the net to the frame of Aphrodite's bed, making sure it was completely hidden. Then he told his wife that he was going on a trip to the island of Lemnos. The moment her husband was gone, Aphrodite invited Ares over.

The lovers went to bed. In the middle of their lovemaking session, the bronze net fell on them. Trapped, naked, and helpless, the lovers could do nothing but wait for Hephaestus to return.

When Hephaestus returned, he wasn't alone—he'd brought the other Olympian deities with him to witness the adulterous couple's shameful behavior. The other deities ridiculed Aphrodite and Ares, but they also made fun of Hephaestus, which he hadn't expected.

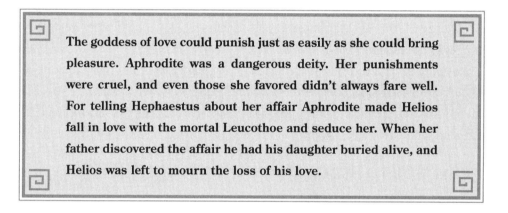

The goddess of love could punish just as easily as she could bring pleasure. Aphrodite was a dangerous deity. Her punishments were cruel, and even those she favored didn't always fare well. For telling Hephaestus about her affair Aphrodite made Helios fall in love with the mortal Leucothoe and seduce her. When her father discovered the affair he had his daughter buried alive, and Helios was left to mourn the loss of his love.

Poseidon looked at the beautiful, naked, embarrassed Aphrodite and pitied her. He begged Hephaestus to reconcile with his wife and set the couple free. Whether because of Poseidon's intervention or because the Olympians' teasing made Hephaestus feel like a fool, he released the couple.

A GODDESS IN LOVE

Hephaestus genuinely loved and desired his beautiful wife and never wanted to be apart from her. But Aphrodite couldn't help her nature, and she continued to cheat on her husband—not just with Ares, but with others as well.

TELL-ALL ANCHISES

This love affair was all Zeus's doing. Aphrodite sometimes teased the other deities for succumbing to her love spells, so Zeus decided to teach her a lesson by making her fall in love with the mortal Anchises, king of Dardania.

Aphrodite encountered Anchises as he was herding sheep on Mount Ida. Zeus's love spell made Aphrodite fall head over heels in love. She approached Anchises as a beautiful mortal girl and seduced him easily. Their union produced a son, Aeneas.

Thinking that Anchises would be pleased to know that he was a consort of the goddess of love, Aphrodite revealed her true identity to him. Anchises, however, reacted in a way she hadn't anticipated. He'd heard stories about love affairs between gods and mortals, and he knew that such relationships often ended badly for the mortal involved. He was frightened of the repercussions of making love to a goddess.

Aphrodite quieted Anchises' fears by promising to protect him as long as he never told anyone about their affair. This news was too exciting to keep secret, and before long Anchises forgot his fears and bragged about his relationship with Aphrodite. As punishment, Zeus struck him with a thunderbolt. The strike didn't kill Anchises, but it made him lame. Since he'd broken his promise, Aphrodite abandoned him. Anchises had been right—dallying with the gods usually spelled disaster for a mortal.

SIREN-SEDUCED BUTES

Butes' mother was Zeuxippe, daughter of the river-god Eridanus; his father was either Teleon or Poseidon. Butes was one of the Argonauts who accompanied Jason on his quest for the Golden Fleece (see Chapter 19). He was also a priest of Athena.

Sailing on the *Argo*, the Argonauts encountered the Sirens, bird-women with beautiful voices. The Sirens' alluring songs mesmerized sailors and caused them to run their ships onto the treacherous rocks. When the Argonauts heard the Sirens, the entire crew resisted their call—except Butes, who fell completely under their spell. When the crew wouldn't steer the *Argo* toward their music, Butes jumped overboard and tried to swim to the Sirens.

Butes would have perished, but Aphrodite saw his plight and took pity on him. She rescued Butes from the sea and took him to Sicily, where the two made love. Aphrodite and Butes had a son, Eryx. (Some myths name Poseidon as Eryx's father.)

PRETTY-BOY ADONIS

Aphrodite's most famous mortal lover was Adonis, an incredibly handsome man who was born as the result of an incestuous relationship between Myrrha and her father, King Theias of Assyria. (Other myths name other men as her father, including King Cinyras of Cyprus.) When Myrrha's mother bragged that her daughter was more beautiful than Aphrodite, the goddess caused the girl to feel an unquenchable lust for her own father. King Theias repulsed his daughter's advances but was fooled one night when she disguised herself as a concubine and managed to seduce him. When Theias learned that his daughter was pregnant with his child, he chased her with a knife, intending to kill her. As she fled, Myrrha prayed to the gods for help and was changed into a myrrh tree.

Adonis was born from the tree's trunk. When Aphrodite came across the baby, she was taken with the child's beauty. She put him in a box and delivered him to Persephone in the Underworld. Adonis grew into a handsome young man, and Aphrodite wanted him back, but Persephone didn't want to give up the boy she'd raised. Zeus intervened, saying that Adonis would split his time between the two goddesses.

Aphrodite was so obsessed with her beautiful lover that she wanted to spend every moment with him. Ares grew jealous, took the form of a boar, and killed Adonis. (Some myths say that Artemis sent the boar to avenge Hippolytus, one of her favorite huntsmen, whose death Aphrodite had indirectly caused.) The grieving Aphrodite transformed the blood of Adonis into anemone flowers and decreed that an annual festival would be held in his honor. Adonis's shade returned to the Underworld.

IMMORTAL LOVERS

Aphrodite also had love affairs with gods. Some myths claim that Ares and Aphrodite shared more than mere physical desire. Although no one else cared for Ares, he was Aphrodite's true love. Together, they had four children: Anteros, Deimos, Phobos, and Harmonia. Some myths say that Eros was also the child of this divine couple.

Aphrodite had affairs with other Olympian gods. Hermes manipulated her into a sexual liaison (see Chapter 14). She also had affairs with Dionysus (which, according to some myths, resulted in the birth of Priapus) and with Poseidon.

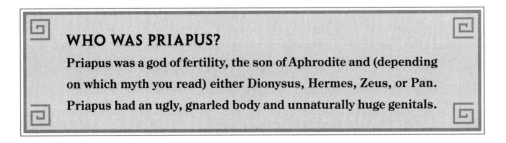

WHO WAS PRIAPUS?

Priapus was a god of fertility, the son of Aphrodite and (depending on which myth you read) either Dionysus, Hermes, Zeus, or Pan. Priapus had an ugly, gnarled body and unnaturally huge genitals.

LOVE'S HELPING HAND

Throughout the ancient Greek myths, Aphrodite uses her divine powers to further the cause of love. When someone (usually a mortal man) was spurned by his beloved, Aphrodite often stepped in to help him— sometimes even when the man didn't want her help.

PARIS AND HELEN

Perhaps the most famous lovers brought together by Aphrodite were Paris, the handsome son of the king of Troy, and Helen, wife of Menelaus and the woman who would become known as Helen of Troy. Why did Aphrodite bring these two together? The answer lies in an event that happened before Paris and Helen ever laid eyes on each other.

At a wedding attended by the Olympians, the goddess Eris (whose name means "strife") threw a golden apple into the midst of the festivities. The apple was desirable in itself, but it was also inscribed with the words "for the fairest." Three goddesses—Aphrodite, Athena, and Hera—claimed the apple. Each believed that she was the fairest, and an argument broke out. Zeus decreed that a judge would settle the dispute. He told Hermes to lead the three goddesses to Paris, who would serve as judge and choose the winner.

Paris couldn't decide who deserved the prize, so each goddess tried to bribe him. Athena offered him wisdom and victory in battle; Hera promised him power and dominion over Asia; and Aphrodite promised him the most beautiful woman in the world. Paris considered each gift and then awarded the golden apple to Aphrodite.

Aphrodite became the young man's protector. She also kept her promise and helped Paris kidnap Helen, who was already married to King Menelaus of Sparta. Paris made his way to Sparta and visited Menelaus's court. There, Aphrodite worked her magic and caused Helen to fall madly in love with the handsome guest. The couple eloped, causing the Trojan War (see Chapter 20).

MILANION AND ATALANTA

Atalanta was a young woman who was often compared to Artemis. A swift runner and a famous hunter, she wanted nothing to do with men. Her beauty, however, attracted many admirers, and her father insisted that she marry. Atalanta agreed on one condition: She would marry the man who could beat her in a foot race—but any man who lost the race would also lose his life. Despite the high price of failure, many men tried to outrun Atalanta, and many men died.

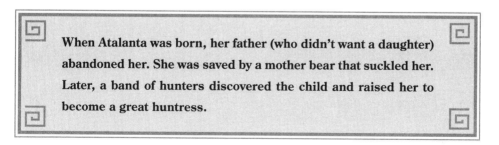

When Atalanta was born, her father (who didn't want a daughter) abandoned her. She was saved by a mother bear that suckled her. Later, a band of hunters discovered the child and raised her to become a great huntress.

Milanion was one of Atalanta's many admirers, but he stood out from the others because he had Aphrodite on his side. Aphrodite saw that no man could ever beat Atalanta in a foot race. So the goddess came up with a plan. She retrieved three golden apples from her orchard and gave them to Milanion to use during the race.

At the start of the race, Milanion had the apples tucked safely away. The race began, and a burst of speed put Milanion briefly ahead of Atalanta. While he had the lead, he tossed one of the apples off the race course. Atalanta ran after the apple to pick it up. The race continued. Each time Atalanta gained on Milanion, he threw another apple. By distracting Atalanta, he won both the race and the woman.

AENEAS AND DIDO

Aeneas was the son of Aphrodite and Anchises. After the Trojan War, Aeneas traveled to the city of Carthage in Africa. Deeply concerned for the safety of her son, Aphrodite caused Dido, queen of Carthage, to fall helplessly in love with him. Dido extended her protection to Aeneas, allowing him and his men time to rest and replenish their supplies. Dido and Aeneas met at a cave to make love.

Dido truly loved Aeneas and wanted to marry him. Aeneas, however, wanted to continue his journey. When the Trojans were ready to leave, Aeneas left with them. Distraught by his departure, Dido threw herself into a fire.

CHAPTER 16

PARTYING WITH DIONYSUS

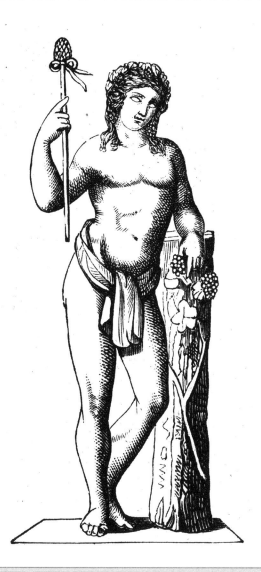

ionysus, the final Olympian to be introduced in these chapters, was the god of wine and revelry. The ultimate party god, he was always ready for a good time—and he wanted to make sure that his followers shared in the fun. Not surprisingly, Dionysus was a popular god, in worship and in the myths. So grab a glass of wine, put on your dancing shoes, and get the party started.

THE TWICE-BORN GOD

Different myths tell different stories of Dionysus's birth. Both versions name Zeus as his father and emphasize Hera's jealousy, but the child's mother and the circumstances of his birth differ.

MYTH 1

As Chapter 6 describes, Zeus seduced Semele disguised as a human male, although he told her that he was actually the ruler of the gods. Hera learned of their affair and was consumed with jealousy. She disguised herself as an old woman and sought out the pregnant Semele, eventually gaining the woman's trust. When Semele confided that Zeus was the father of her child, Hera made her doubt whether her lover had told the truth.

To discover her lover's actual identity, Semele asked him to grant her a wish. Still smitten with the young woman, Zeus promised her anything she wanted, and Semele requested that he reveal his true form to her. Zeus knew that any mortal who looked upon him as he really was would die and begged her to change her mind. She persisted, and he had no choice but to comply. When he presented himself to her in all his glory, Semele burst into flames.

Zeus called on Hermes to rescue his unborn child. Hermes extracted the baby from the mother while Zeus cut a gash in his own thigh. Hermes placed the child inside Zeus's wound and stitched it back up. Three months later, Dionysus was born.

MYTH 2

In this version, Zeus was again Dionysus's father, but Persephone was his mother. Zeus, desiring Persephone, turned himself into a snake and mated with her. From this union, Zagreus was born. The infant boy had horns and came into the world wearing a crown of snakes.

Hera hated Zeus's illegitimate son and wanted to destroy him. She stole the child and handed him over to the Titans, telling them to kill him. In some stories, Zagreus runs from the Titans, changing into different animals as he flees. In the end, though, the Titans tore Zagreus to pieces. They cooked and devoured him—everything except the heart.

Athena intervened, stealing the heart and turning it over to Zeus. Zeus gave Semele the heart and ordered her to eat it. She did as she was told and became pregnant with the child whose heart she'd consumed. When the child was born the second time, he was named Dionysus.

DIONYSUS DRIVEN MAD

Although Hera could not prevent Dionysus's birth, she was determined to seek revenge for her husband's infidelity. Zeus knew his wife, however, and took precautions to protect his son. As soon as Dionysus was born, Zeus placed him in the care of Ino (Semele's sister) and her husband, Athamas, the king of Orchomenus.

To hide Dionysus from Hera's watchful eyes, the couple dressed him as a girl. Eventually, however, Hera saw through the disguise and punished the couple. She drove Ino and Athamas mad, causing them to kill their own sons.

Before Hera could attack Dionysus, Zeus again rescued him. He transformed Dionysus into a young goat and ordered Hermes to take him to Mount

Nysa and place him in the care of some nymphs who lived there. Well hidden, Dionysus grew up happy and healthy.

Time passed, and Dionysus was transformed into his true form. Hera, who hadn't given up searching for him, discovered the young Dionysus and drove him mad. For several years, the mad Dionysus wandered through the world. His aimless travels eventually led to the land of Phrygia, where he was taken in by the earth goddess Cybele (also known as Rhea). Cybele cured Dionysus of his madness and initiated him into her religious cult. He stayed with Cybele for a while, learning her rites and practices. Before long, Dionysus had created his own religious cult, using Cybele's as its foundation.

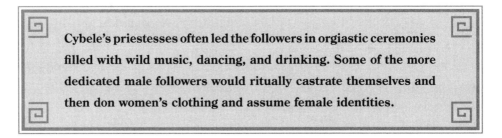

Cybele's priestesses often led the followers in orgiastic ceremonies filled with wild music, dancing, and drinking. Some of the more dedicated male followers would ritually castrate themselves and then don women's clothing and assume female identities.

THE RITES OF DIONYSUS

The religious rites of Dionysus were different from those held to honor other Olympian deities. Traditional rites honored the gods and goddesses in temples specially built for that purpose. Dionysus wandered among the people, and his cults celebrated him in the woods. In Dionysian festivals, worshipers became one with the god. They believed that Dionysus participated actively in his rites. This god loved people; he loved dance; and he loved wine. His festivals were like big parties.

Dionysus was usually accompanied on his travels by the Maenads, wild followers whose name means "madwomen." The Maenads carried a *thyrsus*, a symbol of Dionysus, and incited people to join Dionysus's cult and participate in his rites. Although everyone was invited, women were the most eager participants in Dionysian festivals.

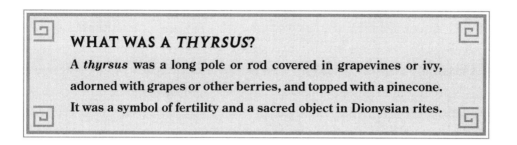

WHAT WAS A *THYRSUS*?

A *thyrsus* was a long pole or rod covered in grapevines or ivy, adorned with grapes or other berries, and topped with a pinecone. It was a symbol of fertility and a sacred object in Dionysian rites.

Dionysus was the god of wine, and his rituals celebrated this drink. It was believed that wine gave people the ability to feel the greatness and power of the gods. Through wine, his worshipers achieved the ecstasy they needed to merge with the god. One of Dionysus's names was Lysios, which meant "the god of letting go." But the excesses of his festivals often led to frenzy and madness.

Dionysian rites were usually held at night. Women dressed in fawn skins, drank wine, wore wreaths of ivy, and participated in wild dances around an image of Dionysus (believed to be the god himself). Sometimes the women would suckle baby animals such as wolves or deer, and sometimes they would hunt down an animal, tear it to pieces, and devour the raw meat. Occasionally, the crazed women would tear apart a man or a child in their rites.

The wine and tumultuous dancing took worshipers to a state of ecstasy, in which they felt the power of the gods. Religious ecstasy was often heightened by sexual ecstasy. The nights were wild and the followers frenzied—and anything was possible.

DIONYSUS TAKES A WIFE

Ariadne, daughter of the Cretan king Minos, was in love with the great hero Theseus. When Theseus came to Crete to kill the Minotaur (read the full story in Chapter 18), Ariadne fell in love with him at first sight. Unfortunately, the feeling wasn't mutual.

Ariadne helped Theseus achieve his quest, thus alienating herself from her father. She ran off with Theseus, who promised to marry her when they reached Athens. On their journey, they stopped at the island of Naxos. As Ariadne lay sleeping on the shore, Theseus sailed away and left her.

She awoke alone and friendless on a strange island, abandoned by her lover. But Dionysus saw her and was struck by her beauty. He fell in love with her instantly, as Ariadne had done with Theseus, and he made her his wife. Some myths say the couple resided on the island of Lemnos; others say he took his bride to Mount Olympus.

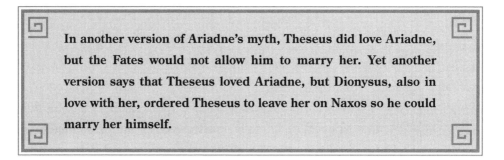

In another version of Ariadne's myth, Theseus did love Ariadne, but the Fates would not allow him to marry her. Yet another version says that Theseus loved Ariadne, but Dionysus, also in love with her, ordered Theseus to leave her on Naxos so he could marry her himself.

Ariadne and Dionysus had many children, including Oenopion, Phanus, Staphylus, and Thoas. Oenopion became the king of Chios. Phanus and Staphylus were Argonauts who accompanied Jason on his quest (see Chapter 19). Thoas became the king of Lemnos.

MADNESS UNLEASHED

Although the Dionysian rites were popular, not everyone accepted them. Some held that Dionysus wasn't truly a god, a claim that stirred his wrath. Just as Hera had punished Dionysus with madness, he punished those who offended him in the same way. Then, he'd watch as the afflicted mortal destroyed himself.

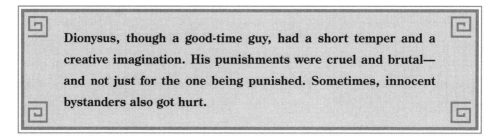

Dionysus, though a good-time guy, had a short temper and a creative imagination. His punishments were cruel and brutal— and not just for the one being punished. Sometimes, innocent bystanders also got hurt.

THE MADNESS OF KING LYCURGUS

Lycurgus, king of Thrace, banned the cult of Dionysus in his kingdom. When he learned that Dionysus and his Maenads had arrived in Thrace, Lycurgus tried to have Dionysus imprisoned, but the god fled to the sea, where he was sheltered by Thetis. The king's forces did manage to capture and imprison some of Dionysus's followers.

In retaliation, Dionysus inflicted Lycurgus with madness. With the king unable to rule, the imprisoned followers were released. But that wasn't the end of the story.

The mad Lycurgus hacked his own son to death, mistaking the boy for a vine of ivy. (Because ivy was sacred to Dionysus, the king wanted to get rid of the plant.) To make matters worse, Dionysus plagued Thrace with a drought and a famine. An oracle revealed that the drought would continue until Lycurgus was put to death. The starving Thracians captured their king and took him to Mount Pangaeus, where they threw him among wild horses, which dismembered and killed him. Dionysus lifted the drought, and the famine ended.

A GOD IN PRISON

In Thebes, the young king Pentheus banned Dionysian rites. In defiance of the king's decree, Dionysus lured the city's women (including Pentheus's mother and aunts) to Mount Cithaeron, where they took part in a frenzied rite. Pentheus refused to recognize Dionysus's divinity and had Dionysus imprisoned in a dungeon. But the dungeon couldn't hold Dionysus; his chains fell off, and the doors opened wide to release him.

Next, Dionysus convinced the king to spy on the rites held on Mount Cithaeron, promising him spectacular sights and a chance to witness sexual acts. Pentheus hid himself in a tree as Dionysus had instructed. The women taking part in the rites saw Pentheus in the tree and mistook the king for a mountain lion. In a wild frenzy and led by Pentheus's own mother, the women pulled him down and tore him to pieces.

> Later, Pentheus's mother came to her senses and realized what she had done. Full of grief, she buried her butchered son herself. Along with her sisters, she was exiled from Thebes.

DIONYSUS'S REVENGE

In Attica, Dionysus encountered a beautiful girl named Erigone, and the two became lovers. Dionysus taught Erigone's father, Icarius, how to cultivate vines and make wine. As an act of generosity, Icarius shared his wine with his neighbors. The neighbors enjoyed the drink, but they overindulged and passed out. When they awoke with terrible hangovers, they believed that Icarius had tried to poison them: What else besides poison could make them feel so wretched? The men banded together and beat Icarius to death.

When her father disappeared, the distraught Erigone roamed the countryside with her dog, searching for him. She discovered her father's badly beaten, lifeless body. In grief and despair, Erigone hanged herself from a nearby tree.

Dionysus was greatly displeased with the ill treatment of his friends. To avenge their deaths, he drove the women of Attica mad; many of them hanged themselves, just as Erigone had done. The men consulted an oracle to find out why their women were committing suicide and learned that they'd offended Dionysus. To appease the god, they established a festival to honor Icarius and Erigone. Dionysus restored sanity to the remaining women, and all was well once again.

THE GOLDEN TOUCH

Although Dionysus could be cruel to those who crossed him, he was also a much-loved god who often rewarded his followers. Dionysus's favorite gift to bestow was wine. From time to time, however, he allowed the recipient to choose the gift. The story of King Midas is one example.

Dionysus's companion and tutor, Silenus, was captured by the people of Lydia and taken to King Midas of Phrygia. Midas recognized Silenus as a companion of Dionysus and welcomed him into his household. The king entertained Silenus for ten days and ten nights, going above and beyond the rules of hospitality. Then, he sent Silenus back to Dionysus, accompanied by an escort.

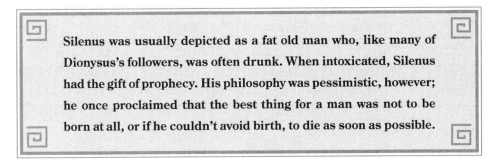

Silenus was usually depicted as a fat old man who, like many of Dionysus's followers, was often drunk. When intoxicated, Silenus had the gift of prophecy. His philosophy was pessimistic, however; he once proclaimed that the best thing for a man was not to be born at all, or if he couldn't avoid birth, to die as soon as possible.

To thank the king for his hospitality to Silenus, Dionysus offered Midas whatever gift he desired. Midas requested that anything he touch turn to gold. Dionysus reluctantly granted the king's wish.

At first, Midas was pleased with his newfound ability. He reveled in his ability to turn ordinary objects like stones and twigs into solid gold. When he sat down to eat, however, Midas realized the problem with his wish. When he tried to eat, his food and drink turned to gold. In despair, Midas realized that his gift was going to kill him.

He called on Dionysus to take back this gift, and the god advised Midas to bathe in the river Pactolus. Midas did as he was told. When he touched the river, his power to turn objects into gold flowed into the water, and the sands of the river became golden. The river became known as a rich source of gold.

JOINING THE OLYMPIANS

Although Dionysus loved to wander the Earth and spend time with mortals, he did take his place on Mount Olympus as one of the twelve great deities. Before he left for the heavens, he undertook a personal quest to retrieve his mother.

In one version of his myth Dionysus's mother Semele died before she could give birth to him. Although Dionysus never knew his mother, he was driven to find her. That was a difficult task because she dwelled in the Underworld.

Still, Dionysus was determined. He consulted a guide, who told him to enter the Underworld through the Alcyonian Lake, a route much faster than traveling by land. When he reached the Underworld, Dionysus had to bargain with Hades to get his mother back. He traded one of his own sacred plants, the myrtle, to Hades in exchange for his mother's freedom. Semele was released from the Underworld and accompanied her son to Mount Olympus, where Dionysus took his place among the great Olympians. Dionysus reconciled with Hera, and Semele was permitted to live in luxury among the gods.

CHAPTER 17
THE LESSER GODS

o the ancients, the world was inhabited by thousands of deities and spirits that controlled nature and interacted with humans. Although the Olympians were unquestionably the most powerful deities, a host of other gods appear throughout the myths. They may have been less powerful and less glorious than the mighty Olympians, but these lesser gods played an important role in classical mythology.

THE MUSES: GODDESSES OF THE ARTS

The Muses, daughters of Zeus and Mnemosyne, were the goddesses of music, art, poetry, dance, and the arts in general. These goddesses were honored by the poets and artists who created through their inspiration.

As Chapter 6 recounts, Zeus and Mnemosyne made love for nine consecutive nights, creating the nine Muses. Each Muse was in charge of a particular domain of the arts:

- **Calliope**: Epic poetry
- **Clio**: History
- **Erato**: Love poetry, lyric poetry, and marriage songs
- **Euterpe**: Music and lyric poetry
- **Melpomene**: Tragedy
- **Polyhymnia (or Polymnia)**: Mime and songs
- **Terpsichore**: Dance
- **Thalia**: Comedy
- **Urania**: Astronomy

The Muses attended celebrations and festivals, singing and dancing for the gods. They were said to be followers of Apollo in his role as the god of music. Although artists invoked the Muses for inspiration, these goddesses had few myths of their own.

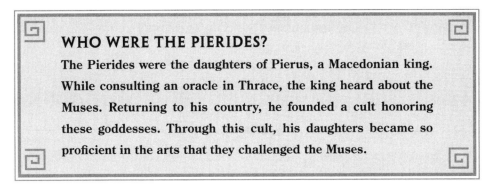

WHO WERE THE PIERIDES?

The Pierides were the daughters of Pierus, a Macedonian king. While consulting an oracle in Thrace, the king heard about the Muses. Returning to his country, he founded a cult honoring these goddesses. Through this cult, his daughters became so proficient in the arts that they challenged the Muses.

Although the Muses were inspirational, they also inflicted punishment. For example, the Pierides (daughters of King Pierus) challenged the Muses to a contest to showcase their own artistic abilities. The Muses were angered by the women's audacity. When the Pierides lost the contest, the Muses turned each of them into a jackdaw (a bird in the crow family). In a similar episode, a bard named Thamyris bragged that he was more skilled than the Muses in the arts of song and poetry. The Muses quickly stifled the man's ego by striking him blind and making him lose his memory.

THE CHARITES: BEAUTY, GRACE, AND FRIENDSHIP

The Charites, also known as the Graces (from their Roman name *Gratiae*), were minor goddesses of beauty, grace, and friendship (and sometimes charm, nature, creativity, and fertility). The myths disagree on their number and their parentage. Usually, though, there were said to be three Charites, daughters of Zeus and Eurynome.

The most common names for the Charites were Aglaia (Splendor), Euphrosyne (Mirth), and Thalia (Festivity—there was also a Muse named Thalia). These names rose to popularity through Hesiod's *Theogony*. Aglaia was said to be the personification of beauty and splendor; Euphrosyne was the personification of joy and merriment; and Thalia personified blossoming and festivity.

The Charites were young, graceful, and beautiful and usually appear in a group. Most commonly seen in art, the Charites in myths are usually in the company of Aphrodite; sometimes they sing and dance in the company of Apollo and the Muses. Like the Muses, the Charites were believed to influence artistic endeavors.

THE SATYRS: LUSTY APPETITES

The satyrs were nature spirits that personified fertility and sexual desire. Originally they were portrayed as mortal men, but later they came to resemble Pan: with horns, a man's torso and face, and the legs and feet of a goat or, in some myths, a horse. (You can read more about Pan later in this chapter.)

The satyrs appear in numerous myths, usually as minor characters and often in the company of the great Olympian deities. Satyrs served as comic relief thanks to their mischievous behavior and blatant sexual desire. They were often in drunken, amorous pursuit of nymphs. In the visual arts, satyrs were depicted with enormous, erect penises.

As followers of Dionysus, satyrs participated in the ecstatic Dionysian festivals. They staggered about drunk, playing music and dancing, and trying to quench their lust.

The best-known satyrs were Marsyas and Silenus. Marsyas, as you may recall, challenged Apollo to a musical contest, lost, and paid a terrible price (see Chapter 13). Silenus was Dionysus's friend and tutor. Known for his wisdom and prophecies, Silenus often overindulged in wine. In fact, he was usually too drunk to walk and had to ride on a donkey instead.

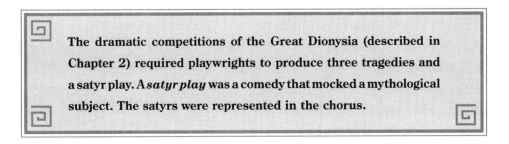

> The dramatic competitions of the Great Dionysia (described in Chapter 2) required playwrights to produce three tragedies and a satyr play. A *satyr play* was a comedy that mocked a mythological subject. The satyrs were represented in the chorus.

THE NYMPHS: BEAUTIFUL SPIRITS OF NATURE

Nymphs appear frequently throughout classical mythology. These beautiful nature-goddesses (often, a nymph was the daughter of Zeus or another deity) were eternally youthful. Most nymphs attended upon a higher deity or a higher-ranking nymph. Personifications of fertility and natural grace, they creatures resided in caves, trees, springs, or other bodies of water. The myths relate numerous love affairs involving nymphs and either men or gods. Examples include Poseidon and Amphitrite (Chapter 7), Ares and Cyrene (Chapter 10), Apollo and Daphne (Chapter 13), and Odysseus and Calypso (Chapter 19). Different kinds of nymphs could be found throughout nature:

- **Crinaeae:** Lived in fountains
- **Dryads:** Lived in trees
- **Hamadryads:** Lived in specific trees and died when the tree died
- **Leimakids:** Lived in meadows
- **Meliae:** Lived in ash trees
- **Naiads:** Lived in fresh water
- **Napaeae:** Lived in valleys
- **Nereids:** Lived in the sea
- **Oreads:** Lived in mountains
- **Pegaeae:** Lived in springs

Although they were goddesses, the nymphs were not immortal; however, they did live very long lives. Nymphs usually appear as minor characters in myths that feature higher-level gods or heroes. Fun-loving and playful, nymphs were sometimes cruel. For example, if a nymph's beloved refused or mistreated her, she could be vindictive. When the river-nymph Nais discovered her lover's infidelity, she struck him blind. He fell into a river, and the other river nymphs let him drown.

PAN: GOD OF WOODS AND PASTURES

Son of Hermes and the god of shepherds and flocks, Pan was half-man and half-goat. When he was born, his mother was so frightened at the sight of her child that she ran away, taking the nurse with her. But Hermes was proud of his son and introduced him to the Olympians.

It is easy to see why Pan's mother was horrified. In art, Pan is shown with two horns on his forehead and with the ears, tail, legs, and hooves of a goat. The young god was raised by nymphs and became a mountain dweller. His physical characteristics made it easy for him to climb rocks and move quickly over the rough terrain.

As a woodland god, Pan was worshiped primarily in rural areas. He was believed to be responsible for the fertility of animals. When a herd's animals did not reproduce, Pan was blamed for their barrenness, and his statues were defaced. (Most gods would erupt with anger over such treatment, but it didn't bother Pan. He grew much angrier if his sleep was interrupted.)

As a fertility god—one whose lower half took the form of an animal renowned for its lust—Pan was famous for his sexual ability and was frequently shown with an erect phallus. He often chased nymphs, trying to catch and violate them. One such nymph was Syrinx.

A follower of Artemis, Syrinx did not want to have sex with Pan and tried to outrun him, but Pan was very fast. He chased her to a river's edge. Trapped, unable to cross the river, Syrinx begged the river nymphs to save her. They granted her wish, transforming her into a bed of reeds, just as Pan reached the scene.

Disappointed, Pan breathed a huge sigh. His breath blew through the hollow reeds and made a delightful, musical sound. Pan cut several different lengths of the reeds and tied them together to make a set of pipes. This instrument became known as panpipes, or syrinxes.

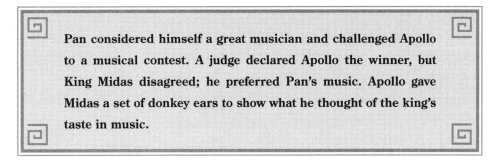

Pan considered himself a great musician and challenged Apollo to a musical contest. A judge declared Apollo the winner, but King Midas disagreed; he preferred Pan's music. Apollo gave Midas a set of donkey ears to show what he thought of the king's taste in music.

HECATE: TITANESS WITH AN ATTITUDE

After the Olympians defeated the Titans, most of the Titans were sent to Tartarus (see Chapter 4). A few, however, were spared this eternal torture because they'd refused to fight against Zeus; Hecate was one of these. After the war, she was able to keep her powers over Earth, sky, and sea (although her powers in these realms were inferior to Zeus's).

Early myths show Hecate as a benevolent goddess associated with the Earth, like Demeter. Hecate oversaw the soil's fertility, ensuring that crops could grow. After the fall of the Titans, her powers became more numerous: She could grant eloquence in speech to orators, material prosperity to any mortal, and victory in battle to warriors. As a goddess of prosperity, she could grant bountiful catches to fishermen and fertile livestock to farmers. Mortals often looked to Hecate for help and blessings, and she was easily persuaded to grant favors.

THE CHANGE

Later, Hecate's character underwent a gradual change, growing darker and more menacing. Hecate transformed from a benevolent earth goddess to a goddess of sorcery and witchcraft. Later myths show her as a goddess of the night, associated with the land of the dead. Some myths say she was an attendant and confidante of Persephone, queen of the Underworld. Although a virgin goddess, Hecate was associated with childbirth and rearing. She was also associated with gates and doorways, the moon, torches, dogs, ghosts, magic and witchcraft, and curses. Worshipers built shrines to Hecate at crossroads because these spots were associated with magical rites.

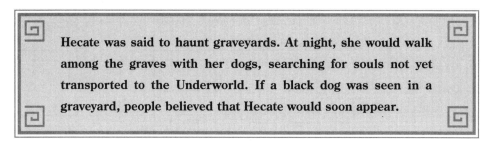

Hecate was said to haunt graveyards. At night, she would walk among the graves with her dogs, searching for souls not yet transported to the Underworld. If a black dog was seen in a graveyard, people believed that Hecate would soon appear.

Hecate sometimes appears in art as a woman with three faces. Usually, she carries torches and has a pack of hellhounds baying at her side. An intimidating presence, Hecate enjoyed the power that comes from causing fear in others.

THE IMPORTANCE OF THREE

The number three was associated with Hecate, who was considered a triple goddess. Her three faces, looking in three different directions, could see past, present, and future. Similarly, she had control over the three phases of existence: birth, life, and death. She had three sacred emblems: a key, a dagger, and a rope. Hecate was also said to appear at crossroads where a traveler faced three choices.

Hecate had different names to indicate the different facets of her character. Here are a few of them:

- **Apotropaia:** Protector
- **Chthonia:** Of the Underworld
- **Kourotrophos:** Nurse
- **Propolos:** Attendant
- **Trimorphe:** Three-formed
- **Trioditis:** Of three roads

Although a minor goddess, Hecate was powerful and influential in the classical mythology. Today, she is still invoked by those interested in witchcraft and magic.

TRITON: SON OF POSEIDON

Triton was Poseidon's son and a minor sea deity. Half-man, half-fish, Triton served as his father's herald and messenger. He possessed powers as well, especially the ability to calm the seas by blowing a conch-shell horn. Triton's conch shell could also instill fear. For example, during the war between the Giants and the Olympians, the loud blasts from Triton's conch shell frightened the Giants; they ran away, thinking that the sound came from a monster. Like his father, Triton carried a trident.

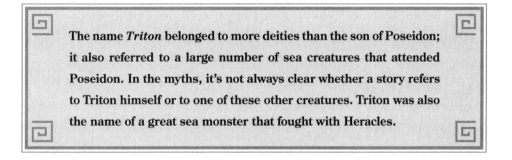

The name *Triton* belonged to more deities than the son of Poseidon; it also referred to a large number of sea creatures that attended Poseidon. In the myths, it's not always clear whether a story refers to Triton himself or to one of these other creatures. Triton was also the name of a great sea monster that fought with Heracles.

Triton appears in several myths. He was the father of Pallas, Athena's young playmate whom she accidentally killed. Another myth tells of the assistance Triton gave to the Argonauts. During the quest for the Golden Fleece (see Chapter 19), a huge tidal wave carried the *Argo* inland, and the Argonauts found themselves on Lake Tritonis. (Some myths say the wave carried them into the desert of Libya.) For days, the Argonauts searched for a way to return to the sea, but to no avail.

Disguised as a mortal named Eurypylus, Triton introduced himself to the Argonauts, who welcomed him with great hospitality. To show his appreciation for their kindness, he showed the men a route that would return them to the sea. Some myths say that Triton pushed the ship along the land, all the way back to the sea.

Triton wasn't always honorable. Like most gods, he had a complex character. According to one myth, during a festival held in honor of Dionysus, Triton came upon some women bathing in the sea in preparation for the rites. Unable to restrain his lust, Triton harassed the women, who called upon Dionysus for help. The god of the vine rushed to their aid, and the two gods fought. Triton lost.

Another myth shows Triton as a thief who stole cattle and attacked ships. To stop him, the local people left out a bowl filled with wine. Triton found the wine and drank it all, and then passed out. As he slept, someone (some say Dionysus) beheaded him with an ax.

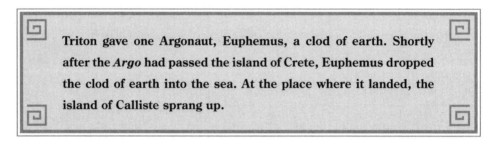

Triton gave one Argonaut, Euphemus, a clod of earth. Shortly after the *Argo* had passed the island of Crete, Euphemus dropped the clod of earth into the sea. At the place where it landed, the island of Calliste sprang up.

LESSER, BUT NOT LEAST

As you read the myths, you're likely to come across numerous other minor deities. Here are a few you should know about:

- **Boreas:** The North Wind, Boreas was often depicted as violent and untrustworthy. Like many other gods, he sometimes abducted and raped mortal women.
- **Eris:** Goddess of discord and strife. She often accompanied Ares on the battlefield. Eris was the source of the golden apple that created conflict among Aphrodite, Athena, and Hera and ultimately led to the Trojan War.

- **Eros:** God of love, particularly sensual love. Eros is often depicted as carrying a bow and arrows; his gold-tipped arrows inspired love, whereas his lead-tipped arrows caused hatred or, at best, indifference. Sometimes, because love is blind, this god was shown blindfolded.
- **Eurus:** The East Wind. He was usually described as being wet and blustery.
- **The Fates:** Three goddesses in charge of determining a person's life-span. These goddesses spun, measured, and cut each individual's thread of life. Some myths say that they could also determine whether a person would be good or evil. Everyone—even the Olympians—was subject to the Fates.
- **Hebe:** Goddess of youth. Daughter of Zeus and Hera, Hebe was the cupbearer to the gods for a time. Later, she became the wife of Heracles when he joined the deities on Mount Olympus.
- **Hymen:** God of marriage. He was normally shown leading a wedding procession.
- **Iris:** Goddess of the rainbow, which connected the sky and Earth. Iris was also a messenger of the gods.
- **Nemesis:** Goddess of vengeance. She was usually called upon to avenge those who had been wronged, but she was also in charge of limiting excess. If someone became too rich or had an unending streak of good luck, for example, Nemesis would take away some of that person's good fortune, to keep the universe in balance.
- **Nike:** Goddess of victory. Often seen in the company of Zeus, Nike also visited conquerors and victors; she would hold a crown of victory above their heads.
- **Notus:** The South Wind. He was normally associated with the warmth and moistness of a gentle wind. In the autumn, however, Notus was thought to turn angry and bring storms that destroyed crops.
- **Thanatos:** God of death. Thanatos was the twin brother of Hypnos, god of sleep. When a person's thread of life had run short, Thanatos would visit that mortal and cut off a lock of his or her hair. When Thanatos

had snipped your hair, there was no going back: You were dedicated to Hades.

- **Tyche:** Goddess of fortune and the personification of luck. She was one of the Oceanids.
- **Zephyrus:** The West Wind. Zephyrus, the god of spring breezes, was considered the gentlest of all of the wind gods. As you read in Chapter 13, however, one myth blames Zephyrus for the death of Hyacinthus, so this god also had his violent side.

In addition to the great gods whose power resounded throughout the universe, every hill, every river, every spring, even every individual tree seemed to have its own god or goddess. This conception of the world makes the universe seem both ordered and chaotic: ordered because each deity has his or her domain, but chaotic because the desires of those many gods sometimes came into conflict.

CHAPTER 18

MONSTER MADNESS

tories about things that go bump in the night have been frightening people for millennia, and the Greek myths certainly have their share of monsters. The mythological monsters in this chapter are some of the best-known and scariest creatures of the ancient world. These monsters challenged the gods, attacked heroes, and terrorized ordinary people—adding goose bump–inducing thrills to their myths.

CHIMAERA: FIRE-BREATHING AND MERCILESS

The Chimaera was the monstrous daughter of Typhon and Echidna. She breathed fire and had the head of a lion (Hesiod said she had three heads), the body of a goat, and the tail of a snake. This monster terrorized the people of Lycia and was defeated by the hero Bellerophon.

A mortal, Bellerophon was famous for having tamed Pegasus, a winged horse. Bellerophon accidentally killed his brother (although some myths say the victim wasn't his brother at all, but a tyrant) and was exiled from his homeland. He went to Argos to be purified. There, King Proetus welcomed Bellerophon into his kingdom and purified him of the murder.

Things were going well for the young man until the king's wife fell in love with him. He refused her advances; in retaliation, she falsely accused him of attempted rape. King Proetus was torn: He couldn't let such a crime against his wife go unpunished, but he liked the young man. Besides, Bellerophon was a guest in his home, and he would be breaking the laws of hospitality if he put his guest to death. Proetus decided to send Bellerophon to his father-in-law's kingdom with a sealed letter ordering his execution.

Ignorant of the contents of the letter, Bellerophon left Argos and made his way to Lycia. King Iobates greeted him warmly and entertained his guest for a week before he remembered the letter. When the king opened the letter and saw what it demanded, he found himself in the same predicament as Proetus. He had accepted Bellerophon as a guest in his home, and he didn't want the young man's blood on his hands. Instead of executing Bellerophon, the king ordered him to kill the Chimaera, which had been terrorizing his kingdom.

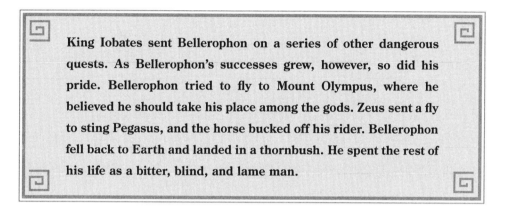

King Iobates sent Bellerophon on a series of other dangerous quests. As Bellerophon's successes grew, however, so did his pride. Bellerophon tried to fly to Mount Olympus, where he believed he should take his place among the gods. Zeus sent a fly to sting Pegasus, and the horse bucked off his rider. Bellerophon fell back to Earth and landed in a thornbush. He spent the rest of his life as a bitter, blind, and lame man.

The king was sure that Bellerophon would be killed in this quest; no one could stand up to the Chimaera. The monster was merciless and destroyed everything in her path. No single person could withstand it.

But Bellerophon wasn't an ordinary person. He had tamed Pegasus, so he had an ally in the battle. The Chimaera's fire-breath was her most deadly weapon, and Pegasus flew Bellerophon out of range. The hero swooped down on the Chimaera, showering her with arrows. According to one version of this myth, Bellerophon attached a block of lead to the end of his spear. He managed to thrust the lead into the Chimaera's throat, where her fiery breath melted it, causing her to suffocate. Bellerophon returned to King Iobates with news of his triumph.

SCYLLA: BEAUTY TRANSFORMED TO TERROR

Unlike other monsters, Scylla wasn't born hideous. She began her life a beautiful sea nymph, happy and carefree. Scylla enjoyed the company of the other sea nymphs, but she did not share their enthusiasm for lust and love. In fact, she wanted nothing to do with men and lovemaking. She was happy as she was and rejected all suitors—until she caught the attention of Glaucus.

Glaucus was a sea deity who fell in love with the beautiful Scylla. He knew she disliked men, and he also knew he'd need the help of magic to have his way with her. Glaucus went to the witch Circe and asked her to create a love potion that would leave Scylla helpless against him, but his plan backfired.

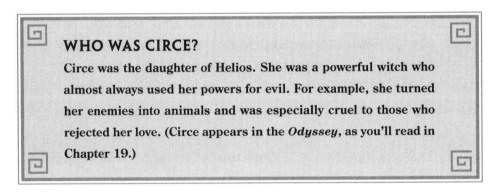

WHO WAS CIRCE?

Circe was the daughter of Helios. She was a powerful witch who almost always used her powers for evil. For example, she turned her enemies into animals and was especially cruel to those who rejected her love. (Circe appears in the *Odyssey*, as you'll read in Chapter 19.)

Circe fell in love with Glaucus, but Glaucus cared for no one but Scylla. When Circe declared her love for Glaucus, he rejected her. Furious, Circe decided to take her rival out of the running. She concocted a potion of poisonous herbs and added it to Scylla's bathwater.

Different myths describe the potion's effect in different ways. One myth says that it transformed Scylla only from the waist down, affecting the part of her body that was submerged in the water. Scylla's upper body remained that of a beautiful woman, but her lower body was hideously changed: The heads of six vicious dogs encircled her waist. These dogs, constantly barking and hungry for prey, would attack anything that got close to Scylla.

In another account, Scylla's entire body was transformed so that no trace of her former beauty remained. Scylla now had six heads (each with three rows of teeth) and twelve feet. Now, Scylla inspired fear in all who saw her.

The monstrous Scylla made her home by the sea between Italy and Sicily, where she lived in a cave next to the whirlpool of Charybdis. There, Scylla waited for sailors to pass. Ships trying to navigate the strait had to maneuver to avoid the whirlpool. This caused the ship to sail closer to the rocky cliffs where Scylla lurked in her cave. While the sailors were preoccupied with avoiding the whirlpool, Scylla would strike, snatching as many men as she could from the deck of the ship and devouring them.

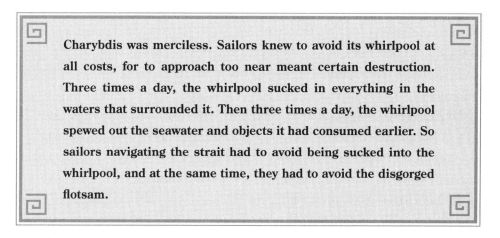

Charybdis was merciless. Sailors knew to avoid its whirlpool at all costs, for to approach too near meant certain destruction. Three times a day, the whirlpool sucked in everything in the waters that surrounded it. Then three times a day, the whirlpool spewed out the seawater and objects it had consumed earlier. So sailors navigating the strait had to avoid being sucked into the whirlpool, and at the same time, they had to avoid the disgorged flotsam.

THE MINOTAUR: MONSTER IN A MAZE

Chapter 7 tells of the conflict between King Minos of Crete and Poseidon over the sacrifice of a beautiful bull. Poseidon had sent the bull to Minos, expecting the king to sacrifice the animal in his honor. But Minos was so enthralled by the bull's beauty that he refused to go through with the sacrifice. The king's wife, Pasiphae, was also taken with the bull; in fact, she fell in love with it. (Some myths claim that Poseidon made Pasiphae fall in love with the bull to get back at Minos for denying the god his sacrifice.)

Pasiphae was consumed by physical desire for the bull; she ordered the craftsman Daedalus to build a hollowed-out cow form. She hid herself within this form and was mounted by the beautiful bull. Pasiphae conceived a child through this union; her son was called Minotaur.

The Minotaur was a monster with the body of a man and the head of a bull. Pasiphae suckled the creature when it was a baby, but it grew into a ferocious, man-eating monster. Not quite sure what to do with this creature, Minos consulted the oracle at Delphi, and then ordered Daedalus to construct an extremely complicated maze, or labyrinth.

The labyrinth that Daedalus built was so intricate that no one who entered was able to find the way out. The labyrinth became the Minotaur's prison. Shut away in this maze, the Minotaur wandered its passageways, killing and eating any living creature it found.

Minos made a name for himself as a conqueror of many lands. He declared himself ruler of the seas and was in constant pursuit of new territory. He made war on Athens because his son Androgeus had died there. But Athens was too well defended, and Minos's army was unable to take the city. So Minos changed tactics. He prayed for a great plague to sweep over Athens. (Since Minos was the son of Zeus, his prayers were usually well-received.)

The gods answered his prayers, and Athens was struck with a pestilence so fierce that King Aegeus was forced to bargain with Minos. Minos said that he would ask the gods to lift the plague if King Aegeus would send him a tribute of fourteen youths: seven men and seven maidens. (Some myths say the tribute was to be sent every year; some myths say every nine years.) Aegeus consulted the Delphic Oracle and learned that this was the only way to end the plague. He agreed to the tribute Minos demanded.

At the appointed time, Athens sent seven young men and seven young women to Crete. Their fate was to become food for the Minotaur; they were thrown into the labyrinth, where they were trapped until the Minotaur found and devoured them. Entering the labyrinth meant certain death at the hands of a terrifying, merciless monster.

Twice, Athens sent young people to Crete to be sacrificed to the Minotaur. When it was time for the third tribute, Theseus, King Aegeus's son, volunteered to go so that he could kill the Minotaur and end the slaughter of young Athenians. When he arrived in Crete, Theseus won the love of Ariadne,

Minos's daughter, and she taught him how to escape the labyrinth: There was one path to the center, where the Minotaur dwelled. Ariadne gave Theseus a ball of thread, so he could unwind it as he made his way through the labyrinth and then retrace his path to the entrance. Theseus killed the Minotaur with his father's sword and led the other Athenians out of the maze, following the thread.

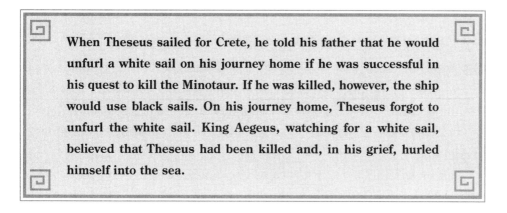

When Theseus sailed for Crete, he told his father that he would unfurl a white sail on his journey home if he was successful in his quest to kill the Minotaur. If he was killed, however, the ship would use black sails. On his journey home, Theseus forgot to unfurl the white sail. King Aegeus, watching for a white sail, believed that Theseus had been killed and, in his grief, hurled himself into the sea.

THE SPHINX: RIDDLE ME THIS

The Sphinx was another monstrous daughter of Typhon and Echidna. She had the head and breasts of a woman, the body of a lion, and the wings of a bird of prey. A vicious, man-eating monster, the Sphinx enjoyed playing with her food like a cat toying with a mouse. Her favorite game offered her victims a riddle to solve. If the victim could solve the riddle, the Sphinx promised to let the person go. Although many tried, they all failed and were devoured.

The Sphinx lived in the mountains outside Thebes, where she harassed travelers and residents of the city. Oedipus, traveling to Thebes, encountered the Sphinx, who stopped him and demanded that he try to answer her riddle: "What creature walks on four legs in the morning, two at noon, and three in the evening?"

Unlike those who'd tried and failed to answer this puzzling riddle, Oedipus answered, "Man." In the "morning" of life (that is, in infancy), a baby crawls on all fours; at "noon," or the prime of life, a person walks upright on two legs; in the "evening" of life, an old person relies on a cane.

Oedipus gave the correct answer. The Sphinx was so shocked and furious that she threw herself off a cliff. The city of Thebes was saved. In gratitude, the people made Oedipus their king and gave him the hand of Jocasta, the recently widowed queen. (To find out why Oedipus's reward was actually a huge problem for him, read Chapter 19.)

CACUS VERSUS HERACLES

Cacus was the son of Hephaestus and Medusa. Inheriting the properties of fire from his father and monstrousness from his mother, Cacus was a fire-breathing monster who was sometimes described as a three-headed giant. He lived on human flesh and decorated his cave with the bones and skulls of his victims.

The most famous myth involving Cacus tells of his encounter with the hero Heracles. For one of his twelve labors, Heracles had to steal cattle from Geryon (another monster) and drive them back to Greece. Heracles success-fully stole the cattle and was on his way home when he stopped to rest by a river. As the hero slept, Cacus spotted the magnificent herd and decided he wanted the cattle. He stole four bulls and four heifers. As Hermes had done in another myth (see Chapter 14), Cacus drove the cattle backward to mask their trail.

When Heracles awoke and saw that some of the cattle were missing, he searched for them, but Cacus's trick sent him in the wrong direction. Just when Heracles had almost given up, some of the cattle in his herd mooed, and a cow hidden in Cacus's cave answered their calls.

Realizing that his hiding place had been discovered, Cacus blocked the cave's entrance with a giant boulder. But that didn't stop Heracles; he broke off the mountaintop to expose the cave's interior. Cacus and Heracles fought; Cacus used fire and Heracles used boulders and tree branches. Cacus pro-duced so much smoke that it was difficult for Heracles to see his target. He jumped into the cave where the smoke was thickest. He found Cacus there and strangled the monster to death.

CENTAURS: EQUINE DEPRAVITY

The Centaurs were a race of beings that had the head and torso of a man and the body and legs of a horse. With a few notable exceptions, the race was brutal and savage. Centaurs enjoyed devouring raw flesh and were constantly on the hunt for it. Usually violent and looking for a fight, Centaurs represented savagery and uncivilized life. Caught between the human and animal world, their human side couldn't overcome their wild animal nature.

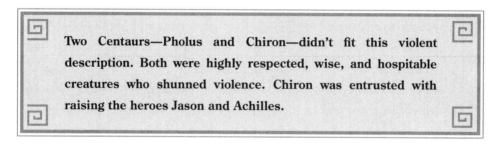

Two Centaurs—Pholus and Chiron—didn't fit this violent description. Both were highly respected, wise, and hospitable creatures who shunned violence. Chiron was entrusted with raising the heroes Jason and Achilles.

The most famous myth involving the Centaurs tells of their battle with the Lapithae, people who lived in Thessaly. Pirithous, the Lapith king, invited the Centaurs to his wedding. All went well until the Centaurs got drunk and began trying to rape the women, including the bride. A great fight broke out between the Centaurs and the Lapithae, with casualties on both sides. Eventually, the Lapithae drove out the Centaurs. Both the *Iliad* and the *Odyssey* refer to this fight, which was also a frequent subject in ancient Greek art.

MORE MYTHOLOGICAL MONSTERS

Myths tell larger-than-life stories of heroes and explore primal fears. So it's not surprising that they're populated by monsters. This chapter has introduced a few of the better-known monsters, but as you read the myths, you're sure to encounter others. Here are some of the monsters you might meet:

- **Cyclopes:** The Cyclopes were a race of one-eyed giants. In Chapter 4, you read about the three Cyclopes who were the sons of Gaia and Uranus. These Cyclopes were skilled craftsmen who designed the thunderbolt and gave it to Zeus as a weapon. In later myths, the Cyclopes are savage man-eaters. The most famous was Polyphemos, son of Poseidon, who threatened Odysseus on his long journey home (more about that in Chapter 19).

- **Erinyes:** Also known by their Roman name, the Furies, the Erinyes were born from drops of blood when Cronus threw his father's severed genitals into the sea. The Erinyes had snakes for hair, their eyes dripped blood, and their bodies looked like winged dogs. Their name means "angry ones," and it was their job to torment people who broke the laws of nature. In the *Oresteia*, the Erinyes pursue Orestes for murdering his mother, until Athena intervenes.
- **Gorgons:** These three monstrous sisters had serpents for hair (like the Erinyes), claws, and long, sharp teeth. Some say they had wings and impenetrable scales covering their bodies. Looking at a Gorgon would turn any being to stone. Medusa was the most famous Gorgon.
- **Griffins:** These monsters guarded treasure and were often employed by the gods and goddesses. A griffin had the head and wings of an eagle and the body of a lion. When these creatures were on guard, a treasure was almost always protected.
- **Harpies:** Harpies were birds with women's faces. Fierce creatures with sharp claws, they were often sent by the deities to punish criminals. When anything was missing—including children—the Harpies were thought to be responsible.
- **Hydra of Lerna:** The Hydra was a giant serpent with numerous heads and poisonous breath; different myths say that this monster had anywhere from five to a hundred heads. Whenever one head was cut off, two more grew in its place. The Hydra fought against Heracles, aided by a giant crab.
- **Stymphalian Birds:** These birds had very long legs, steel-tipped feathers, and razor-sharp claws. They preyed on humans, shooting them with sharp feathers or attacking them with their beaks and claws.

CHAPTER 19

THE LEADING MEN
OF CLASSICAL MYTHOLOGY

Today, people use the word *hero* to describe any person who does something brave or admirable. The ancients, however, had different ideas about what makes a hero—and bravery was just the beginning. Heroes had to satisfy a long list of requirements, some of which modern people would find surprising. This chapter defines what heroism meant to the ancients and tells the stories of some of classical mythology's most illustrious heroes.

WHAT MADE A HERO?

When you think of a hero, you probably imagine someone who risks his or her own interests—or even life—to help someone else. Today, a hero can be anyone who acts with courage or integrity. Most people would say that heroism is defined more by how a person acts than by who that person is.

The ancient Greeks would agree with some parts of that definition but would scratch their heads at others. To the ancients, a hero had to be a certain kind of person *and* act in a certain way. Here are some of the qualities that defined a hero:

- **Noble:** Heroes were of high birth. Often, at least one parent was divine.
- **Courageous:** Heroes didn't show fear in the face of a challenge.
- **Strong:** Heroes possessed great physical strength—in some cases, to an almost supernatural degree.
- **Bold:** Without hesitation, heroes undertook difficult quests, adventures, and exploits to prove themselves.

- **Skillful:** Often the skill mastered by heroes was warfare, but they were expected to excel in some pursuit.
- **Hospitable:** The laws of hospitality were important to the ancients, and heroes were expected to follow them, whether as host or as guest.
- **Favored by the gods:** The gods took an interest in heroes—sometimes opposing them and sometimes supporting them. But usually a hero had at least one powerful god on his side.

Heroes often performed amazing feats that no ordinary person could accomplish. They were mortal, and they were rewarded by the gods after death. Heroes also had very human flaws, such as pride, rage, or jealousy. Unlike modern heroes, classical heroes could be self-centered; they were concerned with their reputation and sometimes put themselves ahead of others. Finally, heroes had to be able to help their friends (showing loyalty) and hurt their enemies (showing bravery and fierceness).

HERACLES

Heracles is probably the most famous hero of Greek mythology. He is so prominent in the myths that previous chapters have already mentioned him several times; it's impossible to talk about some of the gods or monsters without mentioning Heracles. He was a hero who gained immortality by shedding blood, sweat, and tears.

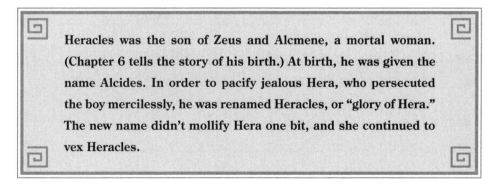

Heracles was the son of Zeus and Alcmene, a mortal woman. (Chapter 6 tells the story of his birth.) At birth, he was given the name Alcides. In order to pacify jealous Hera, who persecuted the boy mercilessly, he was renamed Heracles, or "glory of Hera." The new name didn't mollify Hera one bit, and she continued to vex Heracles.

GOING HOME

On his way back to Thebes, his native city, Heracles ran into a group of men sent from the ruling Minyans to collect the annual tribute of one hundred cattle from the defeated Thebans. He cut off their ears, noses, and hands and tied the severed parts around their necks. He sent them back to their king with the message that Thebes was no longer under his control.

Of course, the Minyans retaliated, but due to Heracles' skill in warfare, Thebes was ready. Heracles gathered an army of Thebans and attacked the Minyan city. The Thebans won the war, and in gratitude, the king of Thebes gave Heracles his daughter Megara in marriage.

Megara and Heracles had three sons and lived happily together—until Hera found them. Hera hadn't given up her quest to destroy Zeus's illegitimate son and struck Heracles with a fit of madness. Heracles murdered his three sons and Megara, who had tried to shield one of her sons with her body. Next, Heracles tried to kill his foster father Amphitryon, but Athena hit Heracles with a rock and knocked him unconscious. When the young man came to, he was horrified to realize what he had done.

To purify himself and purge his guilt for murdering his family, Heracles consulted the Delphic Oracle, which ordered him to go to King Eurystheus of Tiryns and there accomplish ten tasks given to him by the king. Successfully completing these tasks would purify Heracles and give him immortality so that he could take his place among the gods. More anxious to atone for his sins than for immortality, Heracles complied.

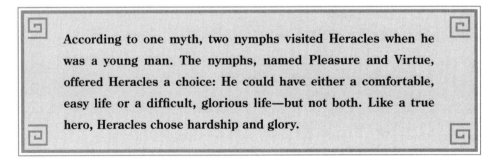

According to one myth, two nymphs visited Heracles when he was a young man. The nymphs, named Pleasure and Virtue, offered Heracles a choice: He could have either a comfortable, easy life or a difficult, glorious life—but not both. Like a true hero, Heracles chose hardship and glory.

THE TWELVE LABORS

Although the oracle specified that Heracles must complete ten tasks, Eurystheus judged that he had not successfully completed two of them. Heracles had twice received aid, so he did not complete those two labors on his own. So Eurystheus created two more labors, bringing the total to twelve:

1. **Kill the Nemean Lion.** This lion had a hide so thick that arrows and spears could not pierce it. Heracles had to fight the lion with his bare hands. Thanks to his incredible strength, he was able to wrestle the lion to the ground and strangle it.

2. **Kill the Hydra of Lerna.** As you know from Chapter 18, the Hydra was a great serpent with many heads. Heracles attacked the monster, but each time he cut off one head, two more grew in its place. He had to call on his nephew Iolaus for help. When Heracles chopped off a head, Iolaus cauterized the stump, preventing new heads from growing. The Hydra had one immortal head, which Heracles buried under a rock. Although Heracles defeated the Hydra, Eurystheus deemed that he hadn't completed this task successfully because he'd had assistance.

3. **Capture the Cerynitian Hind.** This deer with golden antlers was sacred to Artemis. To avoid offending that goddess, Heracles had to capture it unharmed. He hunted the hind for a full year and finally caught it in a net as it slept.

4. **Capture the Erymanthian Boar.** For years, a vicious boar had plagued the countryside of Psophis. Heracles stood outside the boar's lair and shouted loudly. The boar ran out of the lair, straight into a snowdrift. Heracles caught the boar in chains and took it back to Eurystheus.

5. **Clean the Augean Stables.** Heracles' first four tasks had brought him glory; the fifth was intended to be both humiliating and impossible. These stables, which belonged to King Augeas, were home to thousands of cattle and hadn't been cleaned in thirty years. Heracles was charged with cleaning the stables in a single day. To accomplish this task, Heracles diverted the courses of two rivers to make them run through the stables. The rivers washed away all the dung and thus completed the task in a day.

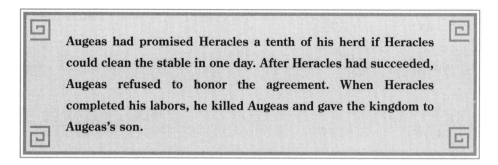

Augeas had promised Heracles a tenth of his herd if Heracles could clean the stable in one day. After Heracles had succeeded, Augeas refused to honor the agreement. When Heracles completed his labors, he killed Augeas and gave the kingdom to Augeas's son.

6. **Drive out the Stymphalian Birds.** These man-eating birds had taken over a forest in Arcadia. Heracles got rid of them by using a giant bronze rattle made by Hephaestus. The rattle's noise scared the birds and drove them from the forest. Because Hephaestus had helped him, though, Heracles didn't get credit for this feat.

7. **Capture the Cretan Bull.** The Cretan Bull was the beautiful bull given to Minos by Poseidon. After a long struggle, Heracles subdued the beast. Then he took it back to Tiryns and released it there.

8. **Capture the Mares of Diomedes.** Diomedes' mares were dangerous man-eating horses. Heracles succeeded in rounding up the mares. As he was driving them back to Tiryns, however, he was attacked by Diomedes. Heracles defeated Diomedes and fed him to his own horses. After they'd eaten their former owner, the horses became tame.

9. **Fetch Hippolyte's Girdle.** This girdle was a belt or sash owned by the queen of the Amazons, a fierce, warlike race of women. Heracles simply asked for the girdle, and Hippolyte gave it to him—an easy victory.

10. **Steal the Cattle of Geryon.** To complete this task, Heracles had to kill a two-headed watchdog and Eurytion the herdsman, a son of Ares who guarded the cattle. Then he had to engage in battle with Geryon, a monster with multiple heads and bodies; Heracles killed him with an arrow that had been dipped in the Lernaean Hydra's poisonous blood. Heracles encountered further obstacles as he drove the cattle back to Tiryns: The monster Cacus stole eight of the herd, and Hera sent a gadfly to scatter the cattle and a flood to swell a river they had to cross.

11. **Retrieve the Golden Apples of the Hesperides.** These apples belonged to Atlas's daughters, so Heracles convinced Atlas to get the apples for him. While Atlas retrieved the apples, Heracles would hold the world on his own shoulders. Glad to be relieved of his heavy burden, Atlas agreed. When he returned with the apples, however, Atlas wasn't willing to take the world back upon his own shoulders. Heracles said he'd continue to bear the burden, but asked Atlas to take it back for just a moment so he could make himself more comfortable. Atlas did—and Heracles ran away with the apples.

12. **Fetch Cerberus from the Underworld.** Eurystheus charged Heracles with bringing the Underworld's three-headed guard dog back alive. With guidance from Athena, Hermes, and Hestia, Heracles entered the Underworld and crossed the river Styx. He asked Hades for permission to take Cerberus back to the world of the living. Hades agreed, but only if Heracles could overpower the monstrous dog without the use of weapons. (In some myths, Heracles must fight Hades before he can try to catch Cerberus.) Heracles wrestled Cerberus barehanded, subdued the creature, and carried it out of the Underworld. Eurystheus was terrified of the monster, however, and Heracles returned Cerberus to the Underworld.

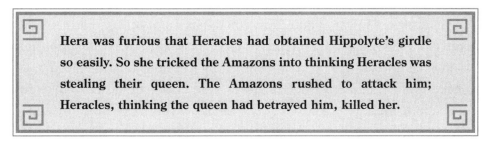

Hera was furious that Heracles had obtained Hippolyte's girdle so easily. So she tricked the Amazons into thinking Heracles was stealing their queen. The Amazons rushed to attack him; Heracles, thinking the queen had betrayed him, killed her.

After many years of laboring at near-impossible tasks, Heracles was finally purified of his family's murder. As the oracle had foretold, he'd also gained immortality. First, however, he had to live out the span of his mortal life. Before he became fully immortal, Heracles had several more adventures. He joined the Argonauts, killed several Giants, challenged Dionysus to a drinking contest (and lost), founded a city, and more.

DEATH AND IMMORTALITY

Heracles' mortal life ended tragically. He married a woman named Deianeira, and while the couple was traveling, a Centaur named Nessus tried to abduct her. Heracles shot Nessus with poisoned arrows. The dying Centaur gave Deianeira his blood-soaked shirt and told her that, if her husband wore it, he would become passionate for her. Later, Deianeira came to believe that Heracles was having an affair, and she gave him the shirt, hoping to rekindle his interest in her. As soon as the poison touched his skin, Heracles began writhing in pain as the flesh was ripped off his bones. He tore up trees to build his own funeral pyre and asked to be burned alive there. Heracles' mortal body burned, but his immortal body ascended to Mount Olympus.

PERSEUS

The poet Homer referred to Perseus as the "most renowned of all men"— and with good reason. Perseus was kind, faithful to his wife, and loyal to his mother and his family. He was also a fearsome slayer of monsters. Perseus was a model man and the epitome of a hero.

MAMA'S BOY

Perseus was born to Danae and Zeus. When Danae was still a virgin, her father heard a prophecy that Danae's son would one day kill him, so he imprisoned his daughter in a tower to keep her away from men. But Zeus managed to get to her and their union produced Perseus. Danae's father locked Danae and her son in a chest and cast them out to sea, but they were saved by a kind fisherman.

Later, King Polydectes wanted a sexual relationship with Danae, but she wanted nothing to do with him. He was relentless in his pursuit, however, and Perseus defended his mother. Polydectes knew that he was no match for Perseus, so he devised a plan to get the young man out of the way. He pretended he was going to marry another woman and demanded lavish wedding gifts from his subjects. Perseus couldn't afford such a gift, but he offered to get the king anything he wanted. Polydectes told Perseus to bring him Medusa's head. This Gorgon was such a formidable monster that Polydectes was sure that Perseus's quest would kill him.

However, Perseus was favored by the gods; he had both Athena and Hermes on his side, and they helped him to overcome and kill Medusa. (Chapter 11 gives the details of how Perseus accomplished his task.) When Perseus returned home, he found that Polydectes was still persecuting Danae, forcing her to work as a slave in his palace. Perseus showed Polydectes the head of Medusa and turned the king to stone.

A DAMSEL IN DISTRESS

Perseus met his bride in the true fashion of a hero—he rescued her. Andromeda was a beautiful young woman, daughter of the king of Joppa. Her mother Cassiopeia was proud of her daughter's beauty, but she went too far and declared that her daughter was more beautiful than the Nereids. The offended sea nymphs complained to Poseidon, who sent Cetus, a sea monster, to attack the coast.

In great distress, the king consulted an oracle and learned that the only way to stop Cetus was to offer his daughter as a sacrifice to the monster. The king reluctantly complied and ordered that Andromeda be chained to the foot of a cliff by the sea. As Cetus approached Andromeda to devour her, Perseus flew in on winged sandals and used Hermes' sword to kill the monster.

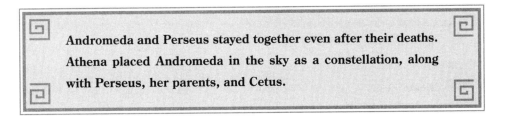

Andromeda and Perseus stayed together even after their deaths. Athena placed Andromeda in the sky as a constellation, along with Perseus, her parents, and Cetus.

Andromeda and Perseus were married and lived happily together. Unlike most husbands in mythology, Perseus was faithful to his wife for as long as he lived. Together they had a son, Perses.

A PROPHECY NOT FORGOTTEN

Perseus, a family man through and through, went to Argos to visit his grandfather, Acrisius. Even though his grandfather had tried to have him and his mother killed, Perseus had no hard feelings. Acrisius, on the other hand, hearing about his grandson's journey to Argos and remembering the prophecy that Danae's son would kill him, fled in fear.

Perseus followed Acrisius to Larissa, a city in Thessaly. Upon his arrival, he learned that the local king's father had died and funeral games were being held in his honor. Perseus joined in the funeral games, entering the discus-throwing competition. During the games, Perseus threw a discus that struck Acrisius, accidentally killing him. The old prophecy had been fulfilled.

With the death of Acrisius, Perseus gained the throne of Argos. He was so ashamed of the fact that he'd killed his own grandfather, however, that he wanted nothing to do with Argos. He traded kingdoms and became king of Tiryns instead.

JASON

Jason was the son of Aeson, who should have been the king of Iolcus. When Aeson's father died, however, Aeson's half-brother Pelias usurped the throne. He spared Aeson but killed his sons. One son, Jason, was saved when his mother and her attendants encircled the new baby, crying and pretending that the child had been born dead. Jason was secretly sent to be raised by Chiron, a wise Centaur. Pelias still feared being overthrown, so he consulted an oracle, which warned him that a man with one sandal would cause his downfall.

When Jason grew up, he learned of his heritage and was determined to claim the throne. He left Chiron and journeyed to Iolcus. On the way, Jason had to cross a river. When he came to the river's edge, he met an old woman who asked him to carry her across. Jason agreed, but he lost a sandal in the process.

When Jason arrived in Iolcus, he wore his lone remaining sandal when he was presented to Pelias. Jason told the king that he had come to claim his birthright. Pelias could not kill Jason outright because of the laws of hospitality, plus he did not want to start a riot among Aeson's supporters. Therefore, Pelias replied that Jason could have the throne if he brought back the Golden Fleece of Chrysomallos, a magnificent winged ram. Jason agreed, and thus began the famous quest for the Golden Fleece.

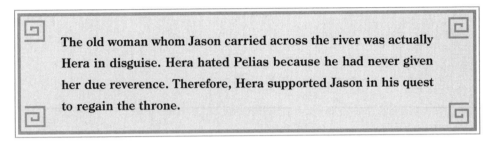

The old woman whom Jason carried across the river was actually Hera in disguise. Hera hated Pelias because he had never given her due reverence. Therefore, Hera supported Jason in his quest to regain the throne.

THE QUEST FOR THE GOLDEN FLEECE

Jason gathered some of the noblest and greatest heroes of Greece, including Heracles, to join him on his quest. Under the direction of Athena, they had a great ship built and named it the *Argo*. The band of heroes called themselves the Argonauts, or "sailors of the *Argo*." They set sail for Colchis, where the fleece was located, but the journey was long and fraught with many obstacles. The Argonauts dallied with the women of the island of Lemnos (Jason fathered twins there), got lost, fought battles, rescued the prophet Phineus from some Harpies, and got through the Symplegades (cliffs that crashed together, crushing any ships that attempted to sail between them).

Finally, the Argonauts landed in Colchis, where Jason claimed the fleece. Aeetes, King of Colchis, told Jason he could have the fleece if he accomplished three tasks:

- Yoke a team of fire-breathing oxen and use them to plow a field.
- Plant a dragon's teeth in the plowed field.
- Conquer the never-sleeping dragon that guarded the fleece.

Jason was favored by both Hera and Athena, who helped him on his quest. Athena summoned Eros to make Medea, a witch who was Aeetes' daughter, fall madly in love with Jason. Medea became infatuated with the hero and helped him in each task:

- She gave him an ointment to protect his skin from the fire-breathing oxen.
- She warned Jason that the dragon's teeth, once planted, would create an army of warriors and told him how to defeat them. Jason threw a rock into the crowd of warriors. Confused, they attacked and killed each other.
- She gave Jason a sleeping potion that put the guardian dragon to sleep, and he was able to grab the fleece.

As soon as Jason had the fleece, the Argonauts left Colchis, taking Medea with them.

Aeetes sent his son Apsyrtus and a fleet of ships to pursue the fleeing Argonauts. Again, Medea acted to help her lover. She sent word to her brother that she had been kidnapped and told him that he must rescue her at a particular location. When Apsyrtus went there to rescue his sister, Jason ambushed and killed him. At the same time, the Argonauts attacked and killed Apsyrtus's crew.

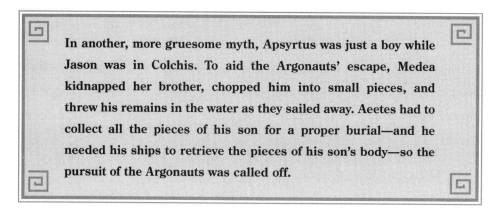

In another, more gruesome myth, Apsyrtus was just a boy while Jason was in Colchis. To aid the Argonauts' escape, Medea kidnapped her brother, chopped him into small pieces, and threw his remains in the water as they sailed away. Aeetes had to collect all the pieces of his son for a proper burial—and he needed his ships to retrieve the pieces of his son's body—so the pursuit of the Argonauts was called off.

The Argonauts faced more challenges on the way home. They had to navigate between the whirlpool Charybdis and the cave-dwelling monster Scylla

(Chapter 18), face terrible sea storms, find their way back to the Mediterranean after being blown far off course, and defeat a terrible bronze Giant. But they eventually made it home to Iolcus.

AN UNSUCCESSFUL MISSION

While the Argonauts were on their quest, a rumor spread in Iolcus that their ship had sunk. Thinking that Jason was dead, Pelias killed Jason's younger brother and his father Aeson. This upset Jason's mother so much that she killed herself.

Faced with the deaths of his parents and brother, Jason knew that Pelias would never give up the throne. He agreed to let Medea get rid of him. Medea convinced Pelias's daughters that they could restore their father's youth and demonstrated what they needed to do: She killed a ram, cut it into pieces, and boiled those pieces. A little while later, a lamb leaped from the pot. Pelias's daughters did the same thing to their father. They cut him into pieces and boiled the pieces. But no young boy emerged from the pot; Pelias had been killed by his own family.

Even with Pelias out of the way, Jason did not get the throne. He and Medea were exiled from Iolcus due to the ghastly way in which they had disposed of Pelias. They fled to Corinth. There, Jason fell in love with Glauce, daughter of the king of Corinth, and planned to leave Medea to marry her. Medea gave Jason's new bride-to-be a poisoned dress and crown; when Glauce put them on, she was killed, along with her father, who rushed to save her. Medea then murdered the two children she'd had with Jason and escaped to Athens, leaving Jason to mourn his losses.

Because Jason had abandoned his wife, he lost Hera's favor. Although he did regain the throne of Iolcus for his son Thessalus, the rest of his life was unhappy. Eventually, Jason died when a timber from the *Argo* fell on him.

THESEUS

Theseus, the greatest Athenian hero, was the son of Aethra, a mortal woman. His father was either Aegeus (king of Athens) or Poseidon—or both. As

Chapter 7 explains, Aethra lay with both Aegeus and Poseidon on the same night, and some myths hold that the son she bore had an immortal father *and* a mortal one.

Aethra lived in Troezen. When she was pregnant with Theseus, Aegeus showed her a great boulder. Beneath the boulder, he said, he had placed his sword and sandals. He told her that if her child was a boy, he could become heir to the Athenian throne if he could lift the boulder, remove the sword and sandals, and bring them to him. Then Aegeus returned to Athens.

When Theseus reached manhood, his mother showed him the boulder. He easily picked it up and retrieved the sword and sandals. Saying goodbye to his mother, he set out for Athens to meet his father for the first time.

THE JOURNEY TO ATHENS

Theseus could travel to Athens by sea or by land. The sea route was easier and safer, but—young hero that he was—Theseus chose the more dangerous land route. Along the way, he overcame many challenges from robbers, murderers, and monsters. In each case, Theseus delivered justice by turning the tables on those who attacked him.

At Epidaurus, Theseus encountered Periphetes, son of Hephaestus, who possessed a huge club that he used to attack and kill passersby. When Periphetes attacked him, Theseus managed to wrestle away the club and kill the bandit with his own weapon. Theseus kept the club, which became one of his emblematic weapons.

Theseus next came upon a vicious Giant named Sinis, who robbed and killed travelers. The Giant would bend down two pine trees, tie his victim between the two trees, and then let the trees spring upright, ripping the traveler in half. Theseus overcame the Giant and killed him by his own method. He also raped Sinis's daughter, Perigune, who later gave birth to Theseus's son Melanippus.

At Crommyon, Theseus was attacked by a huge, monstrous sow. Most mortals ran away in terror from this beast, but Theseus stood his ground and killed the sow with Aegeus's sword.

Next to block Theseus's way was Sciron, a robber who waited for travelers on a narrow path along a cliff's edge. He demanded that travelers wash his feet before he'd allow them to pass. When a traveler bent down before him, Sciron kicked the person over the cliff, where a sea monster (in some versions, a giant turtle) consumed the unfortunate traveler. Theseus, however, didn't fall for Sciron's trick. He pretended to comply, but as soon as he positioned himself in front of Sciron, Theseus took hold of Sciron's legs and threw the robber over the cliff.

Theseus's next assailant was Cercyon, king of Eleusis. This man challenged all passersby to a wrestling match, promising his kingdom to anyone who could beat him. His opponent always lost, however, and was always put to death. Theseus, a great wrestler, won the match, killing Cercyon and winning his kingdom.

> **Cercyon had divine blood: According to different myths, he was the son of Poseidon or Hephaestus or the grandson of Apollo. He won his wrestling matches due to his incredible strength. Theseus, though not as strong, had better technique, so their contest illustrates the triumph of skill over brute strength.**

Finally, Theseus happened upon an innkeeper named Procrustes. At first, the innkeeper seemed kind and hospitable, telling travelers that he had a marvelous bed that was a perfect fit for whoever slept in it. When a traveler lay down, however, Procrustes made that traveler fit the bed: A tall traveler would have his legs cut off, and a short traveler would be stretched or hammered like metal to fit. (Some myths say he had two beds, a long one and a short one, to ensure he could always murder his guests by this method.) Theseus turned the tables on Procrustes by making him fit his own bed (the myths don't say whether Procrustes was too tall or too short), killing him in the process.

CLAIMING THE THRONE

After a long and dangerous journey, Theseus finally reached Athens, but his trials were not over. Although he was welcomed warmly, he had not yet revealed himself to Aegeus. Aegeus was married to Medea, a skillful witch who wanted her own son to take over the throne. When Theseus arrived in Athens, Medea immediately recognized him as the rightful heir to the throne. She convinced her husband to distrust the newcomer.

Aegeus sent Theseus on a mission to kill the Cretan Bull, an exploit he believed would kill the young man. Always hungry for adventure, Theseus eagerly accepted the mission. Because he was such a skilled wrestler, Theseus overcame the bull by wrestling it to the ground. Then he tied a rope around its neck and led it back to Athens, where he presented the bull to Aegeus.

Of course, Medea was furious that the young man was still alive, so she decided to take matters into her own hands. At a banquet to celebrate Theseus's success, she poisoned the hero's cup. Just as Theseus was about to drink, Aegeus, who knew the cup was poisoned, recognized the sandals Theseus was wearing. The king dashed the cup from his son's hand.

Aegeus officially recognized Theseus as his son and named him as his successor. Medea was exiled (or fled) from Athens.

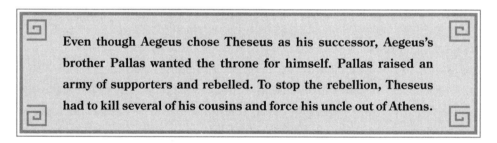

Even though Aegeus chose Theseus as his successor, Aegeus's brother Pallas wanted the throne for himself. Pallas raised an army of supporters and rebelled. To stop the rebellion, Theseus had to kill several of his cousins and force his uncle out of Athens.

Theseus had many other adventures. He slew the Minotaur (Chapter 18), abducted Helen, and was trapped in the Underworld with his friend Pirithous until he was rescued by Heracles (Chapter 8). Some myths name him as one of the Argonauts. Theseus abducted and married Hippolyte, queen of the Amazons. (The abduction caused a war between the Amazons and Athens.)

Aphrodite caused his second wife, Phaedra, to fall in love with her stepson Hippolytus, who rejected her. Phaedra falsely told Theseus that Hippolytus had tried to rape her, and Theseus either killed his son directly or cursed him, causing a sea monster to frighten Hippolytus's horses, which bolted and dragged him to his death.

ACHILLES

Achilles was the greatest hero on the Greek side of the Trojan War. He was the son of Peleus, king of the Myrmidons, and Thetis, a sea nymph. Zeus and Poseidon had both wooed Thetis, until Prometheus warned them that Thetis would give birth to a son who would become far greater than his father. Hearing that prophecy, the gods decided to leave Thetis alone.

When Achilles was born, his mother tried to make him immortal. According to one myth, she rubbed the baby with ambrosia and placed him on a fire to burn away his mortality, but she was interrupted by her husband before she was finished. The more famous story is that she dipped her son into the river Styx, holding him by one foot. The water made the boy impervious to harm—everywhere except for the heel that his mother grasped as she lowered him into the water. This is where the phrase *Achilles' heel*—a small but serious weakness—comes from.

Achilles was raised by Chiron the Centaur, who'd also brought up Jason. He is a central figure of Homer's epic poem the *Iliad* (turn to Chapter 20 to read more of Achilles' story).

ODYSSEUS

Odysseus was king of the island of Ithaca. Renowned for his cleverness, he fought on the Greek side during the Trojan War and came up with the ruse of the Trojan horse. The Homeric epic the *Odyssey* tells the story of Odysseus's long voyage home after the ten-year Trojan War. Trying to return to his faithful wife and son, Odysseus faced ten years of obstacles and adventures. His journey was so long and arduous because he had offended Poseidon—not a good idea if you're going to travel by sea.

During the first part of Odysseus's journey home, his men battled the Cicones. Although they won the fight, they sustained some casualties, losing six men from each ship. At another stop, Odysseus sent three men to scout the location. The scouting party encountered the lotus-eaters and joined them in a feast. The lotus put the men in a dream state that made them stop caring about going home; all they wanted was to eat more of the lotus. Odysseus had the men dragged back to the ships and tied down so they wouldn't jump overboard and swim back to the lotus-eaters' land.

ENCOUNTERING POLYPHEMUS

Things took a serious turn for the worse when Odysseus's ships landed on an island inhabited by the Cyclopes—one-eyed, man-eating Giants. The Cyclops Polyphemus was Poseidon's son. When Odysseus and twelve of his men explored the island, they found a cave with a large amount of food stored in the back. Odysseus and his men settled in to wait for the cave's owner to return to ask him to share his food. But the cave's owner was Polyphemus.

Around dusk, Polyphemus returned with his flock of sheep. As was his routine, he drove the flock into the cave and blocked the entrance with a massive boulder. Odysseus asked the Cyclops for the hospitality due to him by the laws of the gods. Polyphemus answered Odysseus's request by seizing two of his men and devouring them.

The men could not kill Polyphemus because he was the only one strong enough to move the boulder away from the cave's entrance. In the morning, Polyphemus ate two more of Odysseus's men and then drove his flock outside. He then replaced the boulder, keeping the men trapped inside the cave, awaiting their turn to become a meal for the Cyclops. But clever Odysseus devised a plan.

When Polyphemus returned with his flock that night, he ate two more men. Odysseus gave the Cyclops some strong wine the hero had with him. Polyphemus got drunk and asked Odysseus his name, to which Odysseus replied, "No-one." Polyphemus was grateful for the wine and promised to eat

No-one last as his reward. Then he passed out. As the monster lay sleeping, Odysseus drove a stake through his single eye, blinding him. Polyphemus cried out that he was being murdered, and the other Cyclopes came running. When they asked who was attacking him, he answered, "No-one!" This answer made no sense, and the other Cyclopes left him alone.

In the morning, Polyphemus needed to let his flock out to graze, but he worried that the men would take advantage of his blindness and escape. So, after he'd moved the boulder, he blocked the entrance with his own body. As his sheep filed out one by one, he felt their backs to make sure that only the sheep were leaving. Because he couldn't see, however, he didn't notice that Odysseus and his six surviving men had tied themselves under the sheep's bellies. In this way, they escaped from the Cyclops's cave. They drove the sheep to their ship, loaded them on board, and set sail from the island.

As they sailed away, Polyphemus threw huge boulders at their ship, but because of his blindness he missed. Odysseus couldn't resist telling the Cyclops the real name of the hero who'd tricked him, shouting that it was the great Odysseus. In a rage, Polyphemus asked his father, Poseidon, to prevent Odysseus from ever getting home—or, if that wasn't possible, that all his men would be killed and his fleet destroyed. Poseidon took his son's prayers to heart and bedeviled Odysseus for the rest of his journey.

THAT OLD WINDBAG

Odysseus and his men visited Aeolus, a mortal to whom the gods had granted control of the winds, on his floating island, Aeolia. They stayed there for several days, and Odysseus entertained Aeolus with stories of his adventures. As a parting gift, Aeolus gave Odysseus a bag that held all of the winds except for the wind that blew toward Ithaca. As long as the other winds remained in the bag, Odysseus's ships would head straight home.

Odysseus guarded the bag day and night. When his fleet was almost at Ithaca, his men began to wonder what was in the bag. Since Odysseus kept such close watch on it, they reasoned it probably held a treasure. As Odysseus slept, the crew opened the bag, releasing all the winds it held. A violent storm blew them back to Aeolia. This time, Aeolus could not offer any help because he did not want to offend the god who opposed Odysseus.

NEVER TRUST A GIANT

Odysseus arrived at the land of the Laestrygonians: savage, man-eating Giants. At first, the locals seemed friendly; a young girl even gave the men directions to her parents' house. When the men arrived, they were met by a Giantess, who called for her husband. As soon as he arrived, he snatched one of the men and ate him.

The other men escaped and rushed back to their ships, with the Laestrygonians in hot pursuit. Before the fleet could sail away, the Giants hurled huge boulders at the ships, causing them to sink. They speared the men like fish and ate them. The only ship that got away was Odysseus's, which had been at a distance from the others.

TURNING MEN INTO SWINE

With just one ship remaining, Odysseus was wary of the other dangers he might encounter. The next time he landed on an island, the men drew lots to determine who would explore the island. Odysseus stayed on the ship.

The explorers came upon the witch Circe, who invited them to dine with her; she turned all the men into swine. One man escaped and told Odysseus what had happened. Determined to save his men, Odysseus went ashore alone. Hermes intercepted him and gave him a magic herb to protect him from Circe's magic. When her magic failed, Odysseus threatened to kill her for what she'd done. She begged him for mercy and offered to sleep with him. But Hermes had warned Odysseus that she would try to steal his manhood in bed, so the hero made her swear by the gods that she would not harm either him or his crew. He also demanded that she return his crew to their true form. She did as she was told and, surprisingly, became a gracious and hospitable hostess. Odysseus and his men stayed with her for an entire year.

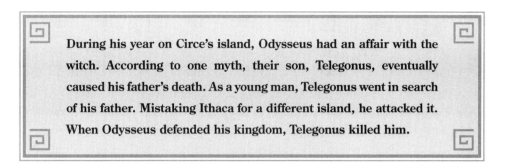

During his year on Circe's island, Odysseus had an affair with the witch. According to one myth, their son, Telegonus, eventually caused his father's death. As a young man, Telegonus went in search of his father. Mistaking Ithaca for a different island, he attacked it. When Odysseus defended his kingdom, Telegonus killed him.

ODYSSEUS'S OBSTACLE COURSE

Poseidon was determined to do whatever he could to prevent Odysseus from getting home. Before Odysseus returned to Ithaca, he encountered many other obstacles, adventures, and trials, including:

- **A Journey to the Underworld.** Odysseus decided to speak with the shade of the prophet Tiresias to find out how to avoid other dangers on his trip home. Tiresias told him how to get safely past the cattle of Helios, Scylla, and Charybdis. He also told Odysseus how to make peace with Poseidon after he'd made it back to Ithaca. While he was in the Underworld, Odysseus also spoke with the shades of his mother, Agamemnon, and Achilles.
- **The Sirens.** These female creatures sang beautiful, alluring songs as ships sailed past. When sailors steered closer, their ships were dashed against hidden rocks. On Circe's advice, Odysseus had his men plug their ears with wax so they wouldn't be tempted by the Sirens' singing. Odysseus wanted to hear the beautiful songs, so he had his men tie him to the ship's mast. When he heard the Sirens singing, he struggled to break free so he could go to them, but his bonds prevented him, keeping him and his ship safe.

After his ship passed them by and not a single sailor succumbed to their music, the Sirens became distraught. Thinking their spell had lost its power, they threw themselves into the sea and were never heard from again.

- **Scylla and Charybdis.** As Chapter 18 describes, Scylla was a man-eating monster that lived in a cave in some sea cliffs, and Charybdis was a dangerous whirlpool. Sailors trying to pass them were usually caught by one or the other. When Odysseus's ship arrived at these dangers, he judged Scylla to be the lesser of the two evils and steered his ship closer to her side. Unfortunately, he got too close, and Scylla seized and devoured six of his crew.

- **The Cattle of Helios.** Odysseus had been warned by both Circe and Tiresias not to touch the cattle on a certain island because they were sacred to Helios. When they approached this island, Odysseus told his men that they would not stop there, but the men threatened to mutiny and Odysseus was forced to give in. While they were ashore, the winds changed, and they couldn't leave. After a while, they ran out of food. Odysseus warned the men not to touch the sun god's cattle, but his crew figured it would be better to feast on the cattle and be killed by the gods than to die of starvation. Helios was furious and complained to Zeus, threatening to hide the sun in the Underworld if he wasn't avenged. When Odysseus's men set out to sea again, Zeus sent a storm that killed the entire crew. Odysseus's ship was pulled into Charybdis, and the hero barely escaped.

- **Calypso's Island.** After Odysseus's ship was destroyed, he clung to a piece of wood and drifted for nine days. He landed on an island inhabited by the nymph Calypso. Calypso fell in love with Odysseus and kept him with her for seven years, promising him immortality if he stayed. But Odysseus yearned for home. Eventually, at Athena's request, Zeus sent Hermes to order Calypso to release Odysseus.

- **Return to Ithaca.** Odysseus left Calypso's island on a raft and was nearly killed when Poseidon sent a storm. He washed up on the island of Scheria, where he was hospitably received by the Phaeacians, who eventually gave him passage home on one of their ships. When Odysseus finally reached Ithaca, he had to fight the suitors who had been living in his palace and trying to win the hand of his faithful wife Penelope (and with it his throne). He won the battle, with Athena's aid, and reclaimed both his wife and his kingdom.

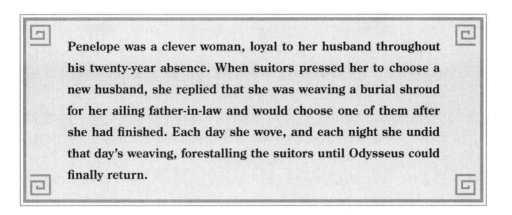

Penelope was a clever woman, loyal to her husband throughout his twenty-year absence. When suitors pressed her to choose a new husband, she replied that she was weaving a burial shroud for her ailing father-in-law and would choose one of them after she had finished. Each day she wove, and each night she undid that day's weaving, forestalling the suitors until Odysseus could finally return.

OTHER HEROES YOU SHOULD KNOW

Classical mythology tells of the exploits and adventures of many heroes. Here are some other heroes you're likely to meet in the myths:

- **Agamemnon:** He sacrificed his daughter Iphigenia to bring the winds that would allow his fleet to sail to Troy. During the Trojan War, Agamemnon commanded the Greek forces. After he returned home, he was murdered in his bath by his wife Clytemnestra and her lover Aegisthus.
- **Meleager:** The hero who killed the Calydonian Boar, Meleager was also listed among the Argonauts.
- **Narcissus:** A devastatingly handsome man, Narcissus scorned all who loved him. As punishment, the gods caused him to fall in love with his own reflection in a pool of water. When he realized that the object of his desire was a mere reflection and could not love him back, Narcissus committed suicide.
- **Oedipus:** Before Oedipus's birth, his parents, Laius and Jocasta, king and queen of Thebes, learned through an oracle that their son would kill his father and marry his mother. At the child's birth, Laius ordered a servant to abandon the child on a hillside to die, but the servant gave the helpless baby to a shepherd instead. When Oedipus came of age, he heard the same prophecy. Trying to avoid his fate, he left the city

where he'd grown up and the people he believed were his parents, traveling toward Thebes. At a crossroads, he fought with a stranger and killed him; the man was Laius, his biological father. After Oedipus solved the riddle of the Sphinx (Chapter 18), he became king of Thebes and married the recently widowed queen Jocasta, his biological mother. When Oedipus learned that he'd actually fulfilled the prophecy he'd tried to avoid, he blinded himself.

- **Orestes:** Son of Agamemnon, Orestes avenged his father's death by murdering his own mother, Clytemnestra. He was pursued by the Erinyes for his crime until Athena cast a tie-breaking vote in Orestes' favor at his trial.

- **Orpheus:** A master musician, Orpheus ventured into the Underworld to rescue his wife, Eurydice, who'd been killed by a poisonous snake. (Chapter 8 tells you how that worked out.)

- **Pelops:** When Pelops was a child, his father, Tantalus, cut him to pieces and made a stew of his flesh, offering it to the gods as a feast. The gods weren't fooled and restored the boy to life. Only Demeter, distracted by the absence of Persephone, took a bite of meat; this missing piece of Pelops's shoulder was replaced by a piece of ivory. The gods taught Pelops how to drive a chariot, and he won his wife in a chariot race (although he cheated by having the linchpins removed from his opponent's chariot to make the wheels fall off). A great warrior, Pelops conquered the area known as the Peloponnese. Later, the Greeks carried his bones to Troy because of a prophecy that they would win the war if they did so.

CHAPTER 20

THE TROJAN WAR

he Trojan War—a ten-year conflict between the Achaeans (a collective name for the various Greek forces) and the Trojans—was one of the most famous events in classical mythology. It was a long, bloody, and destructive war that caused numerous tragedies. Yet it was also an occasion for warriors to prove their heroism and for the gods to help their favorites.

CAUSES OF THE WAR

Several seemingly unrelated events fit together like a jigsaw puzzle and caused the Trojan War. It all began at the wedding of Peleus and Thetis—parents of the Greek hero Achilles.

A MARRIAGE CELEBRATION GONE AWRY

The wedding of Peleus, a mortal king, and Thetis, a sea goddess, was a grand affair. Nearly all the gods and goddesses attended, as did many mortals.

Eris, the goddess of strife and discord, was not invited to the wedding. In fact, Zeus instructed Hermes to stop Eris at the door if she appeared. When Eris was prevented from entering, she threw a golden apple inscribed with the words "for the fairest" into the crowd. Athena, Aphrodite, and Hera each considered herself to be the fairest and therefore the apple's rightful owner. A dispute broke out among the goddesses. None of the other deities wanted to get involved; if they chose one goddess, the other two would be angry and out for revenge. So Zeus ordered Hermes to lead them to the handsome young prince Paris, and he would settle the dispute. Paris chose Aphrodite because she promised him the most beautiful woman in the world—who happened to be Helen of Troy (see Chapter 15).

HELEN OF TROY

Helen, the daughter of Zeus and Leda, always had numerous suitors, and her stepfather, King Tyndareus of Sparta, worried that this competition would start a war among the princes of Greece. So Tyndareus, advised by the clever Odysseus, made all of Helen's suitors swear that they would support and defend whoever became her husband. The suitors drew straws, and the winner was Menelaus. He married Helen and, after the death of Tyndareus, became king of Sparta.

PARIS WANTS HIS PRIZE

Even though Helen was already married, Paris was determined to collect the prize promised to him by Aphrodite. Against everyone's advice, Paris traveled to Sparta. When he arrived, he was welcomed warmly by Menelaus.

While Paris was visiting, Menelaus had to leave Sparta to attend a funeral. He left Helen behind, never imagining she could be in danger. Paris saw his chance. He grabbed Helen and fled Sparta. (Some myths say he also stole treasure from the palace.)

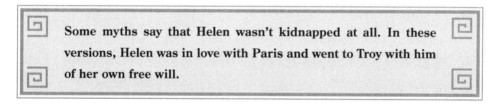

Some myths say that Helen wasn't kidnapped at all. In these versions, Helen was in love with Paris and went to Troy with him of her own free will.

Menelaus and Odysseus traveled to Troy to demand Helen's return. King Priam did not want war with the Greeks, but his fifty sons appealed to him to protect Paris's right to Helen, who had been promised to him by Aphrodite herself. Outvoted, Priam refused to return Helen and the stolen treasure.

BOUND FOR TROY

When Menelaus returned to Sparta, he immediately called upon Helen's former suitors who had sworn to support him. Though wary of the situation, they agreed to abide by the oath. An army of Greek forces was assembled, and Menelaus named his brother Agamemnon commander-in-chief.

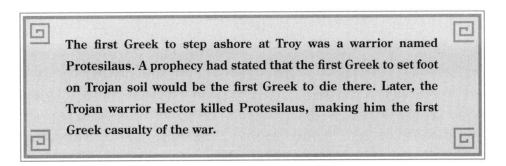

The first Greek to step ashore at Troy was a warrior named Protesilaus. A prophecy had stated that the first Greek to set foot on Trojan soil would be the first Greek to die there. Later, the Trojan warrior Hector killed Protesilaus, making him the first Greek casualty of the war.

Menelaus rounded up more than a thousand ships to sail for Troy. The winds were not in their favor, however, and the ships could not leave the harbor. As you read in Chapter 12, Agamemnon had previously offended Artemis. A seer told Agamemnon that he must sacrifice his daughter Iphigenia to appease Artemis and gain favorable winds. Agamemnon complied, an act that would cause trouble for him later.

The Greek fleet arrived at Troy. Deciding that the best tactic would be to cut off the supply of provisions to the city, the Greeks attacked the surrounding towns. These battles took place over the course of nine years. It was only during the war's tenth year that the Greeks attacked Troy directly.

ENTER THE OLYMPIANS

The gods and goddesses took an intense interest in the Trojan War. Many of them chose sides and helped their favorites when they could. The gods were split in their choices, though, which is one reason the war dragged on for so long.

Many of the Olympians supported the Greeks. Poseidon sided with the Greeks because he still held an old grudge against Troy; he never forgot that an earlier king had refused to pay him for helping to build the city's protective walls. Hera and Athena also had a grudge against Troy; Paris had given the golden apple to Aphrodite and not to one of them. Hermes and Hephaestus also supported the Greeks.

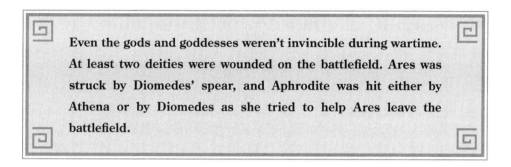

Even the gods and goddesses weren't invincible during wartime. At least two deities were wounded on the battlefield. Ares was struck by Diomedes' spear, and Aphrodite was hit either by Athena or by Diomedes as she tried to help Ares leave the battlefield.

The Trojans also had the support of several gods. Aphrodite, winner of the golden apple, stuck with Paris and sided with the Trojans. Apollo and Artemis also favored the Trojans. Ares had no particular allegiance but was most often seen fighting with the Trojans, probably because his lover Aphrodite supported them.

Other Olympians—including Hades, Hestia, Demeter, and Zeus— remained neutral.

HEROES OF THE WAR

The Trojan War brought together some of the most famous heroes of classical mythology. There were legendary fighters on both sides:

- **Hector.** The oldest son of King Priam, Hector was the best warrior on the Trojan side. A brave, noble man, he had been in favor of returning Helen to her husband. But when war became inevitable, Hector was a vigorous and formidable defender of his city. He killed Protesilaus, the first Greek to die in the war. He also killed Achilles' best friend, Patroclus, an act that led to his own downfall. Hector was favored and protected by Apollo, but even Apollo couldn't protect him from Achilles.
- **Achilles.** He was the greatest warrior among the Greeks during this war. Chapter 19 describes Achilles' birth and his mother's attempts to make him invulnerable. Achilles killed a great number of enemies, but when he came into conflict with Agamemnon over a concubine, he got angry and refused to fight. When Achilles heard of his friend

Patroclus's death, he swore an oath to kill Hector. He rejoined the war with a fury that drove him to kill countless Trojans, including Hector. Achilles defiled Hector's body. For days, he dragged Hector's corpse behind his chariot as he drove around and around the walls of Troy. Later, Achilles was killed by an arrow shot by Paris, which hit him in the one spot where he was vulnerable: his heel. Some myths say that Apollo guided the arrow to the fatal spot.

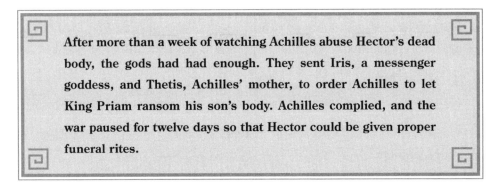

After more than a week of watching Achilles abuse Hector's dead body, the gods had had enough. They sent Iris, a messenger goddess, and Thetis, Achilles' mother, to order Achilles to let King Priam ransom his son's body. Achilles complied, and the war paused for twelve days so that Hector could be given proper funeral rites.

- **Patroclus.** Achilles' best friend, he had been raised in the wilderness with Achilles by the centaur Chiron. During the Trojan War, he was a warrior on the Greek side. When Achilles refused to fight, Patroclus wore Achilles' armor and took his place in battle. Patroclus fought well, but he was eventually killed by Hector.
- **Aeneas.** A son of Aphrodite, he was second only to Hector on the Trojan side. A valiant warrior with many successes on the battlefield, Aeneas fought to the bitter end, even as Troy burned around him. He was one of the few Trojans to survive the war, and he led the other survivors to their new home.
- **Diomedes.** Besides Achilles, he was the best warrior on the Greek side. One of Helen's former suitors, he was bound by his oath to fight with the Greeks. Diomedes killed the Trojan prince Pandarus, wounded Aeneas, and wounded both Ares and Aphrodite—in just one day on the field.

- **Agamemnon.** He was commander-in-chief of the Greek forces. He killed Antiphus, one of Priam's sons. Although Agamemnon was an authoritative leader, he came into conflict with Achilles during the war's last year, over a woman, Briseis, whom Achilles felt he'd won as a war prize.

- **Odysseus.** A skilled tactician and diplomat, he often soothed tempers when different Greek factions fell into conflict. Along with Ajax, Odysseus retrieved the slain Achilles' body and armor from the middle of a fierce battle. He was favored by Athena, who often helped him.

- **Ajax of Salamis.** Often referred to as Ajax the Great, this Greek warrior twice fought Hector. Zeus declared the first battle a draw; in the second battle, Hector disarmed Ajax, who had to withdraw from the fighting. After Ajax and Odysseus retrieved Achilles' body, Odysseus was awarded Achilles' armor. Athena struck the furious Ajax mad, and he slaughtered a herd of sheep, believing that they were the Greeks who had denied him the honor of Achilles' armor. When he regained his senses and realized what he'd done, he committed suicide.

- **Ajax of Locris.** Also known as Ajax the Lesser, he defiled a temple of Athena after Troy fell. The Trojan princess Cassandra had sought sanctuary in the temple and was clinging to a statue of the goddess. Ajax dragged her from the temple (in some versions, he raped her first). He was killed by Athena on his journey home from Troy.

- **Nestor.** On the Greek side, Nestor was an older man known for his wise advice. Although too old to engage in actual combat, he led his troops in a chariot and carried a golden shield. Nestor's son Antilochus, who had been one of Helen's suitors, was killed in the war.

- **Teucer.** Although he was King Priam's nephew, he fought with his half-brother Ajax of Salamis on the Greek side of the war. He was known as a skilled archer, yet every time he shot an arrow at Hector, Apollo deflected it.

THE TENTH YEAR

For nine long years, the Greeks succeeded in conquering the towns around Troy, but they hadn't conquered the city itself. The siege dragged on. So much blood had already been spilled; men missed their families; and exhaustion was taking its toll. Something had to give. The tenth year was the turning point of the war. Just as several factors combined to cause the war, a number of different events worked together to bring the war to its close.

TROJANS AHEAD

Hector's death was a severe blow to the Trojans. Soon after, however, the Greeks lost Achilles (killed by Paris with Apollo's help) and Ajax of Salamis, who killed himself. Also, Amazon warriors arrived to help the Trojan cause. These events did not bode well for the Greeks. However, they were far from giving up. If anything, they became even more motivated.

AN INSIDER'S SECRETS

Led by Odysseus, the Greeks captured Helenus, Priam's son and one of Troy's chief prophets. Helenus revealed that the Greek forces would never defeat Troy without the help of Achilles' son Neoptolemus, and Philoctetes, who owned the bow and arrows of Heracles. Helenus also told the Greeks that Troy could not fall as long as the Palladium stood within the city.

Odysseus and Diomedes volunteered to fetch Neoptolemus and Philoctetes. First they went to Scyrus to recruit the young Neoptolemus. This was an easy task, for the young man was eager to join the army and live up to his father's honorable name. Next they traveled to the island of Lemnos to get Philoctetes, who proved to be more difficult to recruit. Philoctetes was bitter toward the Greeks, especially Odysseus, for abandoning him on the island years before. But the ghost of Heracles visited Philoctetes and told him it was his duty to help the Greeks, so he agreed to join the Greek cause.

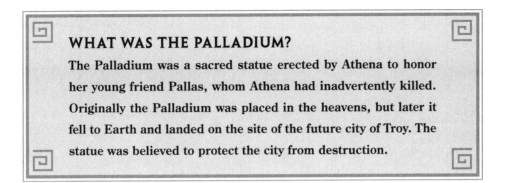

WHAT WAS THE PALLADIUM?

The Palladium was a sacred statue erected by Athena to honor her young friend Pallas, whom Athena had inadvertently killed. Originally the Palladium was placed in the heavens, but later it fell to Earth and landed on the site of the future city of Troy. The statue was believed to protect the city from destruction.

When the group returned to Troy, Odysseus and Diomedes devised a scheme to steal the Palladium from inside the city walls. They disguised themselves, and under cover of night, snuck into Troy and removed the statue unchallenged.

Although the Greeks accomplished the tasks outlined by Helenus, Troy did not fall. They still needed a plan.

THE FALL OF TROY

Odysseus came up with a plan to get the Greeks into Troy. Under Athena's direction, the Greeks built a gigantic wooden horse with a hollow body. Odysseus and an elite group of Greek warriors hid inside the horse. Their Greek companions took the horse to the city gates and left it there with an inscription explaining it was dedicated to Athena.

The Greek army then withdrew from sight, pretending to sail away. The Trojans weren't quite sure what to do with the horse. Some wanted to destroy it. Others wanted to bring it inside, and still others could hardly contain their curiosity.

A raggedly dressed Greek soldier appeared. He said his name was Sinon and that the Greek army had planned to sacrifice him to Athena, but he had escaped. Athena was furious with the Greeks, he explained, because they had stolen the Palladium. As if disclosing a great secret, Sinon told the Trojans that the Greeks had built the great wooden horse as an offering to Athena, but that they'd purposely built it to be too big to fit through the city's gates. The horse would replace the Palladium and bring the Trojans victory.

Most of the Trojans agreed that they should try to get the horse inside the city walls. One man, however, spoke out against the idea. The prophet Laocoon, wary of what the horse would bring, warned the Trojans not to trust the Greeks. To emphasize his point, Laocoon threw his spear at the horse. Just then a huge monster rose up from the sea and devoured Laocoon and his sons.

To the Trojans, Laocoon's death appeared to be a direct result of his attack on the horse. They reasoned that the horse must indeed be an offering to Athena; when Laocoon attacked the horse, she was offended and sent the sea monster to punish him. Athena did send the sea monster to kill Laocoon, but not because he had desecrated her monument—she just wanted to shut him up.

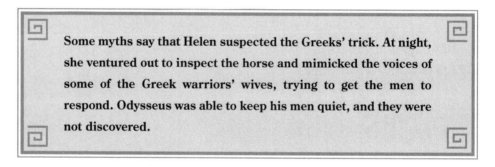

Some myths say that Helen suspected the Greeks' trick. At night, she ventured out to inspect the horse and mimicked the voices of some of the Greek warriors' wives, trying to get the men to respond. Odysseus was able to keep his men quiet, and they were not discovered.

The Trojans decided to bring the horse into the city. When the horse was inside Troy's walls, they celebrated what they believed was their sure victory. No one noticed Sinon release the Greek warriors who hid inside the horse.

Outside Troy, the Greek army, which had only pretended to sail away, quickly reassembled. The warriors who'd hidden in the horse opened the city gates—and in rushed the Greeks. They sacked Troy, destroying the city completely and killing or capturing all the Trojans they could find. Priam tried to take refuge at the altar of Zeus, but he was brutally murdered by Neoptolemus, Achilles' son. Hector's infant son Astyanax was thrown from Troy's high walls. Trojan women—including Hecuba (the queen), Andromache (Hector's wife), and Cassandra (a Trojan princess)—were enslaved. Some myths say that Ajax of Locris raped Cassandra on the altar of Athena.

THE GODS ARE NOT PLEASED

After they'd helped the Greeks defeat Troy, several of the Olympians were appalled at the warriors' sacrilegious behavior. The gods and goddesses who'd once supported the Greeks decided to punish them. Even though the Greeks had won the war, they didn't fare much better than the Trojans. After ten years of fighting, not many Greek soldiers made it home alive.

Poseidon called up a great storm, which destroyed much of the Greek fleet. Some of the remaining ships were wrecked on the rocky shores of Euboea, where they had been guided by a false beacon. Other ships, blown far off course by the storm, were lost for years. Some Greeks did make it home—and later wished they hadn't:

- Diomedes returned home to Argos to find that his wife had taken another man as her lover. He was exiled from his own country.
- Teucer arrived home safely but was not allowed to land. His father forbade him to enter the country because of his deeds during the war.
- In order to arrive home safely, Idomeneus promised Poseidon he would sacrifice the first living creature he encountered after reaching his homeland. Poseidon allowed him safe passage, but when the ship landed, the first to meet Idomeneus was his son, happy and excited that his father was home. Bound by his promise, Idomeneus sacrificed his son to Poseidon. For this act, Idomeneus was banished from his homeland.
- Agamemnon returned home to find that his wife, Clytemnestra, had taken a lover. Clytemnestra, still furious over the sacrifice of her daughter Iphigenia, murdered Agamemnon in his bath.
- It took Odysseus ten years to get home to Ithaca (see Chapter 19). Although Odysseus was supported by Athena, he was opposed by Poseidon—and his journey home was fraught with dangers.

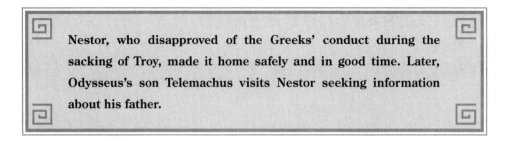

Nestor, who disapproved of the Greeks' conduct during the sacking of Troy, made it home safely and in good time. Later, Odysseus's son Telemachus visits Nestor seeking information about his father.

The Trojan War was a long, bloody, and vicious conflict that destroyed a city and wasted many lives. It was the occasion for great acts of heroism and horrifying acts of brutality. The losses were catastrophic, and victory meant very little. In some ways, the fall of Troy signaled the end of the world the Greeks had known, because the city's destruction eventually led to the founding of Rome.

CHAPTER 21

WHEN IN ROME . . .

o far, the mythology discussed in this book has been primarily Greek. Much of Roman mythology was borrowed from the Greeks. While many of the stories are essentially the same, the names are different. However, the Romans also had their own myths, separate from those of the Greeks. This chapter shows you the deities as the Romans knew them and introduces some uniquely Roman myths.

GREEK VERSUS ROMAN

Early in Rome's history, the ancient Romans had a religion that was completely their own. As time passed, however, extensive changes occurred within this religion. As Romans conquered neighboring territories, they absorbed some aspects of local religions, and as Greek literature became known in Rome, it influenced Roman religion. Greek mythology was assimilated into Roman mythology to fill in gaps in the latter; eventually, Romans adopted (and adapted) Greek myths on a broad scale.

Although the Romans borrowed heavily from Greek mythology, they kept their own names for the gods and goddesses. To gain a very basic knowledge of Roman mythology, just examine the Roman and Greek counterparts in the following table. Because Roman myths are so similar to Greek ones, knowing the Roman equivalents of Greek names gives you a head start in understanding Roman mythology.

GREEK NAME	ROMAN NAME	GREEK NAME	ROMAN NAME
APHRODITE	VENUS	HERA	JUNO
APOLLO	SOL	HERACLES	HERCULES
ARES	MARS	HERMES	MERCURY
ARTEMIS	DIANA	HESTIA	VESTA
ATHENA	MINERVA	MUSES	CAMENAE
CRONUS	SATURN	ODYSSEUS	ULYSSES
DEMETER	CERES	PAN	FAUNUS
DIONYSUS	BACCHUS	PARCAE (FATES)	MOIRAI
EOS	AURORA	PERSEPHONE	PROSERPINE
ERIS	DISCORDIA	POSEIDON	NEPTUNE
EROS	CUPID	RHEA	OPS
HADES	PLUTO	ZEUS	JUPITER
HEPHAESTUS	VULCAN		

AENEAS'S JOURNEY TO ITALY

The Romans didn't borrow everything from the Greeks, of course. They had their own stories about the beginnings of their culture and the founding of their city. The Romans believed that their ancestor was the Trojan hero Aeneas.

Aeneas was one of the few who survived the Trojan War. He was the leader of those Trojans who managed to escape the war with their lives. With their city destroyed, the Trojans needed a new home. They wandered, unable to find a suitable place, until they received a prophecy that they should make their home in the place of their "ancient mother." At first, the prophecy was interpreted as referring to Crete, but when the displaced Trojans went there, they suffered a famine. They had to reconsider the prophecy.

The prophecy referred to Italy, the homeland of Dardanus, an ancestor of the Trojans. So the Trojans set out for Italy, but their journey was not an easy one. They suffered terrible sea storms and an encounter with Harpies—and they had Juno to deal with.

JUNO'S WRATH

Juno (you've known her throughout this book as Hera) could be ruthless, especially when she took things personally. Juno had favored the Greeks during the Trojan War and saw no reason to change her mind about the Trojans after the war had ended. One of the reasons she hated the Trojans was that Dardanus, their ancestor, was the illegitimate son of Jupiter (the Greek Zeus) and Electra—and Juno's anger at her husband's extramarital affairs could last for generations.

Juno wanted the Trojans to fail and tried to prevent them from finding a new home. First, she tried to make the winds destroy the Trojans' ships. But without the cooperation of Neptune (Poseidon), little damage was done. In fact, angry that Juno had invaded his domain, Neptune stopped the storm, but the winds had already blown the Trojan fleet far off course.

Trying to get back on course, the fleet made numerous stops. During a stop in Carthage, the queen, Dido, fell in love with Aeneas and committed suicide when he left her. (Chapter 15 tells you their story.)

Many of the Trojans, who had been wandering for years, grew tired of traveling and wanted to settle down. Juno incited some of the women to mutiny. When the fleet stopped in Sicily, Juno convinced the women to set fire to the ships. Some ships were destroyed, but Jupiter intervened to save the rest. Even with a reduced fleet, Aeneas refused to give up his quest for a new homeland. The remaining ships couldn't carry everyone, so he allowed some of the refugees to stay in Sicily, but the others continued with him on the journey.

REACHING ITALY

Finally, more than seven years after the fall of Troy, Aeneas and his companions landed in Italy. Now that they'd reached their destination, however, they weren't sure what to do next. Until this point, Aeneas had relied on visions and prophecies, but now he needed further guidance.

As you read in Chapter 8, Aeneas decided to travel to the Underworld and seek advice from his father's shade. He met his father in the Elysian Fields, who told him that he would found the Roman race and his descendants would found the city of Rome.

Aeneas returned to the world of the living and set out again. This time, he and his followers landed in Latium, a region on the Tiber River. Latium was ruled by King Latinus, a son of Faunus (Pan). He had received an oracle saying that his daughter, Lavinia, would marry a man from abroad. Latinus recognized Aeneas as the man whose arrival the oracle had foretold, so the Trojans received a warm welcome.

JUNO STEPS IN AGAIN

Of course, Juno couldn't leave it alone. She decided to stir up trouble between the Trojans and the Latins by taking advantage of a prearranged marriage between Lavinia and Turnus, king of the Rutulians. King Latinus and his wife, Amata, had already promised their daughter in marriage to Turnus, who also happened to be Amata's nephew. Oracle or no, he wasn't willing to be pushed aside for some stranger.

Juno sent a Fury to turn Amata against a marriage between Aeneas and Lavinia. Next, the Fury incited Turnus to declare war.

The Trojans fought valiantly against the Rutulians. Many casualties occurred on both sides. Because each commander was losing so many men, the two leaders agreed to solve the dispute through one-on-one combat. Aeneas was a better fighter than Turnus, and Juno knew this. She persuaded Turnus to back out of the agreement at the last minute.

Furious, Aeneas launched a vicious attack on the Rutulians. So many men were killed that Turnus was rumored to be among the slain. Distraught over her nephew's death, Amata killed herself.

Turnus, however, had not died. Once again, the two leaders agreed to meet in single combat. This time, Juno was nowhere to be seen. Aeneas easily defeated Turnus and ended the war.

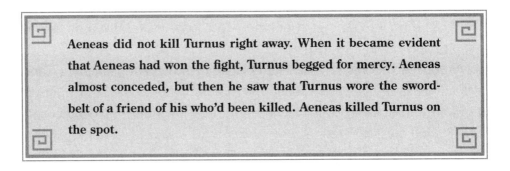

Aeneas did not kill Turnus right away. When it became evident that Aeneas had won the fight, Turnus begged for mercy. Aeneas almost conceded, but then he saw that Turnus wore the sword-belt of a friend of his who'd been killed. Aeneas killed Turnus on the spot.

ORIGINS OF THE ROMAN PEOPLE

Following the war with the Rutulians, Aeneas negotiated terms with the Latins who agreed to follow the Trojans' rule and worship their gods. In return, the Trojans agreed to call themselves Latins and learn the Latin language.

Aeneas fulfilled the oracle's prophecy and married Lavinia. They had a son named Silvius, the first child born of the Roman race. However, Silvius did not succeed his father as ruler of Latium. Aeneas had a son from his first marriage named Ascanius, whose name later changed to Iulus.

Iulus wandered inland and founded a city called Alba Longa, which would become the capital of the Latins and remain so for many years. Each new ruler of Latium took his place on the throne in Alba Longa. Throughout the first twelve generations of rulers (all descendants of Aeneas), the Latins enjoyed peace and prosperity.

It was this combination of Trojans and Latins that would begin the new Roman race. However, they weren't called Romans yet—because there wasn't yet a city named Rome.

PEACE DISRUPTED

Although the Latins enjoyed a peaceful succession of rulers for several generations, that contentment ended when Numitor ascended the throne. Numitor's rule was usurped by his brother, Amulius, who took steps to ensure no one would challenge him. Amulius killed Numitor's two sons and forced his only daughter, Rhea Silvia, to become a Vestal Virgin.

Rhea Silvia became pregnant and gave birth to twin boys. (Though a Vestal Virgin, she was unable to protect herself from the amorous advances of Mars [Ares].) Furious at this threat to his power, Amulius had Rhea Silvia imprisoned and ordered his servants to drown the two boys in a nearby river. The servants couldn't bring themselves to kill the two helpless infants, however, and set them adrift instead.

Even though the servants didn't drown the boys, the children surely would have died if Mars hadn't come to their rescue. Mars sent a wolf to suckle the infants, and after they were weaned, he sent a woodpecker to bring them food. Eventually, a shepherd named Faustulus found them, took them home, and raised them in secret.

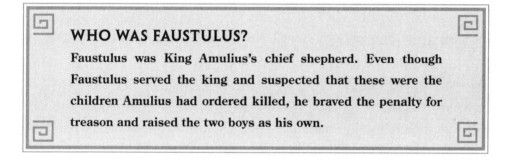

WHO WAS FAUSTULUS?

Faustulus was King Amulius's chief shepherd. Even though Faustulus served the king and suspected that these were the children Amulius had ordered killed, he braved the penalty for treason and raised the two boys as his own.

The boys, named Romulus and Remus, grew up well-educated, strong, and brave. They were friends with the local shepherds, who looked to the two young men as their leaders. Their foster father eventually revealed the details of their infancy, and told them of his suspicions that they were Rhea Silvia's lost twins and therefore heirs to the throne.

After Romulus and Remus had discovered their true identity, they visited Numitor and formed a plan to remove Amulius from the throne. The brothers organized a rebellion with the support of their shepherd friends and those who remained faithful to Numitor. They killed Amulius and returned Numitor to his throne.

FOUNDING ROME

Romulus and Remus were too adventurous to sit back and wait for their inheritance, so they ventured out to found their own city. They agreed on a location (on the Tiber River near the site of their rescue by the wolf), but that's where their agreements ended. They argued over every other detail: Who would oversee the design of the city? Who would name it? And most important, who would rule?

Since they couldn't agree about any of these matters, the brothers turned to the gods, asking for an omen to settle their dispute. Each man positioned himself on a hill overlooking the location they'd chosen. Remus saw the six vultures, and then Romulus saw twelve vultures. Each proclaimed himself the winner: Remus saw the birds first, but Romulus saw more birds. The argument became heated and a fight broke out. Remus was killed, and Romulus became the ruler of the new city and named it Rome after himself.

WOMEN WANTED

Romulus needed to populate his city, so he encouraged fugitives and runaways to take refuge in Rome. The city's population grew quickly, but there was a problem—virtually no women lived there, because no man from the surrounding area would allow his daughter to marry the rogues who inhabited Rome. Romulus decided he would have to take women by force.

He planned a great festival, complete with games and theatrical performances, and invited everyone to attend. Once the guests were inside the city, the Romans barred its gates. They attacked their guests, seizing the women and girls, and wounding or killing the men and boys. Once they had a good supply of women, they drove the remaining men out of the city.

The kidnapped women were terrified, but Romulus made a great speech to soothe and reassure them. He won over the women, who became content to stay in Rome.

Of course, the men weren't willing to give up their wives and daughters so easily, and several attacks were made on Rome. Most of the attacks were disorganized and mounted by small bands of men, and the Romans had little difficulty in repelling them. But the Sabine tribe was a different story.

The Sabine men banded together and organized themselves with a strategic plan of attack. Under their king, Titus Tatius, the Sabine men blockaded the city and bribed the daughter of a Roman commander to open the gates to the citadel. When the Sabine men seemed to be winning, the abducted women put themselves and their children between the two armies. The fighting stopped—no one on either side wanted to harm the women, and of course, the women did not want to see their Sabine fathers or their new Roman husbands harmed.

Unable to continue fighting without killing the very thing they were fighting for, the two armies had no choice but to call a truce. The two sides agreed to merge their populations to create a single federation. Romulus and Titus Tatius would rule jointly.

THE DEATH OF ROMULUS

Romulus and Titus Tatius expanded the Roman Kingdom and built a powerful army. The city was growing and flourishing in peace. Then, after nearly forty years as a successful ruler, Romulus suddenly disappeared.

During one of Romulus's routine inspections of his army on the Campus Martius, a violent thunderstorm occurred. Romulus was surrounded by a cloud and vanished from sight.

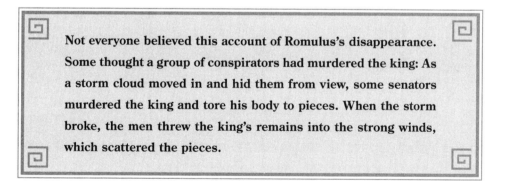

Not everyone believed this account of Romulus's disappearance. Some thought a group of conspirators had murdered the king: As a storm cloud moved in and hid them from view, some senators murdered the king and tore his body to pieces. When the storm broke, the men threw the king's remains into the strong winds, which scattered the pieces.

Those who witnessed his disappearing act claimed that the gods had reached down and lifted Romulus into the heavens. Most of Rome accepted this as truth and honored Romulus's divinity. He was thereafter worshiped as Quirinus, a god of war.

THE AGE OF KINGS

After Romulus, six other kings rose to power. Each played a role in expanding the city and making the city's influence known throughout the world.

NUMA POMPILIUS

Numa was the son-in-law of Titus Tatius. A peaceful man, Numa was known as "the Lawgiver." He instituted new laws and kept the peace with neighboring cities and tribes. Celebrated for his wisdom and piety, Numa credited his mistress, the nymph Egeria, with giving him counsel. Although Numa would propose new laws, it was said he would not introduce them until Egeria had given them her approval.

TULLUS HOSTILIUS

After Numa came Tullus Hostilius. Whereas Numa had championed peace, Tullus was more interested in expansion. He worked hard to train and exercise Rome's army—and his hard work paid off. Under Tullus's rule, Rome conquered several cities and gained a reputation as a formidable power. Tullus also conquered Alba Longa and forced its people to live in Rome, which doubled Rome's population.

For thirty-two years, Rome's expansion was his main concern. Unfortunately, Tullus neglected to pay proper tribute to the gods, so they sent a plague to Rome. Ill and near death, Tullus tried to appease the gods, but it was too late: A lightning strike finished him off.

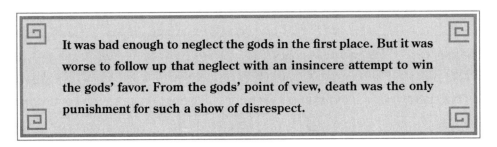

It was bad enough to neglect the gods in the first place. But it was worse to follow up that neglect with an insincere attempt to win the gods' favor. From the gods' point of view, death was the only punishment for such a show of disrespect.

ANCUS MARCIUS

Ancus Marcius, Numa's grandson, inherited his grandfather's preference for peace. This king was best known for building the first wooden bridge over the Tiber River. He also established Ostia as a port at the Tiber's mouth.

Although known as a peaceful ruler, Ancus, like his predecessors, did expand the kingdom of Rome. He pushed the city boundaries farther south and west, gaining the land of Latium.

LUCIUS TARQUINIUS PRISCUS

Lucius Tarquinius Priscus was an Etruscan who had no blood right to the throne. But he changed his name to Lucius Tarquinius Priscus (from the Etruscan name Lucumo) and made himself indispensable to King Ancus. When the king died, Tarquinius was elected king despite the fact Ancus had left behind two sons.

Tarquinius ruled for thirty-eight years and was credited with several improvements to Rome. He expanded the kingdom even more, conquering several Latin towns. He began the construction of a temple to Jupiter and a great stone wall to surround the city. He is also believed to have drained the marshy land that would later become the Roman Forum.

The sons of Ancus never forgave Tarquinius for taking the throne. They felt they were the rightful rulers of Rome and hired two shepherds to murder him.

SERVIUS TULLIUS

Servius Tullius was the child of one of the queen's slaves. The queen recognized the child's greatness, however, and, worked with Tarquinius to ensure that the child would succeed to the throne. When Servius was of age, he married Tarquinius's daughter, becoming next in line to rule.

> **Some myths say that Servius's daughter was the mastermind behind the plot to overthrow her father. When Servius was killed, Superbus would not allow a burial, and Servius's daughter drove her carriage over her father's corpse.**

Servius was a successful ruler, admired and respected by the people of Rome. Like his predecessors, he expanded the kingdom; he also built a wall, called the Servian Wall, around the perimeter of the city. He was said to have divided the citizens into classes based on ownership of property and introduced the worship of Diana (Artemis).

Servius was murdered by his son-in-law, Lucius Tarquinius Superbus, who wanted the throne. Legend has it that Superbus forced Servius from his throne and threw him out of the Senate House. He then sent assassins to stab Servius to death.

LUCIUS TARQUINIUS SUPERBUS

Compared to his predecessors, Lucius Tarquinius Superbus was a poor ruler. He had no interest in winning the people's respect; he merely wanted power. For twenty-five years, he hung on to his throne through a reign of terror. He expanded Rome's kingdom by conquering several Latin states and Rutulian towns. His son Sextus, who would have been the next king, caused an uproar that led to the end of the monarchy.

Sextus was every bit as ruthless as his father, taking whatever he wanted with little regard for anyone else. One night he decided he wanted his friend's wife, Lucretia. While her husband was away, Sextus visited Lucretia's home and made advances to her. Lucretia rejected him, but Sextus threatened to dishonor her family by claiming he found Lucretia and her servant in bed together. Fearing for her family's honor, Lucretia gave in.

When her husband returned, Lucretia told him the whole story. Lucretia made her husband, her father, and a friend, Lucius Junius Brutus, swear that they would avenge her death, and then she killed herself. The men gathered a small army of rebels and killed Sextus. They drove Superbus from Rome and abolished the monarchy. This was the beginning of the Roman Republic.

CHAPTER 22

THE GODS AND
GODDESSES LIVE ON

lthough Greece's Golden Age and Rome's empire ended centuries ago, the myths that arose from these cultures continue to be told and retold. Take a look around you. Classical mythology abounds in everyday life. From common words and phrases to novels and films to video games, references to mythology are everywhere. Now that you're familiar with the main myths of ancient Greece and Rome, you'll see the influence of those myths in today's world.

MYTHS IN EVERYDAY LIFE

One way that the ancient myths of Greece and Rome live on is in the English language. Many words and phrases have their origins in classical mythology. Earlier chapters have mentioned some of these terms; this section describes others you might recognize.

WORDS AND PHRASES

Here are a few words and phrases that originated in classical mythology:

- An *odyssey* is a long, often difficult journey filled with adventures—just like Odysseus's trip home from Troy.
- The word *panic*, which means a sudden, overwhelming fear, traces its origins back to the god Pan. During battle, Pan would let out a terrifying shriek that made the enemy frantic with fear.
- An *arachnid* is a spider. This word comes from Arachne, the mortal woman who foolishly challenged Athena to a weaving contest and was transformed into a spider.

- A *phobia* is a fear, often an irrational one. The word comes from Phobos, a son of Ares who caused terror on the battlefield.
- The word *aphrodisiac* refers to a food or potion that causes sexual desire. Chapter 15 described how Aphrodite liked to stir up sexual desire among both mortals and immortals.
- An *Adonis* is a handsome young man—just like the Adonis who was loved by Aphrodite.
- When someone is consistently lucky, that person is said to have *the Midas touch*. As in the myth of King Midas, everything the person touches turns to gold.
- In Chapter 14, you read about Hermaphroditus, a son of Hermes and Aphrodite who merged physically with a nymph, becoming both male and female. Today, the word *hermaphrodite* refers to an animal or person born with both male and female sex organs.
- The element *titanium*, which takes its name from the Titans, is known for its strength. *Titanic* means gigantic and powerful, just like the ancient Titans.
- Another element with a mythological name is *mercury* (the Roman name for Hermes). A person with a *mercurial* nature is quick-witted, lively, and volatile.
- The names of several months come from Roman mythology: January is named for Janus, a double-faced god of doorways and beginnings; March is named for Mars, the god of war; April may come from a variant of Aphrodite; May's name comes from Maia, an earth goddess; and June is named in honor of Juno. Although many of the days of the week take their names from Norse mythology, Saturday is named in honor of the Roman god Saturn.

Psychology draws some of its terms from classical mythology. For example, *narcissism*, a personality disorder characterized by excessive self-love, draws its name from the story of Narcissus (Chapter 19). Psychoanalysis teaches that people have two drives, one toward life and one toward death; these drives are sometimes referred to as the *Eros* instinct (life) and the *Thanatos* instinct (death).

> The word *psychology* has its roots in Greek myth. *Psyche* means mind, soul, or spirit, but Psyche was also a mythological character who had a love affair with Eros, the god of love.

Probably the most famous psychological term derived from classical mythology came from Sigmund Freud, the Austrian neurologist who founded psychoanalysis. Freud coined the phrase *Oedipal complex* based on the myth of Oedipus, which you read about in Chapter 19. An oracle proclaimed that Oedipus would kill his father and marry his mother, and Freud believed that these feelings of jealousy toward the same-sex parent and love for the opposite-sex parent were a phase that all children go through.

The world of sports also has references to classical mythology. The Olympic Games, which began in ancient Greece, are the most obvious example. Nike, a popular brand of athletic shoes, is the name of the Greek goddess of victory. And the word *marathon* comes from the myth of Pheidippides, an Athenian messenger. During the Battle of Marathon, Pheidippides ran from Athens to Sparta to ask the Spartans to join the Athenians in repelling an invasion. To get from Athens to Sparta (and then back to Athens again with the Spartans' reply), Pheidippides ran more than 250 miles in just three days.

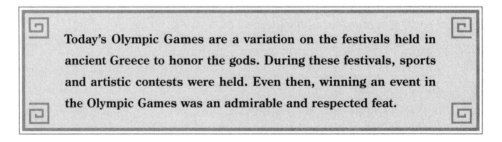

> Today's Olympic Games are a variation on the festivals held in ancient Greece to honor the gods. During these festivals, sports and artistic contests were held. Even then, winning an event in the Olympic Games was an admirable and respected feat.

References to myths can appear where you least expect them, such as in the world of computer science. In general usage, a *Trojan horse*—just like the one that led to the defeat of Troy—is something that appears desirable but in fact presents a threat. In computer science, a *Trojan horse* (often called a

Trojan for short) is a computer program that looks useful and innocent, such as a free computer game, but allows unauthorized access to your computer.

WRITTEN IN THE STARS

Throughout this book are stories of heroes and other mortals who were honored by the gods after death by being turned into constellations. For example, as you read in Chapter 12, after the great hunter Orion was slain, he was placed in the sky. Other constellations include Ursa Major and Ursa Minor (Callisto and her son Arcas, whose story also appears in Chapter 12); Andromeda, Perseus, and Cetus (see Chapter 19); and Hercules (see Chapter 19).

The zodiac signs also come from classical mythology:

- Aries is the golden-fleeced ram.
- Taurus is the white bull who carried Europa to Crete.
- Gemini is Castor and Pollux, twin sons of Zeus and Leda.
- Cancer is the crab that Heracles faced.
- Leo is another enemy of Heracles, the Nemean Lion.
- Virgo is Astraea, the Roman goddess of justice.
- Libra represents Astraea's scales.
- Scorpio is the scorpion that killed Orion.
- Sagittarius is the centaur Chiron, a great archer.
- Capricorn is the goat Amalthea, who nursed Zeus.
- Aquarius is Ganymede, the gods' cupbearer.
- Pisces is the fish that served as a disguise for both Aphrodite and Eros.

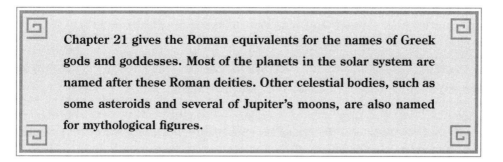

Chapter 21 gives the Roman equivalents for the names of Greek gods and goddesses. Most of the planets in the solar system are named after these Roman deities. Other celestial bodies, such as some asteroids and several of Jupiter's moons, are also named for mythological figures.

MYTHS IN LITERATURE

Myths tell such interesting and fundamental stories that it's no surprise that mythology has been a rich source of inspiration for authors. Its influence has been evident ever since the ancient Greeks and Romans began telling stories about the gods.

Authors work with mythology in many ways. Some refer to mythological characters or scenes to add flavor to their own works. Some writers will rework mythological styles or themes. Others use ancient myths as a starting point for their own stories. Now that you've begun to study classical mythology, you'll enjoy finding allusions to it in other books and stories.

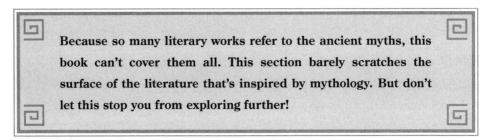

Because so many literary works refer to the ancient myths, this book can't cover them all. This section barely scratches the surface of the literature that's inspired by mythology. But don't let this stop you from exploring further!

Much literature of the medieval and Renaissance period refers to classical mythology. For example, the medieval English poet Geoffrey Chaucer and the Renaissance playwright William Shakespeare both wrote versions of the tragic love story of Troilus and Cressida, set during the Trojan War. Shakespeare also wrote a poem titled *Venus and Adonis* in 1593. *The Divine Comedy*, written by Dante Alighieri between 1308 and 1321, is packed with classical allusions. For example, in *The Inferno*, the narrator's guide is Virgil, author of the *Aeneid*, and the poem is loaded with references to Apollo, Minerva (Athena), the Muses, and the hero Jason, to name just a few.

Later, John Milton adapted the form and themes of classical epic poetry to create his great poem *Paradise Lost* (1667). Although *Paradise Lost* is a Christian poem that tells the story of the fall of Adam and Eve, Milton admired classical poetry and used it to create a heroic Christian epic. Alexander Pope's poem *The Rape of the Lock* (1712) parodies classical conventions.

In the nineteenth century, classical mythology continued its influence on literature. Percy Bysshe Shelley's play *Prometheus Unbound* (1820) was inspired by a play of Aeschylus of the same name, but Shelley takes the story in a different direction to reflect the humanism of his own era. Shelley's wife, Mary, wrote the novel *Frankenstein* (1818), but did you know that her book's subtitle is *The Modern Prometheus*? The Romantic poet John Keats wrote poems such as "On First Looking into Chapman's Homer" (1816) and "Ode on a Grecian Urn" (1820), which deal with mythological themes. His well-known poem "Endymion" (1818) begins with the famous line "A thing of beauty is a joy for ever."

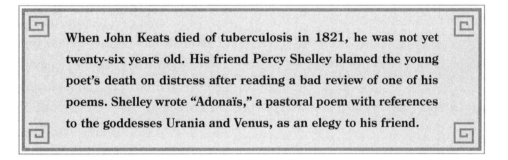

When John Keats died of tuberculosis in 1821, he was not yet twenty-six years old. His friend Percy Shelley blamed the young poet's death on distress after reading a bad review of one of his poems. Shelley wrote "Adonaïs," a pastoral poem with references to the goddesses Urania and Venus, as an elegy to his friend.

In the twentieth century, James Joyce's *Ulysses* (1922) used classical mythology in a new way. Joyce based the plot of his novel on the *Odyssey* (the Roman version of Odysseus's name is Ulysses), creating a modern story that parallels the characters and themes of the ancient epic. Although *Ulysses* is set in Dublin and takes place over the course of a single day instead of ten years, it patterns itself on the *Odyssey*. Although the characters have different names, they are reinterpretations of the main characters of the *Odyssey*. Joyce's novel is brilliant but difficult; a familiarity with classical mythology is essential to understand it.

Many contemporary authors have used classical mythology as a source for their stories. Here's a list of some recent novels inspired by the myths of ancient Greece and Rome:

- *The King Must Die* (1958) by Mary Renault. Read this novel for a retelling of the adventures of the young hero Theseus.
- *The Firebrand* (1987) by Marion Zimmer Bradley. The main character of this novel is Kassandra, daughter of Priam and unheeded prophetess, who recounts the story of the fall of Troy.
- *The Secret History* (1992) by Donna Tartt. This psychological thriller tells the story of a group of students fascinated by their Classics professor and the world of ancient Greece. Their re-enactment of the Dionysian rites leads to tragic results.
- *Troy* (2000) by Adèle Geras. This young adult novel (ages fourteen and older) imagines life inside Troy during the Trojan War.
- *Goddess of Yesterday: A Tale of Troy* (2002) by Caroline B. Cooney. Another young adult novel, written for readers ages twelve and up, this book retells the events leading up to the Trojan War from the perspective of Anaxandra, a young girl who comes to the court of Menelaus.
- *Last of the Amazons* (2002) by Steven Pressfield. The context for this novel is the conflict between the Amazons and Theseus, leader of the Athenians.
- *Ilium* (2003) and *Olympos* (2005) by Dan Simmons. If you like science fiction, take a look at these novels, which are packed with classical allusions and set the events of the *Iliad* and its aftermath on Mars and an alternate Earth.
- *The Songs of the Kings* (2004) by Barry Unsworth. This novel retells the story of Agamemnon's sacrifice of his daughter Iphigenia. Unsworth imaginatively probes ancient politics and heroes' desire to be immortalized in poetry.
- The Troy trilogy by David Gemmell. These three novels retell the story of the Trojan War, as familiar mythological characters interact with characters of the author's creation: *Lord of the Silver Bow* (2006), *Shield of Thunder* (2007), and *Fall of Kings* (2009, with Stella Gemmell).
- *Helen of Troy* (2006) by Margaret George. This novel imagines the story of Helen's life and the Trojan War from her own point of view.

- The Cassandra Palmer series by Karen Chance. This contemporary fantasy series, beginning with *Touch the Dark* (2006), is set amidst conflict between vampires and mages. Cassandra Palmer must learn to deal with the challenges and dangers of being Pythia, the world's foremost clairvoyant.
- *Lavinia* (2008) by Ursula K. LeGuin. This novel tells the story of the arrival of Aeneas and the Trojan refugees in Italy from the point of view of the Italian princess who will marry Aeneas.

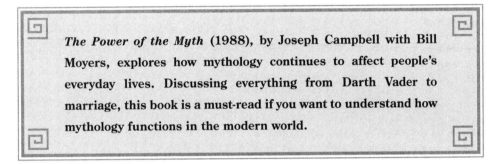

The Power of the Myth (1988), by Joseph Campbell with Bill Moyers, explores how mythology continues to affect people's everyday lives. Discussing everything from Darth Vader to marriage, this book is a must-read if you want to understand how mythology functions in the modern world.

MYTHS IN ART

From its very beginnings to today, mythology has inspired visual artists. Almost any museum you visit will have at least one piece of art—perhaps a painting, a sculpture, or an engraving—related to classical mythology. At its root, mythology formed a basis for ancient religion, and art was an important way to express piety. Statues were erected to honor the gods and goddesses, carvings adorned temple walls, and images were painted on household items such as cups, vases, and plates.

Several Greek and Roman buildings that survive from ancient times are adorned with carvings that depict mythological scenes and characters. Examples include the Parthenon and the Erechtheum in Athens and the temples of the Roman Forum. With a little imagination, you can visualize the scene as it appeared at the height of its popularity.

Numerous classical statues and sculptures still exist today, although many of these have sustained some damage. One of the best-known sculptures is the *Venus de Milo*, currently on display at the Louvre in Paris, which was created between 130 and 100 B.C. Other famous sculptures of gods and goddesses from the classical era that you can see at the Louvre include *Apollo Belvedere* (fourth century B.C.) and the *Winged Victory of Samothrace* (third century B.C.).

During late antiquity and the Middle Ages, the emergence of Christianity replaced mythological subjects in art with images of Jesus, the Virgin Mary, and the saints. With the Renaissance, interest in mythological subjects re-emerged, and artists brought the gods and goddesses back to life in their works. From this period on, many famous works of art depict mythological characters and scenes. Perhaps you're familiar with some of these paintings and sculptures:

- *School of Pan* by Luca Signorelli (1441–1523)
- *The Birth of Venus*; *Venus and Mars* by Sandro Botticelli (1445–1510)
- *Judgment of Paris*; *Venus and Cupid* by Lucas Cranach the Elder (1472–1553)
- *Bacchus and Ariadne*; *The Rape of Europa*; *Danaë*; *The Death of Actaeon* by Titian (c. 1488–1576)
- *Bacchus*; *Medusa*; *Jupiter, Neptune, and Pluto*; *Narcissus* by Caravaggio (1571–1610)
- *Venus and Adonis*; *Prometheus Bound*; *The Rape of Proserpine*; *Venus at the Mirror* by Peter Paul Rubens (1577–1640)
- *Apollo and Daphne*; *The Rape of Proserpina*; *Medusa*; *Aeneas, Anchises, and Ascanius* by Gian Lorenzo Bernini (1598–1680)
- *Penelope at Her Loom*; *Penelope Awakened by Eurycleia* by Angelica Kauffman (1741–1807)
- *Perseus with the Head of Medusa*; *Cupid and Psyche* by Antonio Canova (1757–1822)
- *La Minotaurmachia* by Pablo Picasso (1881–1973)
- *Perseus* by Salvador Dalí (1904–1989)

MYTHS IN MUSIC

Just like artists and writers, musicians and composers have been inspired by classical mythology. Pop songs by artists as diverse as Rush, U2, the Police, the Indigo Girls, Anthrax, and Suzanne Vega make classical allusions. Bands such as Muse, Throwing Muses, and Venus take their names from classical deities.

In classical music, opera retells the stories of many myths. For example, the story of Orpheus, that consummate musician, has been set to music by Claudio Monteverdi (*L'Orfeo*, 1607), Christoph Willibald Gluck (*Orfeo ed Euridice*, 1762), and Jacques Offenbach (*Orphée aux Enfers* [*Orpheus in the Underworld*], 1858).

The story of Troy has also been popular with composers. Hector Berlioz's *Les Troyans* (1858) is a sprawling, five-act grand opera based on the *Aeneid*. Henry Purcell's *Dido and Aeneas* (c. 1689) sets to music the ill-fated love affair of the father of Rome and the queen of Carthage. Other operas that depict events following the Trojan War include Gluck's *Iphigénie en Tauride* (1779), Mozart's *Idomeneo* (1781), and Richard Strauss's *Elektra* (1909).

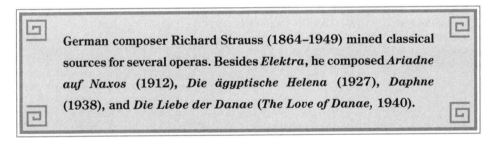

German composer Richard Strauss (1864–1949) mined classical sources for several operas. Besides *Elektra*, he composed *Ariadne auf Naxos* (1912), *Die ägyptische Helena* (1927), *Daphne* (1938), and *Die Liebe der Danae* (*The Love of Danae*, 1940).

MYTHS IN MOVIES

Filmmakers are always in search of compelling stories to bring to the big screen. With the variety of subjects, themes, and plots offered within classical mythology, it's surprising that few movies adhere closely to mythological storylines. Many films make allusions to mythology, but few tell the actual stories.

In 1956, director Robert Wise released *Helen of Troy* (1956), an ambitious attempt to depict the events of the Trojan War. This lavish spectacle tried to be as authentic as possible. The film focuses on Helen (Rossana Podesta) and her love affair with Paris (Jacques Sernas) in the context of the Trojan War.

A more recent cinematic depiction of the Trojan War is *Troy* (2004), directed by Wolfgang Petersen. A star-studded cast was led by Brad Pitt (Achilles), Eric Bana (Hector), Diane Kruger (Helen), Orlando Bloom (Paris), and Peter O'Toole (Priam). The film uses the *Iliad*, the *Aeneid*, and other ancient texts as its sources, but the film departs from those sources in many ways. For example, it leaves out the judgment of Paris as the starting point of the conflict and does not show the gods and goddesses as active participants. Some characters who survived the war in the ancient myths get killed during battle on screen, including Menelaus and Agamemnon.

Other movies based on the stories of classical mythology include these:

- *Orpheus* (1949), directed by Jean Cocteau
- *Ulysses* (1955), directed by Mario Camerini
- *Hercules* (1957), directed by Pietro Francisci
- *Jason and the Argonauts* (1963), directed by Don Chaffey
- *Clash of the Titans* (1981), directed by Desmond Davis
- *Mighty Aphrodite* (1995), directed by Woody Allen
- *O Brother, Where Art Thou?* (2000), directed by Ethan Coen and Joel Coen
- *Clash of the Titans* (2010), directed by Louis Leterrier (remake of the 1981 film)

MYTHS IN POPULAR CULTURE

Mythology doesn't belong exclusively to the world of "high art." It's appeared in television shows, cartoons, comic books, toys, and video games. In myths, the stories are action-packed, the monsters terrifying, and the heroes larger than life.

From 1995 through 1999, *Hercules: The Legendary Journeys* was a popular television series loosely based on myths of Heracles, his labors and his adventures. Kevin Sorbo played Hercules, and the series spun off action figures and other memorabilia. Its most popular spinoff was another television series *Xena: Warrior Princess*, which ran between 1995 and 2001. Xena, played by Lucy Lawless, wasn't a mythological figure, but she represented an Amazon-like female warrior.

Another popular spinoff featuring Hercules and Xena was the full-length animated film *Hercules & Xena: The Battle for Olympus* (1997). In this film, voiced by the television shows' actors, Hercules and Xena team up to overcome the Titans, who've been freed by Hera in a bid to become ruler of the universe.

The year 1997 also saw the release of Walt Disney Pictures' animated film *Hercules*. Although somewhat watered down for its young audience, the film kept the essence of the Heracles myths portraying the hero as a man who, through his ambition and accomplishments, achieved the highest reward: immortality.

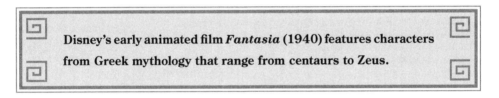

Disney's early animated film *Fantasia* (1940) features characters from Greek mythology that range from centaurs to Zeus.

Comic books also depict mythological themes and characters. Marvel Comics featured the adventures of Zeus beginning in 1940. Selene, whose name comes from the ancient moon goddess, is a villainess in Marvel's *X-Men* comic books. In the world of DC Comics, *Wonder Woman* is a modern version of an Amazon, and one of her main enemies is named Circe. The Erinyes (Furies) appear in several volumes of DC Comics' *Sandman* series.

Want to live the life of an ancient hero? Video games put you right in the middle of the action. *God of War*, for PlayStation 2, is an award-winning video game whose main character, Kratos, is sent on a quest by Athena to kill Ares. Other games in this popular series include *God of War II* (2007), *God of War: Chains of Olympus* (2008), and *God of War III* (2010). Gamers with a taste for mythology can also try *Age of Mythology* (2002), *Titan Quest* (2006), and *Rise of the Argonauts* (2008).

CAST OF CHARACTERS

Achilles: Greatest Greek warrior of the Trojan War; killed Hector and other Trojans, and was killed by an arrow shot by Paris and guided by Apollo

Acrisius: Grandfather of Perseus; accidentally killed by Perseus in fulfillment of a prophecy

Actaeon: Grandson of Apollo; great hunter; killed after he saw Artemis bathing naked

Admetus: King of Pheres; neglected to sacrifice to Artemis and found his bedchamber filled with snakes on his wedding night

Adonis: A beautiful young boy loved by Aphrodite and killed by Ares out of jealousy

Aeacus: Son of Aegina and Zeus; fair ruler of the island Aegina; became a Judge of the Dead

Aeetes: Father of Medea

Aegeus: King of Athens; foster father of Theseus

Aegina: Daughter of the river-god Asopus; mother of Aeacus by Zeus; namesake of the island Aegina

Aeneas: Trojan warrior; founder of the Roman race

Aerope: A lover of Ares; died giving birth to Ares' son

Aether: Air; son of Nyx and Erebus

Aethra: Daughter of the king of Troezen; wife of Aegeus

Agamemnon: Commander-in-chief of the Greeks during the Trojan War; killed by his wife Clytemnestra upon his return from the war

Aglaia: A Charite; the personification of beauty and radiance or splendor

Aglaurus: Daughter of Cecrops; mother of Alcippe by Ares

Agrius: A Giant; killed by the Fates and Heracles during the war with the Olympians

Alcmene: Mother of Heracles by Zeus

Alcyoneus: A Giant; one of the leaders of the Giants during the war with the Olympians; killed by Athena and Heracles

Alirrothius: Son of Poseidon and Euryte; was killed by Ares for raping his daughter

Amalthea: A goat-nymph who suckled Zeus; she was turned into the constellation Capricorn

Amata: Wife of Latinus

Amazons: A race of warrior women; said to be descendants of Ares

Amphitrite: Daughter of Nereus; wife of Poseidon; mother of Benthesicyme, Rhode, and Triton

Amphitryon: Heracles' foster father

Amymone: One of the fifty daughters of King Danaus; mother of Nauplius by Poseidon

Anchises: King of Dardania; father of Aeneas by Aphrodite

Ancus Marcius: Fourth king of Rome

Andromeda: Daughter of the king of Joppa; wife of Perseus

Anteros: God of passion; son of Aphrodite and Ares

Antiope: Daughter of the king of Thebes; mother of Amphion and Zethus by Zeus

Apemosyne: A daughter of the king of Crete; loved and impregnated by Hermes; killed by her brother when he learned of her pregnancy

Aphrodite: Goddess of love; one of the twelve great Olympians

Apollo: God of archery, music, and poetry; brother of Artemis; son of Leto and Zeus; one of the twelve great Olympians

Apsyrtus: Brother of Medea; killed when Medea fled with Jason

Arachne: A young woman who challenged Athena to a weaving contest and was turned into a spider

Ares: God of war; son of Zeus and Hera; one of the twelve great Olympians

Arges: One of the three Cyclopes; known as the Shiner or Thunderbolt

Argus: A monster with a hundred eyes; placed as guardian of Io by Hera; killed by Hermes to rescue Io

Ariadne: Daughter of King Minos; helped Theseus to escape the labyrinth; wife of Dionysus

Artemis: Virgin goddess of the hunt; sister of Apollo; daughter of Leto and Zeus; one of the twelve great Olympians

Asclepius: Son of Apollo; god of healing

Asteria: Sister of Leto; gave Leto refuge from Hera

Atalanta: A famous hunter who would marry only if a man could beat her in a foot race; wife of Milanion

Athamas: King of Orchomenus; husband of Ino; driven mad by Hera for having sheltered Dionysus, causing him to kill his own children

Athena: Goddess of wisdom, war, crafts, and skill; born from the head of Zeus; one of the twelve great Olympians

Atlas: A Titan; condemned to support the heavens on his shoulders

Atropos: One of the Fates; responsible for cutting the thread of life; daughter of Zeus and Themis

Augeas: King of Elis whose filthy stables were cleaned by Heracles in a single day as his fifth labor

Aurora: Roman goddess of the dawn; counterpart of Eos

Autolycus: Son of Hermes and Chione; one of the most famous thieves of ancient Greece

Bacchus: Roman god of wine; counterpart of Dionysus

Battus: A shepherd who witnessed Hermes stealing Apollo's cattle; was turned to stone when he betrayed Hermes

Bellerophon: Mortal man who tamed Pegasus

Boreas: The North Wind

Brontes: One of the three Cyclopes; known as Thunder or Thunderer

Butes: An Argonaut; a priest of one of Athena's temples; fell victim to the Sirens and was saved by Aphrodite

Cacus: Son of Hephaestus and Medusa; a fire-breathing, three-headed monster

Cadmus: Founder of the city of Thebes; became Ares' slave for eight years; husband of Harmonia

Calliope: The Muse of epic poetry

Callisto: An attendant of Artemis; raped by Zeus; bore him a son, Arcas

Camenae: Roman counterpart of the Muses

Campe: A monster appointed by Cronus to guard the Hecatoncheires and the Cyclopes in Tartarus

Cassandra: Daughter of King Priam and Hecuba; tricked Apollo into granting her the gift of prophecy

Cecrops: Half-man, half-serpent; son of Gaia; first king of Attica

Centaurs: A savage race of beings with the head and torso of a man and the body and legs of a horse

Cerberus: The many-headed dog of Hades; guarded the Underworld to prevent the living from entering and the dead from leaving; was captured by Heracles as his twelfth labor

Cercyon: A monster killed by Theseus

Ceres: Roman goddess of agriculture; counterpart of Demeter

Cerynitian Hind: Deer with golden antlers sacred to Artemis; captured by Heracles as his third labor

Ceto: Daughter of Gaia and Pontus; a sea monster

Charites: Known as the Graces; minor goddesses of beauty, grace, and friendship; three daughters of Zeus and Eurynome

Charon: The ferryman who took the dead across the River Styx

Charybdis: A monster that swallowed ships by creating a whirlpool

Chimaera: Daughter of Typhon and Echidna; fire-breathing monster with the head of a lion, the body of a goat, and the tail of a snake

Chione: Lover of Hermes and Apollo; mother of Philammon by Apollo; mother of Autolycus by Hermes

Chiron: A wise Centaur; tutor of several heroes

Chryse: Mother of Phlegyas by Ares

Circe: Daughter of Helios; powerful witch who usually used her powers for evil; hosted Odysseus on his journey home

Clio: The Muse of history

Clito: An orphan girl who became a lover of Poseidon and bore him five pairs of twin sons; mother of Atlas

Clotho: One of the Fates; responsible for spinning the thread of life; daughter of Zeus and Themis

Clytemnestra: Wife of Agamemnon; killed her husband

Clytius: A Giant; killed by Hecate and Heracles during the war with the Olympians

Coeus: A Titan; husband of Phoebe; father of Leto

Coronis: A mortal lover of Apollo; was unfaithful to Apollo and was killed by Artemis

Cretan Bull: Sacrificial bull given to King Minos by Poseidon; father of the Minotaur; was captured by Heracles as his seventh labor

Crinaeae: Fountain nymphs

Crius: A Titan; husband of Eurybia; father of Astraeus, Pallas, and Perses

Cronus: A Titan; ruler of the universe following Uranus; husband of Rhea; father of the first Olympians

Cupid: Roman god of love; counterpart of Eros

Cybele: An earth goddess; taught Dionysus religious rites and practices

Cyclopes: Three sons of Gaia and Uranus (Brontes, Arges, Steropes); Giants with only one eye centered in the forehead

Cyparissus: Grandson of Heracles; loved by Apollo; changed into a cypress tree when his best friend was killed

Cyrene: A nymph; mother of Diomedes by Ares

Daedalus: A great architect; built the labyrinth that imprisoned the Minotaur

Danae: Daughter of the king of Argos; mother of Perseus by Zeus

Danaides: The fifty daughters of Danaus; forty-nine killed their husbands on their wedding night

Daphne: A mountain nymph who, running from Apollo's advances, was turned into a laurel tree

Deimos: Personification of fear; son of Aphrodite and Ares

Demeter: Goddess of fertility and agriculture; one of the twelve great Olympians; daughter of Cronus and Rhea

Diana: Roman moon goddess; counterpart of Artemis

Dido: Queen of Carthage; fell in love with Aeneas; committed suicide when he abandoned her

Dike: Personification of justice; daughter of Zeus and Themis

Diomedes: Greek warrior during the Trojan War; king of Aetolia

Diomedes of Thrace: King of Thrace; owner of savage, carnivorous mares rounded up by Heracles as his eighth labor; killed by Heracles and fed to his own horses

Dionysus: God of the vine, wine, and revelry; one of the twelve great Olympians

Discordia: Roman goddess of discord; counterpart of Eris

Dryads: Tree nymphs

Echidna: Monster with the body of a woman and a serpent's tail instead of legs; mother of many monstrous offspring

Echion: Son of Hermes; the herald for the *Argo*

Egeria: A nymph who was a lover of and counseled Numa Pompilius

Eileithyia: A goddess of childbirth; daughter of Zeus and Hera

Eirene: Personification of peace; daughter of Zeus and Themis

Elais: Daughter of King Anius; could turn anything into oil with a touch

Electra: Daughter of Atlas; mother of Dardanus by Zeus

Enceladus: A Giant; killed by Athena and Heracles during the war with the Olympians

Endymion: King of Elis; lover of Selene; wished for eternal youth and was granted immortal sleep

Enyo: Goddess of the battle; often seen in the company of Ares

Eos: The Dawn; sister of Helios and Selene; mother of the Winds

Eosphorus: The Morning Star

Ephialtes: A Giant; killed by Apollo and Heracles during the war with the Olympians

Epimetheus: A Titan; the brother of Prometheus; the husband of Pandora

Erato: The Muse of love poetry, lyric poetry, and marriage songs

Erebus: Darkness; one of the first five elements born of Chaos

Eriecthonius: Son of Gaia and Hephaestus; half-man, half-serpent; raised by Athena as her own son

Erigone: Daughter of Icarius; loved by Dionysus; committed suicide when she discovered her father's corpse

Eris: Goddess of discord, her name means "strife"; daughter of Nyx; indirectly caused the Trojan War by causing Aphrodite, Athena, and Hera to strive for a golden apple inscribed "for the fairest"

Eros: Love; one of the first five elements born of Chaos; alternatively described as a son of Ares and Aphrodite

Erymanthian Boar: Vicious boar captured by Heracles as his fourth labor

Erysichthon: Son of the king of Dotion; disrespected Demeter's sacred trees and was punished with insatiable hunger

Eunomia: Personification of law and order; daughter of Zeus and Themis

Euphrosyne: A Charite; the personification of joy or mirth

Europa: Daughter of the king of Phoenicia; lover of Zeus

Eurus: The East Wind

Eurybia: Daughter of Gaia and Pontus; wife of Crius; mother of three Titan sons: Astraeus, Pallas, and Perses

Eurydice: The wife of Orpheus; died from a snakebite and was almost

retrieved from the Underworld by her husband

Eurynome: Daughter of Oceanus; wife of Ophion; lover of Zeus; mother of the Graces

Eurystheus: The king of Tiryns; ordained the twelve labors of Heracles

Eurytus: A Giant; killed by Dionysus and Heracles during the war with the Olympians

Euterpe: The Muse of music and lyric poetry

Fates: Three goddesses in charge of determining a person's destiny; called the Moirai by the Greeks and the Parcae by the Romans

Faunus: Roman counterpart of Pan

Faustulus: King Amulius's chief shepherd; foster father of Romulus and Remus

Gaia: Mother Earth; one of the first five elements born of Chaos

Ganymede: Son of the Trojan royal family; kidnapped by Zeus and became the gods' cupbearer

Geras: Old Age; son of Nyx

Geryon: A three-headed monster killed by Heracles as his tenth labor

Giants: A race of monsters; challenged the Olympians for control of the universe and lost

Glaucus: A sea deity; loved Scylla and inadvertently caused her transformation into a monster

Gorgons: Three monstrous sisters who had serpents for hair, sharp claws and teeth, and the ability to turn any who looked on them to stone

Gration: A Giant; killed by Artemis and Heracles during the war with the Olympians

Griffins: Monsters with the head of an eagle, the body of a lion, and the wings of a predatory bird; guardians of treasure

Hades: Ruler of the Underworld; son of Cronus and Rhea

Hamadryads: Nymphs who lived in only one specific tree and died when it died

Harmonia: Daughter of Aphrodite and Ares; wife of Cadmus, king of Thebes

Harpies: Monstrous birds with the faces of women; sent by deities to punish criminals

Harpinna: Daughter of the river god Asopus; mother of Oenomaus by Ares

Hebe: Personification of youth; cupbearer to the gods; daughter of Zeus and Hera

Hecate: A Titaness; a triple goddess presiding over magic and spells; an attendant of Persephone

Hecatoncheires: The hundred-handed, fifty-headed sons of Gaia and Uranus (Cottus, Briareus, and Gyges)

Hector: Greatest Trojan warrior of the Trojan War; killed Protesilaus

Hecuba: Wife of King Priam; mother of Troilus by Apollo

Helen: Daughter of Zeus and Leda; wife of Menelaus and the most beautiful woman in the world; kidnapped by Paris

Helenus: Son of Priam; chief prophet of Troy

Helios: The Sun; brother of Eos and Selene

Hemera: Day; daughter of Nyx and Erebus

Hephaestus: God of fire, smithing, craftsmanship, and metalworking; one of the twelve great Olympians

Hera: Queen of the heavens and the gods; goddess of marriage and childbirth; sister and wife of Zeus; one of the twelve great Olympians

Heracles: Son of Zeus and Alcmene; one of the greatest heroes of Greek mythology; undertook the Twelve Labors

Hercules: Roman counterpart of Heracles

Hermes: Messenger of the gods; the god of commerce and travelers; son of Zeus and Maia; one of the twelve great Olympians

Herse: A daughter of Cecrops; mother of Cephalus by Hermes

Hesperides: Three nymphs—Aegle, Erythia, and Hesperarethusa—who lived in the Garden of the Hesperides and protected the golden apples; Heracles obtained some of these apples as his eleventh labor

Hestia: Goddess of the hearth and home; one of the three virgin goddesses; daughter of Cronus and Rhea

Hippolyte: Queen of the Amazons; daughter of Ares; her girdle was the object of Heracles' ninth labor

Hippolytus: A Giant; killed by Hermes and Heracles during the war with the Olympians

Hyacinthus: A beautiful young man loved by Apollo; killed during a game of discus-throwing

Hydra of Lerna: A giant serpent with numerous heads; had a giant crab as its sidekick; was killed by Heracles as his second labor

Hymen: God of marriage

Hyperion: A Titan; husband of Theia; father of Helios, Selene, and Eos

Hypnos: Sleep; son of Nyx

Iacchus: Son of Demeter and Zeus; a minor deity associated with the Eleusinian Mysteries

Iambe: Daughter of Pan; servant in the house of Celeus who made the grieving Demeter smile

Iapetus: A Titan; husband of Themis; father of Prometheus, Epimetheus, Menoetius, and Atlas

Iasion: Son of Zeus and Electra; lover of Demeter; killed by a thunderbolt thrown by Zeus

Icarius: Taught by Dionysus how to cultivate vines and make wine; killed when his neighbors thought he was trying to poison them

Idas: Son of Poseidon; chosen by Marpessa over Apollo

Idomeneus: A Greek warrior during the Trojan War

Ino: Semele's sister; driven mad by Hera for sheltering Dionysus, causing her to kill her own children

Io: Virgin priestess of Hera; lover of Zeus; turned into a white heifer; persecuted by Hera

Iphigenia: Daughter of Agamemnon; sacrificed by her father to Artemis

Iphimedia: Wife of Aloeus; seduced Poseidon and bore him two Giant sons, Ephialtes and Otus

Iris: Goddess of the rainbow; one of the Olympians' messengers

Iulus: Son of Aeneas; founder of the city Alba Longa

Ixion: King of Thessaly; condemned to Tartarus for trying to seduce Zeus's wife

Jason: A great hero; led the Argonauts on the quest for the Golden Fleece; husband of Medea

Juno: Roman goddess of marriage and childbirth; counterpart of Hera

Jupiter: Roman god of the heavens; counterpart of Zeus

Keres: Female spirits of death, sometimes said to be the same as the Furies; daughters of Nyx

Lachesis: One of the Fates; responsible for measuring the thread of life; daughter of Zeus and Themis

Ladon: A hundred-headed dragon; guarded the golden apples in the Garden of the Hesperides

Laocoon: A prophet; warned the Trojans about the wooden horse; was devoured by a sea monster

Laomedon: King of Troy; father of Priam and Hesione

Latinus: King of Latium; son of Faunus

Lavinia: Daughter of Latinus; wife of Aeneas

Leda: Daughter of the king of Aetolia; mother of Polydeuces and Helen by Zeus

Leimakids: Meadow nymphs

Leto: Daughter of Coeus and Phoebe; mother of Apollo and Artemis by Zeus

Leucothoe: Loved by Helios; buried alive by her father when he found out about the affair

Lucius Tarquinius Priscus: Fifth king of Rome

Lucius Tarquinius Superbus: Seventh and final king of Rome; father of Sextus

Lycurgus: King of Thrace; punished by Dionysus for refusing his religious teachings; killed by his own people

Macris: The nymph who nursed the baby Dionysus

Maenads: Wild female followers of Dionysus

Maia: The eldest daughter of Atlas; mother of Hermes by Zeus

Marpessa: Daughter of the river-god Evenus; chose a mortal man over Apollo

Mars: Roman god of war; counterpart of Ares

Marsyas: A satyr; challenged Apollo to a musical contest and lost his life

Medea: A powerful witch; aided Jason on his quest for the Golden Fleece

Medusa: A Gorgon (a monster with snakes for hair whose appearance could turn any being into stone); a lover of Poseidon

Megara: Daughter of the king of Thebes; first wife of Heracles

Melampus: A great seer; cured the women of Argos from madness inflicted upon them by Dionysus

Meliae: Nymphs who lived in ash trees

Melpomene: The Muse of tragedy

Menelaus: King of Sparta; husband of Helen

Mercury: Roman counterpart of Hermes

Metis: An Oceanid known for her wisdom; Zeus's cousin and first wife

Midas: King of Phrygia; granted by Dionysus a touch that could turn anything to gold

Milanion: Young man who beat Atalanta in a foot race, winning her hand in marriage

Mimas: A Giant; killed by Hephaestus and Heracles during the war with the Olympians

Minerva: Roman goddess of wisdom and warfare; counterpart of Athena

Minos: Son of Zeus and Europa; King of Crete; became a Judge of the Dead

Minotaur: A monster with the body of a man and the head of a bull; trapped in the labyrinth and fed sacrifices of young children

Mnemosyne: A Titaness, her name means Memory; mother of the Muses

Moirai: Greek name for the Fates

Momus: God of satire and mockery; son of Nyx

Moros: Doom; son of Nyx

Muses: The daughters of Zeus and Mnemosyne; goddesses of music, art, poetry, dance, and the arts in general

Myrrha: Daughter of the king of Cyprus; Aphrodite caused her to seduce her father; changed into a myrrh tree to escape his wrath

Myrtilus: Son of Hermes; a famous charioteer, known for his swiftness

Naiads: Freshwater nymphs

Napaeae: Valley nymphs

Narcissus: A beautiful young man who fell in love with his own reflection and was turned into the narcissus flower

Nauplius: An Argonaut; founder of the town of Nauplia; famous for his knowledge of the seas and astronomy

Nausicaa: Daughter of the Phaeacian king Alcinous; helped Odysseus after his raft was wrecked at sea

Nemean Lion: Monstrous lion strangled by Heracles as his first labor

Nemesis: Goddess of vengeance; daughter of Nyx

Nemesis: Retribution

Neptune: Roman god of the sea; counterpart of Poseidon

Nereids: Sea nymphs

Nereus: A marine god known as the "Old Man of the Sea"; father of the Nereids; son of Gaia and Pontus

Nike: Goddess of victory

Niobe: The first of Zeus's mortal lovers; daughter of Phoroneus (the first mortal man); mother of Argus by Zeus; the wife of Amphion, her children were killed by Artemis and Apollo because she bragged that her children were greater than Leto's

Notus: The South Wind

Numa Pompilius: Second king of Rome

Nymphs: Nature goddesses; personifications of the fertility and grace of nature; often daughters of Zeus

Nyx: Night; one of the first five elements born of Chaos

Oceanus: A Titan; husband of Tethys; god of the rivers

Odysseus: A great hero; warrior during the Trojan War; famous for his ten-year journey home following the war

Oedipus: King of Thebes; unknowingly fulfilled a prophecy by killing his father and marrying his mother

Oino: Daughter of King Anius; could turn anything into wine with a touch

Oizys: Pain; daughter of Nyx

Oneiroi: Dreams; sons or grandsons of Nyx; sometimes said to be sons of Gaia

Ops: Roman counterpart of Rhea

Oreads: Mountain nymphs

Orestes: Son of Agamemnon and Clytemnestra; killed his mother to avenge his father's murder

Orion: A great hunter; placed in the sky as a constellation after his death

Orpheus: Son of Apollo; talented musician; visited the Underworld to retrieve his dead wife

Otrere: A queen of the Amazons; mother of Penthesilea by Ares

Otus: A Giant; son of Poseidon and Iphimedia

Pallas: Daughter of Triton; a childhood friend of Athena; accidentally killed by Athena

Pallas: A Giant; killed by Athena and Heracles during the war with the Olympians

Pan: Son of Hermes; a minor god of shepherds and flocks

Pandia: Daughter of Selene and Zeus

Pandora: The first mortal woman; wife of Epimetheus; her curiosity drove her to open a box that released all the plagues and ills on the world

Parcae: Roman name for the Fates

Paris: Prince of Troy; judged the beauty contest between Hera, Athena, and Aphrodite; kidnapped Helen

Pasiphae: Wife of King Minos; fell in love with a sacrificial bull and gave birth to the Minotaur

Patroclus: Achilles' best friend; killed by Hector during the Trojan War

Pegaeae: Nymphs who lived in springs

Pegasus: A winged horse, born from the blood of Medusa's severed head

Peina: Personification of hunger

Pelias: King of Iolcus; killed by Medea to place Jason on the throne

Pentheus: King of Thebes; punished by Dionysus for refusing his religious teachings; killed by women taking part in a Dionysian festival

Periphetes: Son of Hephaestus; killed by Theseus

Persephone: Queen of the Underworld; daughter of Demeter and Zeus; abducted by Hades

Perseus: Great Greek hero; son of Zeus and Danae; killed Medusa

Phlegyas: Son of Ares and Chryse; shot and killed by Apollo; condemned to spend eternity in Tartarus

Phobos: Personification of terror; son of Aphrodite and Ares

Phoebe: A Titaness; wife of Coeus; mother of Leto; first goddess of the moon

Phorcys: A sea deity; father of the Sirens; son of Gaia and Pontus

Pierides: The daughters of Pierus, a Macedonian king; challenged the Muses to a contest, lost, and were turned into jackdaws

Pluto: Roman god of hell; counterpart of Hades

Polybotes: A Giant; killed by Poseidon and Heracles during the war with the Olympians

Polydectes: King of Seriphus; loved and persecuted Danae; turned to stone by Perseus

Polyhymnia: The Muse of mime and songs

Polyphemus: A man-eating Cyclops; son of Poseidon; blinded by Odysseus; because of this blinding, Poseidon persecuted Odysseus

Pontus: Sea; born to Gaia during creation

Porphyrion: A Giant; one of the leaders of the Giants during the war with the Olympians; killed by Zeus and Heracles

Poseidon: God of the sea; one of the twelve great Olympians; son of Cronus and Rhea

Priam: King of Troy; father of Paris

Priapus: God of fertility; son of Aphrodite and Dionysus; other sources name Zeus, Hermes, or Pan as his father

Procrustes: A bandit who mutilated passersby to fit his bed; killed by Theseus

Prometheus: A Titan; the champion of mankind; said to be the creator of man; stole fire from the heavens to give to humanity

Proserpine: Roman counterpart of Persephone

Protesilaus: The first Greek to step ashore in Troy; the first Greek to fall during the Trojan War

Python: A great serpent sent by Hera to persecute Leto; strangled to death by Apollo

Remus: Son of Rhea Silvia and Mars; brother of Romulus; killed while fighting his brother over Rome

Rhadamanthys: Son of Zeus and brother of Minos; became a Judge of the Dead

Rhea: A Titaness; a mother deity and earth goddess; wife of Cronus; mother of the original Olympians

Rhea Silvia: Mother of Romulus and Remus by Mars

Rhode: Daughter of Poseidon and Amphitrite; wife of Helios

Romulus: Son of Rhea Silvia and Mars; brother of Remus; founder of Rome

Saturn: Roman counterpart of Cronus

Satyrs: Nature spirits; the personification of fertility and sexual desire; half-man, half-goat

Sciron: Highwayman killed by Theseus

Scylla: Sea nymph who was transformed into a monster that snatched sailors from their ships

Selene: The Moon; sister of Helios and Eos

Semele: Mortal lover of Zeus; mother of Dionysus by Zeus; died when Zeus, at her request, revealed his true form

Servius Tullius: Sixth king of Rome

Sextus: Son of Superbus; raped Lucretia and brought about the downfall of the Roman monarchy

Sibyl: An aged prophetess who helped Aeneas in his journey to the Underworld

Silenus: A satyr; tutor and companion of Dionysus; possessed the gift of prophecy and was known for his drunkenness

Silvius: Son of Aeneas and Lavinia; first to be born of the Roman race

Sinis: Highwayman killed by Theseus

Sinon: Greek soldier of the Trojan War; convinced the Trojans to accept the wooden horse

Sinope: A nymph; pursued by both Zeus and Apollo; tricked the gods into granting her eternal virginity

Sisyphus: Considered the cleverest of mortal men; outwitted Death; committed several crimes against the gods; sent to Tartarus

Sol: Roman Sun god; counterpart of Apollo

Spermo: Daughter of King Anius; could turn anything into corn with a touch

Sphinx: Daughter of Typhon and Echidna; monster with the head and breast of a woman, the body of a lion, and the wings of a bird of prey; asked a riddle of passersby and was defeated by Oedipus

Steropes: One of the three Cyclopes; known as Lightning or the Maker of Lightning

Stymphalian Birds: Monstrous birds with long legs, steel-tipped feathers, and razor-sharp claws; preyed on men; driven away by Heracles as his sixth labor

Syrinx: A nymph loved by Pan; transformed into a bed of reeds to escape Pan's advances

Taygete: Daughter of Atlas; mother of Lacedaemon by Zeus

Terpsichore: The Muse of dance

Tethys: A Titaness; first goddess of the sea; wife of Oceanus; mother of the Oceanids and all the rivers

Teucer: Greek warrior during the Trojan War

Thalia: The Muse of comedy

Thalia: A Charite; the personification of blossoming or good cheer

Thamyris: Son of Philammon; fell in love with Hyacinthus and was said to be the first man to love another man; a musician who boasted he could out-sing the Muses and was punished with blindness and loss of the ability to make music

Thanatos: Death; son of Nyx

Thaumas: A sea deity; father of the Harpies; son of Gaia and Pontus

Theia: A Titaness; wife of Hyperion; mother of Helios, Selene, and Eos

Themis: A Titaness; a mother deity or earth goddess; wife of Iapetus; mother of Prometheus, the Hours, and the Fates

Theopane: Mother of the ram with the Golden Fleece by Poseidon

Theseus: The greatest Athenian hero; son of Poseidon and Aethra; defeated the Minotaur

Thoas: A Giant; killed by the Fates and Heracles during the war with the Olympians

Thoosa: Daughter of Phorcys; lover of Poseidon; mother of the Cyclops Polyphemus

Tiresias: A mortal who had lived as both a man and a woman; one of the greatest prophets of classical mythology; blinded by Hera for taking Zeus's side during an argument

Titus Tatius: King of the Sabines; ruled jointly with Romulus

Tityus: A Giant who tried to rape Leto; killed by Artemis and Apollo

Triton: Poseidon's herald and son; half-man, half-fish; a sea deity

Tullus Hostilius: Third king of Rome

Turnus: King of the Rutulians; battled Aeneas for the hand of Lavinia

Tyche: Goddess of fortune and the personification of luck

Typhon: A monster with a hundred serpentine heads, wings, and a body encircled by snakes

Ulysses: Roman counterpart of Odysseus

Urania: The Muse of astronomy

Uranus: Sky; born to Gaia during creation

Venus: Roman goddess of love; counterpart of Aphrodite

Vesta: Roman goddess of the hearth; counterpart of Hestia

Vestal Virgins: The priestesses of the Temple of Vesta

Vulcan: Roman god of fire; counterpart of Hephaestus

Zagreus: The original name of the infant Dionysus; a child with a crown of snakes and horns

Zephyrus: The West Wind

Zeus: Ruler of the heavens, gods, and men; one of the twelve great Olympians; son of Cronus and Rhea

FAMILY TREE OF THE GREEK GODS

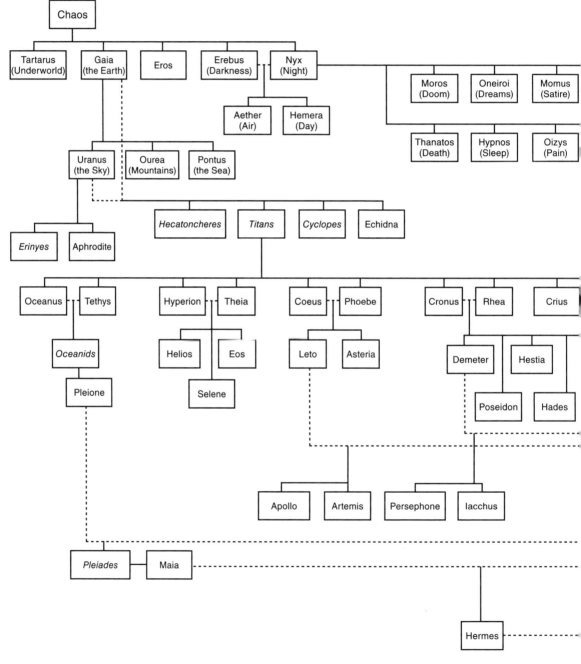

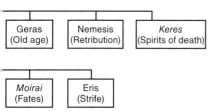

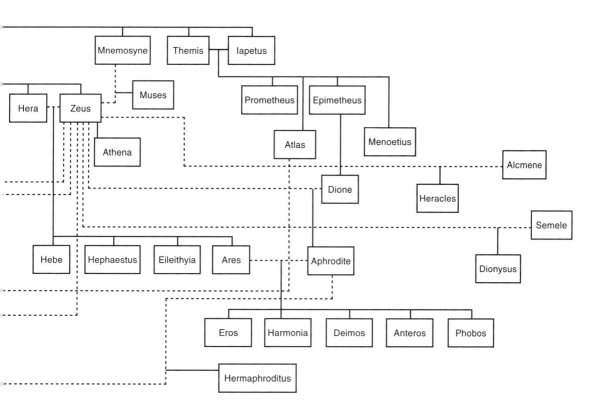

INDEX